BULLY PROOFING
Your School

*A Comprehensive Approach
for Elementary Schools*

Carla Garrity   Kathryn Jens   William Porter
Nancy Sager   Cam Short-Camilli

Editor: Sharon Green
Text layout and design: Graphics West, Inc.
Cover design: Susan Krische and Tracy Katzenberger
"Bullydog" artwork and illustrations: Tom Oling

ISBN #1-57035-279-8

Printed in the United States of America

Published and Distributed by:

Sopris West

4093 Specialty Place   Longmont, Colorado 80504   (303) 651-2829
http://www.sopriswest.com

ABOUT THE AUTHORS

Carla Garrity, Ph.D. practices child psychology at The Neuro-Developmental Center, a multidisciplinary group for the assessment and treatment of children. She has worked for over 25 years developing preventative programs for the well being of children. For many years, Carla supervised and taught at the University of Denver's School of Professional Psychology. The author of numerous books in the field of children and divorce, she developed an interest in recent years in children victimized by bullies. Working with colleagues in the Cherry Creek (CO) School District, *Bully-Proofing Your School* was developed. A companion book, *Bully-Proofing Your Child: A Parent's Guide,* was also co-authored by Carla.

Kathryn Jens, Ph.D. works as a psychologist in the Cherry Creek (CO) School District and has an independent practice with a specialization in psychological trauma. Her graduate study of clinical-community psychology was completed at the State University of New York at Buffalo in 1978.

After years of working with crime victims, Kathryn is particularly excited about this project for its preventative possibilities. She has also developed an interest in the moral development of children and intervention with children exhibiting antisocial personality patterns as a result of this project.

As a single parent, she is grateful to her four children for their input, their patience with her busy life, and for their courageous efforts to stop bullying.

William Porter, Ph.D. received his doctorate in child clinical psychology in 1978 from the University of Denver and has devoted his professional career to developing mental health programming for children and families. He worked in community mental health for Denver (CO) General Hospital prior to joining the Cherry Creek School District, where he has directed a wide variety of student programs for 22 years. Bill has been instrumental in developing outdoor therapeutic, suicide prevention, home alone, adolescent runaway, violence prevention, and a number of other intervention programs. He believes in using every possible "opportunity" to reach a child or family, and his program efforts have received local and national acclaim. Bill is a co-author of *Bully-Proofing Your Child: A Parent's Guide.*

Nancy Sager is an Education and Behavior Consultant with the Cherry Creek (CO) School District. She has worked with special needs children for thirty years. She views the Bully-Proofing program as providing a level of support to children that broadens their repertoire of skills necessary for success today as well as in the future.

Nancy wishes to thank her husband, Don, for his encouragement and unending support.

Cam Short-Camilli is a licensed clinical social worker who has been a school social worker with the Cherry Creek (CO) School District for the past fourteen years. She has worked at both the elementary and middle school levels. She received her B.S.W. from Western Michigan University and her M.S.W. from Michigan State University. Cam's interest in bully-victim problems developed around concerns students and parents brought to her. She has continued to learn from using this program and listening to students.

Cam wishes to thank her husband and two sons for their tremendous support on this project.

PREFACE

Aggressive behavior in students has long been a disruptive element in the educational arena. At a time when violence is so prevalent in our society, bullies have become a (sometimes lethal) threat to the physical and emotional safety of students. Many of us can probably recall personal or professional experiences with bullies. The recall of these memories is intense and awakens strong emotions, especially of fear and helplessness. The pervasiveness of the fear results in a feeling of powerlessness. Bullies bring this imbalance of power and fear to schools, as well. After suffering unchecked bullying, self-destructive acts or desperate retaliation with lethal weapons is not uncommon.

A most discouraging situation is occurring in many schools today. Many children are unwilling to turn to staff for help with bullying because they believe that not only will the staff fail to help them but that telling will make the situation worse. Although we as educators would like to believe that we can simply send children to handle these problems on their own, many need adult support to develop the coping skills necessary to protect themselves from the attack of bullies. The old adage "Just hit 'em back" is one of the myriad of unsuccessful myths surrounding bullying behavior and is in fact probably one of the most dangerous strategies with a true bully. However, there are many approaches that can defuse the situation and lower the potential for aggression. For instance, just having more adults among students has been shown to influence bullying behavior.

Eighty-five percent of the students in schools are neither bullies nor victims. This "caring majority" of students, though, observe the behavior and interactions of bullies, live with an uncomfortable feeling about their own safety, and often believe that if they get involved the aggressive actions will be transferred to them. Fear and power struggles are a reality in elementary schools, and one of the goals within schools must be to bring these issues in line so they are manageable. The actions and influence of this caring majority are a powerful resource with which to maintain the value of kindness and decency. They are the untapped reservoir of strength, the leverage for impacting change in creating a safe school environment for all children.

The *Bully-Proofing Your School* program operates on many levels within a school. It is our belief that developing the caring majority's intervention skills so they feel confident to be involved is crucial. Their power is implicit by number, and explicit by positive acts of kindness toward victims. By developing a strong, reinforced identity, they can help set the tone of a school and dictate its operating environment. This group can give strength and support to the victims and defuse the power of the bullies.

Bullies can occupy an inordinate amount of time from staff, students, and parents. Swift and precise adult interventions that avoid power positions and clearly establish bullying behaviors as unacceptable can prevent the wounds of repeated victimization. Escalating direct power struggles with bullies is exhausting and generally not effective. Intervening calmly and consistently before bullying behavior escalates can strip the bully's power.

Many standard curriculum packages fail after three to four months because there is an expectation inherent to them that all staff members can and will intervene in the same manner. A lack of congruence between an individual and curriculum can cause the program to be undermined—one becomes uncomfortable with the new way and thus returns to one's old style. However, this will not be the case with this program. We strongly believe, and have designed this program around this tenet, that the acknowledgment of personal styles up front is crucial in formulating a team ethic comprised of multiple approaches achieving the same goal. Teachers need to identify and accept the skills they already have that can be implemented in a focused fashion to impact aggressive behavior, support the strength of the caring majority, and soothe the wounds of victims. The wheel doesn't need to be reinvented, just to be mounted and balanced.

The community should also be included in recognizing and supporting a "no-bullying" position. Addressing bullying behavior requires strong support from parents to prevent fractionalizing of the community. Understanding some basic tenets, such as that all parents believe their children are the victims and that very rarely are children self-confessed bullies, helps clarify the picture and enables collaborative relationships with parents to stop bullying.

Developing a comprehensive approach will lead to successful results in identifying and intervening with bullies. Following these plans that address developing the skills and awareness of the staff, intervening with bullies, empowering the caring majority of students, understanding and supporting the victims, and finally, engaging the community of parents will lead to successful intervention that changes the balance of power with value placed upon kindness and inclusion for all students within a school.

ACKNOWLEDGMENTS

We would like to thank the Cherry Creek School District—the Board and Administration—for the opportunity to develop the Bully-Proofing program. We are grateful for their continued commitment to educational excellence and developing a safe school climate where teachers can teach and students can learn.

The program presented in this book was supported in part by funding from Nancy and Sam Gary, as well as from the Rose Community and Cherry Creek Schools Foundations. This financial support allowed us to continue to develop, research, and refine our safe school program and present the second edition of our work. With the professional efforts of Dr. Vicki Meyer, Paul Von Essen and our training team, we were able to reach hundreds of schools across the country to promote safe schools. Drs. Larry Epstein and Amy Plog spearheaded the research component of our program and helped develop the assessment tools, including the Colorado School Climate Survey.

Finally, we want to thank the many students who have demonstrated a commitment to having their schools safe for all students. All have taught us so much and inspired our continued effort to create safe schools for everyone.

CONTENTS

WHY BULLY-PROOF?

Scope of the Problem

In the average elementary school classroom, two to three students spend their day afraid. Some of these children avoid the restroom, cafeteria, and playground because they fear they will be humiliated or picked on by bullies. The United States Department of Justice and the National Association of School Psychologists (NASP) estimate that 160,000 children miss school each day because of fear (Lee, 1993).

Increasingly, children simply do not feel safe at school—safe from violence, safe from humiliation, and safe from bullying. Every seven minutes bullying happens on elementary school playgrounds (Pepler, 1995). Children as young as second grade report that no one helps them; they do not believe that their teachers or the other school staff will help protect them if they report their fear. Indeed, research confirms that what these children are reporting is true. Most of the time no one helps and, if anyone does, it is more likely to be another child than an adult.

Consequently, children are left feeling helpless, afraid, and "on their own" to figure out how to cope with these feelings. Many younger children hide throughout the school day, experience physical symptoms of distress, or even refuse to attend school. As they grow older, children are more likely to take more active measures to protect themselves—often these are not positive measures. Some will begin carrying weapons to school, others will associate with a gang for protection, and still others will drop out of school entirely.

Every day approximately 100,000 children carry guns to school. As many as 6,250 teachers are threatened each day, and of those about 260 are actually attacked (Lee, 1993). School violence is multidetermined and not solely the result of bullying. However, what is bullying behavior in elementary school can easily turn into violence by middle and high school.

This program can be an early, preventative measure against this type of behavior. More importantly, however, it is designed to stop bullying at the elementary level to ensure a safer school environment—one that does not tolerate acts of physical or emotional aggression against children. It is within this type of safe and caring environment that children can learn. And it is within your influence to provide just such an environment.

Underpinnings of the Program

Bully-Proofing Your School provides a "blueprint" for an elementary school to easily implement a bully-proofing program designed to meet one criterion: to make the school environment safe for children both physically and psychologically.

Bully-Proofing Your School encompasses a number of underlying principles:

- ◆ **It is the responsibility of adults to ensure that school is a safe environment in which children can learn.**

    Many children live with fear in daily life at school. This can be incapacitating and can severely affect learning.

    The participation of the staff is an important element in the success of the bully-proofing program.

- ◆ **Bullying is not synonymous with violence.**

    Bullying takes many forms, and school staff must be able to recognize them in order to address them.

- ◆ **The bully-proofing program will be most successful if implemented comprehensively.**

    While the program is somewhat flexible in order to embrace the varying levels of resources from school to school, it will have limited success if implemented piecemeal. Each component of the program is as important as any of the others—it is their combination within a school that will coalesce into a safe learning environment.

- ◆ **Punitive programs are only successful with bullying behavior to a point.**

    Bully-Proofing Your School is not a punitive program. Rather than engaging in power struggles by attempting to discipline bullies, this program focuses on shifting the power away from the bullies.

◆ **Bullies, when confronted with a caring community (a unified group of adults and peers within a school), are defused.**

This program enables the "caring majority" (the majority of students who are neither bullies nor victims) to intervene and thus strip the bullies of their power.

◆ **There are many means to any end.**

Positive training can change the atmosphere of the school. The power of the caring majority can help to make the school a safe learning environment. It can also promote character development and skills for becoming a responsible community member.

Implementing this program will not necessarily present for staff a requirement to learn or relearn conflict resolution strategies. Instead, the program emphasizes the importance of recognizing and utilizing the different styles, strengths, and experience of the staff members. Each individual role is significant, and each contributes to the successful implementation of the bully-proofing program, establishing a positive and safe environment for all.

Program Contents

Bully-Proofing Your School presents both a process and all the materials necessary for the adoption of a school-wide program against bullying.

This school-wide adoption process is comprised of six main components: (1) staff training, (2) student instruction, (3) support of the victims, (4) intervention with the bullies, (5) development of the caring majority, and (6) working with parents.

The sequence of this program manual is as follows:

◆ **Chapter One: Defining Bullying**

This chapter defines the bullying behavior that will be addressed by the program and identifies specific forms which that behavior takes. Also described are the characteristics of both bullies and victims and the dynamics of their relationship within a school.

◆ **Chapter Two: Intervention in Bullying Situations**

This chapter makes the case for the necessity of adults to intervene in bullying situations and provides guidelines for situations requiring adult intervention. A handy "Developmental Guide to Conflict Resolution" is also provided for quick reference.

◆ **Chapter Three: Adoption of a School-Wide Program**

This chapter presents the philosophy and the importance of effective school-wide intervention. It identifies some common attitudinal roadblocks among staff members and provides some suggestions for removing those impediments. The Colorado School Climate Surveys can be found in this chapter as well as the steps to creating a caring and safe climate. Finally, it provides an agenda for the orientation presentation to staff members and parents necessary to introduce this program and obtain support from those involved in implementing it.

◆ Chapter Four: The Staff Training Curriculum

This chapter provides a complete training outline for presentation to the staff, including handouts and transparency masters. The training can be conducted in six sessions, or as a half-day or full-day "workshop," depending upon the time resources available in the particular school.

Besides the information provided with this program for presentation to the staff, a very important process occurs within this component of the program—**staff involvement**. As part of the staff training sessions, staff members are guided in identifying their own predominant styles of conflict resolution (with "The Conflict Resolution Questionnaire"), brainstorming and agreeing upon strategies for addressing bullying situations that are feasible with **their** student body and staff (through role play and discussion), and customizing and fine-tuning the bully-proofing program for the needs of **their** building.

◆ Chapter Five: Student Instruction

This chapter provides a complete classroom curriculum to educate all students about bullying and what they can do about bullying occurring around them. Role play, modeling, class discussion, and classroom materials (posters, etc.) are utilized to teach students specific strategies and techniques to cope with and prevent bullying behavior. Additionally, "The Bully Survey" found in Chapter Three is administered to students to assess the degree of bullying behavior occurring in each classroom.

The curriculum consists of eight weekly sessions with an additional follow-up session, but is meant to be used flexibly to conform to the demands of individual classroom schedules. The classroom curriculum has activities and instructions specified for grades 1–6.

◆ Chapter Six: Creating and Maintaining the Caring Majority

This chapter provides specific techniques for shaping the climate of the school into a safe, respectful, and inclusive environment. Intervention skills for changing the silent majority of children into a caring majority are described. The caring majority provides strength and support to the victims and defuses the power of the bullies. This is the most powerful resource in creating a safe and caring school environment.

- **Chapter Seven: Supporting the Victims**

   This chapter presents a curriculum designed to be used in a one-to-one (individual) or small group format with victimized students. When used in conjunction with the classroom curriculum, these six interrelated sessions assist students being victimized by bullies to increase their self-esteem, decrease their isolation, and improve their social skills and friendship-making behaviors.

- **Chapter Eight: Changing the Bullies**

   This chapter presents a curriculum to be used in individual sessions or in small groups with the bullies. These six sessions focus on changing errors in thinking, learning anger control, and developing empathy. When used as preparation for the classroom curriculum (which is the ideal method), these sessions prime the bullies for the presentation of social skills exercises.

- **Chapter Nine: Effective Prosocial Discipline**

   This chapter shows how to construct a discipline policy that is consistent with bully-proofing. Students who repeatedly use aggression, alienation, and intimidation require specific disciplinary tools. A variety of tools that create prosocial consequences for the bully and protection for the victim are described.

- **Chapter Ten: Collaboration With Parents**

   This chapter details methods for effectively communicating with the parents of both bullies and victims to ensure collaborative relationships between the school and home.

- **Chapter Eleven: Coming From and Going to School
   Conclusion: Maintaining and Supporting the Change**

   A caring community stretches from home to school and back again. A comprehensive plan for building a caring community on the school bus is presented. Surveys for assessing safety on the bus as well as a parent letter and behavioral warning form can be found in this chapter.

- **Resource Guide/Reproducible Materials**

   Recommended resources for teachers, parents, and students on topics such as collaboration, discipline, conflict resolution, coping skills, and assertiveness are referenced throughout the chapters. Reproducible materials are also provided within the appropriate chapters.

Implementing the Program

Bully-Proofing Your School is easy to implement and maintain, and flexible in terms of the time required. If consecutive weekly lessons are presented to the students, the entire program can be completed within a two to three month time frame from start to finish.

The main requirement for implementing the program is enlisting a person (administrator, school psychologist, social worker, counselor, or school team member), persons, or team to fill the role of "facilitator"— to take the initiative within the school building for organizing and guiding the implementation of the six program components. The implementation process would occur as follows:

1. Obtain administrative support for introducing the program into the school. Identify a person (or persons) to act as a facilitator for implementation. *(See Chapter Three.)*

2. The facilitator familiarizes himself or herself with the basic principles and philosophy of the program *(see the Overview, Chapters One and Two)*, and prepares for the program orientation, including a letter to parents inviting them to attend. *(See Chapter Three.)*

3. The facilitator conducts the program orientation presentation to staff members and parents, encouraging their participation in the program. The new school-wide policy regarding bullying behavior and expectations of staff and students are presented. In addition, the Colorado School Staff Climate Survey is administered, scored, and feedback given. Finally, the Five Steps to Creating a Caring and Safe Climate are taught. *(See Chapter Three.)*

4. The facilitator (or designee) familiarizes himself or herself with the classroom curriculum *(see Chapter Five)* and then presents the staff training component to the appropriate school personnel. Within this component, staff members customize the bully-proofing program to the needs of their specific school (i.e., creating classroom rules). *(See Chapter Four.)*

5. The facilitator (or designee) leads the individual/small group sessions with the bullies. *(See Chapter Eight.)*

6. The facilitator (or designee) assists the classroom teachers in presenting the classroom curriculum to their students. *(See Chapter Five.)*

7. The facilitator (or designee) leads the individual/small group sessions with the victims of bullying. *(See Chapter Seven.)*

8. The facilitator (or designee) participates in meetings with parents as the need arises. *(See Chapter Ten.)*

9. The facilitator (or designee) follows up with the classroom teachers approximately one to two months after implementation to troubleshoot and reinforce the program. *(See Chapter Five.)*

Depending on the resources of the adopting school, adaptations can be made to this implementation process. The role of the facilitator can be filled by multiple individuals (division of the responsibilities), or can be downplayed with the classroom teachers assuming more of the responsibilities independently. Additionally, while extremely helpful, the individual/small group student sessions with both the victimized students

(Chapter Seven) and the bullies *(Chapter Eight)* are not **essential** to program implementation. If a school does not have the resources (time and personnel) available for this intensive intervention, the entire program should not be abandoned. The victims will be supported by the caring majority and by the very nature of the program, and the program will still be very effective in empowering all the students to prevent their own and others' bullying behavior even without these components.

April 22, 1999

Dear Mrs. Sager,

Yesterday my class talked about the crisis at Columbine High School, and I said, "I'm glad we're bullyproofed because when we are in high school, we have grown into bullybroofing so if we're bullied, we know of the right way to deal with it, and not the wrong way, which is how the crisis at Columbine High School got started.

Sincerely,

Tim
3rd Grade

CHAPTER ONE

DEFINING BULLYING

All children are the victims of occasional teasing behavior or aggression, but some children are repeatedly targeted. True bullying is **repeated exposure** over time to negative actions. Bullying means there is an **imbalance of power** so that the child being victimized has trouble defending himself or herself. Bullying is aggression. It can take many forms, including physical, verbal, or psychological. **Bullying is when one person uses power in a willful manner with the aim of hurting another individual repeatedly.**

Normal Peer Conflict—What Bullying Is Not

Conflict is an inevitable part of interaction. As children learn the give and take of friendship, of group cooperation, and of social interaction, conflict naturally occurs. Social skills are developmental. Children gain greater capacity for empathy, for compromise, and for kindness to others as they mature cognitively and emotionally. Children in the early elementary years (grades K–2) do not always think of others. Their goal in both friendship and play is egocentric, or self-centered. They pick playmates in order to have a good time and to maximize their own excitement. They believe that a good friend is one who will do what they want. A common response to frustration is one of rejecting the other child. A first grader might say, for example, "If you won't play house with me, I won't invite you to my birthday party."

By the middle elementary grades, children gradually begin to understand friendship and play as a process that involves fun for all participants. Games with rules begin, recess time is spent with others who enjoy the same interests and activities, and sharing is seen. Still, children of this age do not fully understand or engage in mutuality or compromise. Play is fun when everyone gets their needs met, but conflict erupts when access to things or frustration of needs occurs. The capacity to listen to and understand another person's point of view is still not fully developed and only the most mature of children will employ compromise to solve problems during grades 2–4.

By the later elementary grades, children evolve gradually toward a consideration of others. Feelings and personal needs are shared. Having secrets and sharing them through notes and private plans is common. Friendships become exclusive and cliques form. Jealousy and feeling left out are common problems. Mutuality, commitment, and loyalty are hallmarks of social interaction by this age. At this age, compromise is a skill that can be taught and used to solve problems.

Normal peer conflict is typically characterized by the developmental level of the children involved. Aggression and hurtful remarks are part of conflict at all ages; they do not necessarily mean that a bully-victim problem exists. Bullying can be recognized by the following unique social interactional features:

- ◆ Bullying is repetitive negative actions targeted at a specific victim.

- ◆ Bullying is an imbalance of power so that the victim has trouble defending himself or herself. This imbalance can be the result of physical size or the result of emotional or cognitive capacity. Overall, the critical feature is that the victim does not have the skills to cope.

- ◆ Bullying is usually characterized by unequal levels of affect. The child being victimized is typically very upset. This may be manifested by withdrawal, outright crying and anguish, or anger. Regardless of the specific behavior observed, the content and process is one of extraordinary distress on the part of the victim. The child doing the bullying, on the other hand, is typically devoid of affect. He or she is likely to show little outward emotion and to communicate through words or action that the victim provoked or deserved the aggression. Little or no empathy or caring for the victim is evident. The child who bullies feels justified in his or her actions.

Table 1 highlights the main differences between normal peer conflict and bullying.

Who Are the Bullies?

A common myth is that all bullies are boys. This is not true. Both girls and boys are bullies, but boys are more likely to admit to being one and are also easier to spot and identify because of the tactics they generally use.

The common stereotype of a bully as physically large, low achieving, and insecure is also not true. Bullies are not typically children who are failing academically. They are usually not the top students in a class, but they are likely to be average to just slightly below average in their achievement. Nor are they insecure and friendless. Bullies have friends,

TABLE 1 Recognizing the Difference	
Normal Peer Conflict	**Bullying**
Equal power or friends	Imbalance of power; not friends
Happens occasionally	Repeated negative actions
Accidental	Purposeful
Not serious	Serious with threat of physical or emotional harm
Equal emotional reaction	Strong emotional reaction from victim and little or no emotional reaction from bully
Not seeking power or attention	Seeking power, control, or material things
Not trying to get something	Attempt to gain material things or power
Remorse—will take responsibility	No remorse—blames victim
Effort to solve the problem	No effort to solve problem

especially other children who empower them and are empowered by their association with the bully.

Bullies are best identified by their **personality style** rather than by outward manifestations based on appearance, number of friends, or achievement:

- ◆ A bully is a child who values the rewards that aggression can bring.
- ◆ A bully is a child who lacks empathy for his or her victim and has difficulty feeling compassion.
- ◆ A bully tends to lack guilt. He or she fully believes that the victim provoked the attack and deserved the consequences.
- ◆ A bully likes to be in charge, to dominate, and to assert with power. A bully likes to win in all situations.
- ◆ A bully's parent(s) (or other significant role model) often model aggression.
- ◆ A bully thinks in unrealistic ways (e.g., "I should always get what I want.").

Bullying Tactics

Boys tend to bully with aggressive tactics. Physical aggression is frequently used and it tends to be swift and effective. Tripping someone, a quick blow, or a knee in the stomach are all likely behaviors. Verbal aggression often accompanies the physical aggression or is used to threaten later physical consequences.

Girls tend to bully with social alienation and intimidation strategies (but not always—see Figure 1-1). A victim might be teased about her

Depiction of Male Bullying
Drawn by a Sixth
Grade Boy

Depiction of Female Bullying
Drawn by a Sixth
Grade Girl

The New Kid on the Block

Jack Prelutsky

There's a new kid on the block,
and boy, that kid is tough,
that new kid punches hard,
that new kid plays real rough,
that new kid's big and strong,
with muscles everywhere,
that new kid tweaked my arm,
that new kid pulled my hair.

That new kid likes to fight,
and picks on all the guys,
that new kid scares me some,
(that new kid's twice my size),
that new kid stomped my toes,
that new kid swiped my ball,
that new kid's really bad,
I don't care for her at all.

—Prelutsky, 1984

Figure 1-1

clothing, gossiped about in a malicious manner, or become the recipient of intimidating notes. Some girls are targeted by cruel and demeaning extortion tactics with the promise of inclusion in a desired peer group if a specific act is performed. Female bullying is typically more insidious, cunning, and difficult to spot than is male bullying.

The "Bullying Behaviors Chart" (see Figure 1-2 on page 14) describes in more detail the specific tactics which bullies employ. These can range from mild name calling or shoving to very severe acts such as violence and coercion.

Who Are the Victims?

Children who are the victims of peer aggression and bullying are not randomly targeted as once believed, nor are they selected exclusively because of external appearance or disabilities. The victims of bullying are likely to be anxious, insecure children who lack social skills and the ability to defend themselves. They are often physically weak, cry easily, and are easy targets because they yield to bullying. These children are referred to as **passive victims** because they fail to fight back.

BULLYING BEHAVIORS CHART

MILD		MODERATE			SEVERE

PHYSICAL AGGRESSION

◆ Pushing ◆ Shoving ◆ Spitting	◆ Kicking ◆ Hitting	◆ Defacing property ◆ Stealing	◆ Physical acts that are demeaning and humiliating, but not bodily harmful (e.g., de-panting) ◆ Locking in a closed or confined space	◆ Physical violence against family or friends	◆ Threatening with a weapon ◆ Inflicting bodily harm

SOCIAL ALIENATION

◆ Gossiping ◆ Embarrassing	◆ Setting up to look foolish ◆ Spreading rumors about	◆ Ethnic slurs ◆ Setting up to take the blame	◆ Publicly humiliating (e.g., revealing personal information) ◆ Excluding from group ◆ Social rejection	◆ Maliciously excluding ◆ Manipulating social order to achieve rejection ◆ Malicious rumor-mongering	◆ Threatening with total isolation by peer group

VERBAL AGGRESSION

◆ Mocking ◆ Name calling ◆ Dirty looks ◆ Taunting	◆ Teasing about clothing or possessions	◆ Teasing about appearance	◆ Intimidating telephone calls	◆ Verbal threats of aggression against property or possessions	◆ Verbal threats of violence or of inflicting bodily harm

INTIMIDATION

◆ Threatening to reveal personal information ◆ Graffiti ◆ Publicly challenging to do something	◆ Defacing property or clothing ◆ Playing a dirty trick	◆ Taking possessions (e.g., lunch, clothing, toys)	◆ Extortion ◆ Sexual/racial taunting	◆ Threats of using coercion against family or friends	◆ Coercion ◆ Threatening with a weapon

Figure 1-2   Copyright © 1992 by Garrity & Baris.

A passive victim is likely to be a child who:

- ◆ Is isolated or alone during much of the school day.

- ◆ Is anxious, insecure, and lacking in social skills.

- ◆ Is physically weak and therefore unable to defend himself or herself.

- Cries easily, yields when bullied, and is unable to stick up for himself or herself.

- May have suffered past abuse or traumatization.

- May have a learning disorder that compromises his or her ability to process and respond to social interactional cues.

There is another, smaller group of children who are likely to be victimized because of their provocative behavior. **Provocative victims** are children who are often restless, irritable, and who tease and provoke others. While these children will fight back to a point, they are ineffectual aggressors, and more frequently than not they end up losing the power struggle with the bullies and thus are also targets of bullying behavior.

This type of victim is more difficult to recognize than the passive victim, because he or she may be seen engaging the bully. However, the provocative victim is really over his or her head with the bully. Provocative victims are likely to exhibit the following characteristics:

- Are easily emotionally aroused.

- Tend to maintain the conflict and lose with frustration and distress.

- May be diagnosed with Attention Deficit Hyperactive Disorder (ADHD).

Overall, these children are simply impulsive and action oriented. They may look like bullies at first glance but with a closer look it becomes obvious that two characteristics distinguish them. One is that they are not purposefully malicious and mean. Their actions are more impulsively driven than calculated. When they realize they have hurt another child, they will apologize after the fact and quickly resume what they were doing. These children are more oblivious than mean-spirited. Secondly, they typically lose when the bully turns on them. They are not as quick witted, mean-spirited or cunning as the bully. The bully will overpower them and win.

Why, you may wonder, do bullies choose to pick on provocative victims? There appear to be a number of reasons. These children provoke the bully. They irritate others and the bully wants to show them who is boss. Picking on a provocative victim garners a lot of attention on the playground. Unlike the passive victims who cry and tremble, the provocative victims fight back with a great deal of gusto, noise, and bravado. This attracts attention. As one professional put it, "*People's Court* plays itself out right on the playground." Other children come running over to see what all the noise and commotion is about. Soon a crowd has gathered to watch. What could be more satisfying to a bully's need for power and domination than to have a large proportion of the school watch as he or she puts the victim in his or her place.

Simply put, the bully dominates and demonstrates power over both types of victims, passive and provocative. This fuels the sense of power for the bully and he or she will come back again and again to prey on the same child. Sadly, a contagion effect can be put into motion on the school playground. Other children experience excitement and titillation watching the action play out. They watch, anxiously at first, and then seem to experience some vicarious thrill from the malicious behavior of one child against another. This sounds disturbing and hard to believe for many adults but it is not very different from the excitement adults derive from the violence in movies, on television, or on the nightly news. Bullying is exciting news on the childhood playground scene. Being part of the action may be both appealing and appalling at the same time. Some children make the decision to join with the bully both for the thrill of the ride and out of fear for their own well-being. A contagion grows. Soon the bully has far more children on his side and the victim is even more helpless and more at the mercy of the bully than ever. If this scene plays itself out day after day, the victim becomes miserable, desperate, and completely incapable of managing the situation.

The child who is the victim of a bully is probably suffering in silence. Children who are victimized usually don't tell and don't expect help. Many of them are highly vulnerable because of past abuse, loss, or learning disorders.

The consequences of sustained maltreatment over time has not been studied longitudinally, but it is likely that children who are the victims of bullying suffer from lowered self-esteem, fear and anxiety, disrupted academic performance, lack of interest in school, and a lack of trust and friends. Adults who were picked on by a bully during childhood can often recall the details of their traumatization with the same clarity as those who suffer from post-traumatic stress disorder. The effects of being the victim of a childhood bully may last a lifetime for some individuals.

More in-depth information regarding identifying and dealing with bullies and their tactics is provided in Chapter Four: The Staff Training Curriculum and Chapter Eight: Changing the Bullies. Additional information on identifying and assisting both passive and provocative victims is provided in Chapter Seven: Supporting the Victims.

CHAPTER TWO

INTERVENTION IN BULLYING SITUATIONS

The Need to Address the Problem

Children know who the bullies are and who the victims are long before the teachers and staff within a school do. Typically by six weeks into the school year the bully-victim interactional patterns have been established. Yet children do not tell on bullies. They don't tell because they are afraid. They are afraid that the bullying will become worse if they tell or that they might become the victim if they help someone else by telling. And sadly, most victims feel that no one will help them or be able to stop the bully even if they do tell.

Many bullies hide their bullying, especially with passive victims. It goes on "behind closed doors" so to speak, and there is a conspiracy of silence among the children. Most children are afraid to tell. They report that telling is ineffective and it only gets them into worse trouble. Research done in Canada confirms this. When students report on bullying, most teachers and educators immediately confront the bully and demand an explanation of the behavior. Kids are smart. The bully knows who told and he or she will see to it that the student who ratted is certain not to do that again. The innocent bystanders watch and are thankful they were not involved. They, too, have learned the conspiracy of silence— don't tell or you will be next.

Another disturbing fact emerged from the Canadian research. Cameras were hidden on the school playground and certain children wore hidden microphones. It was here that a bullying incident was recorded every seven minutes! In spite of teachers roaming the playground watching for bullying, almost all of it escaped detection by the eyes of the teachers yet the cameras caught it. Why? Because the children were clever. They knew not to bully in front of an adult. They didn't want to get caught. Bullying takes no longer than 10 seconds to happen. A shove off the stairs, a quick punch, a threat, a put-down—any of these can be delivered so fast that an adult could not possibly see or hear from ten feet away.

This, indeed, was how most bullying was accomplished. It was done and over before anyone, other than the victim, even knew it had occurred. Sometimes it was disguised cleverly as playing, which the teachers failed to spot as an unfair game. For example, one girl was being guided about the playground with a jump rope tied around her neck. A group of girls were holding the rope as she walked in front of them. It appeared to be something the girl was acquiescing to and doing willingly. Later it was learned that the group of girls behind her were forcing her to go where they told her with threats of pulling the noose more tightly around her neck if she did not comply.

What is the lesson to be learned from these hidden cameras? They confirmed beyond a doubt that bullying goes on regularly and maliciously. They also confirmed that even the most alert and caring of teachers may not be able to spot it. It is a hidden phenomenon among children and the most efficient way to stop it is to teach the children who are there and aware of it to do something effective to intervene. Children can and will take action to protect the victim if they are part of a group and if they know they have the support of the school staff. A child must know that the bully will be widely identified, that something will be done, and that he or she will not be the only one who stood up for the victim. In other words, children must know that bullying will not be tolerated in their school.

Fears regarding telling are not figments of children's imaginations. Unfortunately, teachers often have difficulty distinguishing between true bullying and normal peer conflict. Thus, they may not realize the severity of a problem and fail to support the victim appropriately.

There is also a firmly held belief among classroom teachers and many parents that children benefit from learning to solve their own problems. Consequently, the most common response a child hears when he or she attempts to tell an adult is, "You are old enough now to solve your own problems." While this response rings true for normal peer conflict, victims of bullies are **not** old enough (or competent enough) to defend themselves.

Children cannot handle true bullying situations, and they do need help. Dr. Dan Olweus (1991), who has researched bully-victim problems for over twenty years, found the **single most effective deterrent to bullying to be adult authority**. The adults in charge within a school need to learn to recognize bullying behavior and to stop it. Bully-proofing your school is essential if school is to be a safe and happy environment in which all the children can learn.

General Guidelines for Intervention

All children will be exposed to peer aggression at some point in their school experience. Most children can handle bullying that is in the mild to moderate range without adult assistance. **All children, however, need help with bullying that is in the moderate to severe range.**

One out of every seven children reports being involved in bullying experiences at school. Six percent are likely to be bullies while 9% of children report being victims (Greenbaum, Turner, & Stephens, 1989). In an average elementary classroom of twenty children, there are most likely three children who need your help.

Help With Mild Bullying

In most cases, mild bullying behavior (refer back to Figure 1-2) can be overlooked by adults without detriment to the children involved. However, some children are not able to cope effectively with even mild bullying, and should be given adult assistance. These children include:

- ◆ Children who are shy or who lack social skills.
- ◆ Children who are isolated.
- ◆ Children who are learning disabled.
- ◆ Children who are repeatedly bullied.
- ◆ Children who have experienced a past trauma.
- ◆ Children who are using money or toys as bribes to protect themselves.

Help With Moderate to Severe Bullying

Adults should always intervene in moderate to severe bullying (refer back to Figure 1-2) situations. This is especially true if the **bullying has occurred more than once** and/or **the two children are not friends**.

Specific techniques for addressing bullying behavior are provided in Chapter Four: Staff Training and Chapter Seven: Changing the Bullies. The "Developmental Guide to Conflict Resolution," shown in Figure 2-1 on page 21, provides a quick reference to intervention.

Developmental Guide to Conflict Resolution

This conflict resolution guide is a general reference to effective intervention tactics with children at various elementary ages involved in varying degrees of bullying. While this guide provides some helpful guidelines, the resolution suggestions are **not rules**—they are suggestions. The goals of conflict resolution as it is defined by this program are to: (1) **become aware of your own predominant style** (e.g., "no-nonsense," "problem solver," "smoother," etc.), (2) **respect it**, (3) **expand your repertoire** of

**Depiction of Moderate/
Severe Bullying**
Drawn by a Fourth
Grade Girl

"Help Mommy."

**Depiction of Moderate/
Severe Bullying**
Drawn by a Fourth
Grade Boy

"Forget it,
I'm going to
kill you."

"Please don't
kill me."

CONFLICT AND RESOLUTION		
Grade Level	**Typical Conflict**	**Preferred Styles of Resolution**
1	Conflict likely over toys, possessions ("It's mine."), going first	◆ Action oriented ◆ Separate the children ◆ Change the topic ◆ **No-Nonsense** or **Smoothing**
1 and 2	Selfishness, wanting own way Threatening with tattling or not playing with again ("I'm not inviting you to my birthday.")	◆ Undo what the offender did ◆ **No-Nonsense** or **Problem Solving**
3, 4, and 5	What's fair and what isn't Teasing, gossiping, feeling superior Putting down, accusing of something not true or distorted	◆ Beginning stage of understanding others' intentions: mutual negotiation possible with help ◆ Compromise for older grade levels ◆ **Problem Solving** or **Compromising**
5 and 6	Bossiness, tattling, put-downs, showing off, betrayal	◆ Compromise can be used: empathy is possible at this age ◆ Talking things out, even if no compromise is reached ◆ **Ignoring** (only if a minor problem) or **Compromising**

Figure 2-1   Copyright © 1991 by Binswanger-Friedman & Ciner.

conflict resolution approaches as much as possible, and (4) **identify and rely upon staff members with styles which complement your own** (e.g., if a "smoothing" approach is necessary in a situation, and you happen to be a very straightforward "problem solver," call upon another staff member to intervene rather than addressing a situation in a manner which violates your predominant style).

Any of these conflict resolution styles may be appropriate with any age or type of conflict, depending upon the circumstances. However, one situation calls for a specific conflict resolution style—an incidence of **physically aggressive or violent behavior** (any situation in which any-one's physical safety is endangered). This type of situation **requires an immediate "no-nonsense" approach**.

Keep in mind that children at certain grade levels exhibit "typical" con-flict behaviors, but some children are more or less mature than others of their age. As children mature, they become increasingly more capable of learning skills such as compromise and problem solving. Use your best judgment when examining a situation and the maturity level of the children involved when selecting a conflict resolution tactic. Modeling these higher level skills by your own interactions with both your peers and students will also promote and facilitate their adoption by the children around you.

Additional strategies for conflict resolution and information concerning delivering consequences and reinforcement is provided in Chapter Four: Staff Training.

CHAPTER THREE

ADOPTION OF A SCHOOL-WIDE PROGRAM

Philosophical Basis

The philosophy behind *Bully-Proofing Your School* is one of shifting the balance of power and fear. Power in most schools rests with the administration and staff, but bullies challenge this traditional power structure by creating fear and apprehension in the school, both at the administration level and at the student level. School bullies muster a great deal of power through the fear they create and schools tend to respond by mounting an administrative "power program." This is often an unsuccessful and unproductive escalation of power forces. Not only does this armament take a great deal of time and energy, it often has little effect on changing the behavior of the bullies. Moreover, there is a clear loss of appropriate focus: the vast majority of the student body—the caring majority—is abandoned for the bullying few. Such a display of bully power evokes great fear in the caring majority of students because they begin to see how much power bullies acquire. It is this imbalance of power that the *Bully-Proofing Your School* program is designed to alleviate.

There are three overall goals in implementing a bully-proofing program. These involve systematic changes as well as individual skill development: (1) shifting the power balance within the entire school system ("Paradigm Shift"), (2) participating in the development of the program by the community of parents, the administration, and the staff, and (3) training in the skills and knowledge base necessary to implement the program. Understanding the theme of shifting the balance of power to the caring majority of students is critical to the success of the program. Since the caring majority sees and experiences bullying behavior but lacks the confidence or knowledge to take action, skill development is essential. The confidence gained from skill development will curb the pervasive fear kindled by the bullies.

It is essential that the adult members of the school network (the community of parents, administration, and staff) understand and support this shift in the balance of power prior to beginning this program. When there is support from all, then each member of the network can see his or her own value in the implementation of the program. Explaining this "Paradigm Shift" is the main goal of the program orientation presentation, which is detailed later in this chapter. Once this shift is accepted by all, implementation of the individual program components can be planned during staff training. Each member of the network has a critical role to play and therefore needs to gain the skills and knowledge that will be taught in the staff training component. See Handout 3-4.

Bully-Proofing Your School is a preventative approach rather than a reactive one. The emphasis is positive rather than punitive. Bullying behaviors are dealt with directly in a matter-of-fact fashion; bullies are held accountable for their behaviors. As a result, the school will become a safe and caring environment for all students. Likewise, consistency in addressing bullying behaviors and supporting positive interactions is essential to effect change within the school. This commitment to safety and caring must come from all. Each conflict that slips by the staff contributes to the feeling students have that they are not protected and allows bullying interactions to escalate. The staff needs to "catch" three supportive, positive behaviors for every correction of a negative behavior to create a caring school environment.

Encouraging Staff Participation

In the next section of this chapter is an agenda for the program orientation presentation to be made to staff members and parents. In addition to introducing the necessity for and the basic principles of this program, a goal of that presentation will be to encourage all staff members to participate in implementing the *Bully-Proofing Your School* program. While the majority of the staff probably believe, in a general sense, that it is good to stop bullies or that something needs to be done in your school, you may still encounter roadblocks (set up by these same staff members) when you begin the process of adopting a school-wide bullying program and request commitment and participation. Some of the most common attitudinal impediments to overcome in your orientation presentation include:

◆ **Some of the staff may not feel that it is necessary to intervene in bullying situations, that "children should learn to solve their own problems."**

The reality is that children are looking to adults to provide a safe environment at school and find it very difficult to cope with aggressive situations themselves. Bullying involves an inequity of power, which must be balanced with adult intervention.

◆ **Staff members will have different comfort levels for intervention. Staff discomfort may be manifested by ignoring bullying behavior.**

Ignoring bullying behavior will not make the problem disappear. The staff should understand that the problem of bullying is going to be a focus within the school, and that with everyone working toward the same goal, progress can be made. All staff members will be fully supported in their intervention efforts.

◆ **Even if staff members are willing to provide intervention, they will not automatically have the skills to do so.**

As part of the staff training component of this program, the staff members will learn tools for intervention in bullying situations that will empower them, and their students, within the classroom.

◆ **Some staff members may be intimidated by student bullies themselves, or have discomfort in general for intervening in conflict-ridden, aggressive situations.**

Teachers express feeling bullied and intimidated by even third, fourth, and fifth grade students because children who ignore staff requests and believe they do not need to respond become intimidating and threatening to the teacher's position. This program, in addition to assisting student victims, will also be helpful for staff members as it focuses on strengthening students, staff members, and parents to become more confident and effective in intervening with bullying behaviors.

◆ **Often staff members feel isolated and unsupported in the classroom and in other areas of the school grounds (e.g., in the hallways, on the playground, in the cafeteria) when it comes to intervening with individual students.**

It is important to acknowledge how, by making a school-wide commitment to the bully-proofing program, all the staff members can support each other in intervening in difficult situations, using their varying conflict resolution styles to complement those of the other staff members.

Introducing the Program Into Your School

You've picked up this book, and read this far, so whether you are an administrator, classroom teacher, other member of a school staff, or a parent, you obviously feel concern about the level of bullying behavior occurring in your school. Now how do you make the leap from your isolated concern to a school-wide program against bullying? It's really not that difficult. Simply take the initiative to talk to other members of the school community about bullying. You will probably be pleasantly surprised: Almost everyone would like schools to be safe. That's a goal most people can agree upon. Then it's really just a matter of obtaining administrative support for introducing this program into the school, and convincing others who will be involved in implementing it to participate. That's what the following agenda for the program orientation presentation will assist you in doing.

To begin the adoption of a school-wide program against bullying, follow these procedures:

1. Obtain administrative support for the *Bully-Proofing Your School* program. This may require first enlisting a number of individuals (teachers and/or parents) to your cause.

   As part of that support, the administration should create a formal policy regarding bullying with the following three minimum standards/expectations for staff and students:

▼ MISSION STATEMENT

Our goal is to make the school environment safe for children both physically and psychologically.

1. Stop the behavior—There will be "no-bullying rules" enforced by staff members.

2. What the students will do—The students will help others by speaking out and getting adult help.

3. How students should treat one another—The students will use extra effort to include everyone.

Note: As you will discover in Chapter Four, these three policy statements directly correspond to the recommended classroom rules.

It should be made clear within the orientation that these three policy standards are not negotiable, but that the specific classroom rules regarding them, intervention strategies, consequences assigned, etc. will be determined by staff member collaboration within the training component of this program. It should also be understood that if some staff members, for some reason, choose not to participate in the staff training, they and their students will still be responsible for meeting the policy objectives by whichever means they choose to employ.

2. Identify, with the assistance of the administration, a person or persons to act as a **facilitator** to spearhead the program adoption

RESOURCE GUIDE

See "Books for Administrators, School-Based Teams, and Specialists" for additional sources of information on policy development.

process. This person could be an administrator, school psychologist, social worker, counselor, school team member, or even a lead teacher.

As described in the Overview of this manual, the facilitator fills many roles in program implementation. But not every responsibility must be undertaken by this one individual. It is unusual to locate one person with all of the many skills necessary to guide each program component, which should not be viewed as a stumbling block to program adoption. The facilitator need only be able to organize the effort; to locate, enlist, and coordinate the contributions of others with the strongest skills in the appropriate areas. The "facilitator" could even be a school-based team. Each human resource situation within each school will be unique.

Helpful skills/characteristics of an individual filling the role of facilitator include:

◆ Strong organizational skills to guide the program adoption process.

◆ Possession of a "network" within the school community from which to locate individuals to assist in the program adoption effort, if necessary.

◆ The respect of the majority of the school community in order to garner support for the program.

◆ Flexibility in time scheduling in order to work with teachers and students in their classrooms during the day.

◆ Some training in or basic knowledge of child development, group processes, social skills training, conflict resolution techniques, and behavioral management.

3. Once the facilitator (for simplicity's sake, the facilitator will be referred to as a single individual within this manual) has been enlisted, he or she should become familiar and comfortable with the principles and procedures of this program, and prepare for the program orientation presentation. To assist in this process, reproducible materials have been provided at the end of this chapter.

After an agreement to adopt the *Bully-Proofing Your School* program has been made, a letter to parents (see Figure 3-1) should be sent, notifying them of the new school policy against bullying and inviting them to attend the orientation presentation in order to express their concerns/opinions and participate in implementation.

Letter 3-1

The facilitator should prepare any handouts/ transparencies to be used as part of the presentation and determine a staff training schedule to be announced which will fit into the schedule of the particular school. Recommendations for scheduling staff training include planning a session per faculty meeting or using a staff development day to conduct a half-day or full-day training session. Monthly follow-up sessions to discuss progress and troubleshoot should also be built in. If training sessions are scheduled for faculty meeting times, approximately six meetings of 45 minutes each will be necessary to train the staff.

▼ SPECIAL NOTE

It is important that a clear philosophy and policy guidelines be developed for a school implementing a school-wide program against bullying. When this task is successfully completed, it provides students, parents, and staff members with a vision for the school, while providing staff with a common direction and guidelines for the day-to-day implementation of this philosophy.

While it is not the purpose of this manual to provide detailed information on the process of establishing philosophy and guidelines, and a recommended policy statement is provided for your use, it is nevertheless an extremely important task that should be given the attention of the administration, particularly, and the staff members and parents as well. In implementing *Bully-Proofing Your School,* it is essential that the school develop the philosophical vision and daily guidelines to the extent that they provide a straight avenue to fulfilling the mission statement of creating a school which is safe for children both physically and psychologically.

There are a number of models which provide schools with detailed road maps for successfully completing the policy-making process. It is suggested that a school examine an appropriate model before undertaking this task. One of the most comprehensive guides available commercially is *Foundations: Establishing Positive Discipline Policies.* The *Foundations* program lists the following as key features of effective school-wide policies:*

1. An effective policy communicates the vision of a positive and invitational school.

2. An effective policy must be designed by staff.

3. An effective policy is written with involvement from parents and students.

4. An effective policy is centered around a school mission statement.

5. An effective policy describes procedures used by staff to achieve consistency in their day-to-day interactions with students.

6. An effective policy outlines expectations and procedures for consistent staff supervision of school-wide areas.

7. While striving for consistency, the policy should provide flexibility for all classroom teachers to set up and run their own classrooms.

8. An effective policy specifies when to involve administration in behavioral problems and outlines procedures to use when severe misbehavior occurs.

9. An effective policy guides staff development and change.

10. An effective policy is systematically evaluated, revised, and updated each year.

11. An effective policy is user friendly.

12. An effective policy is aligned with school board policy and relevant to state or federal laws.

---

* Reprinted with permission from Sprick, Sprick, & Garrison, 1992.

4. The facilitator then conducts the program orientation presentation, the beginning of the adoption process. The main goals of the orientation presentation are to: (1) introduce both the new bullying policy and this program, (2) strongly encourage as many staff members and parents as possible to participate in the program, (3) generate enthusiasm to begin the school-wide program adoption, (4) introduce the Five Steps to Building a Caring and Safe Climate, and (5) administer Colorado School Climate Surveys.

The orientation presentation should take approximately 60 minutes and, ideally, take place before the school year begins. Adult

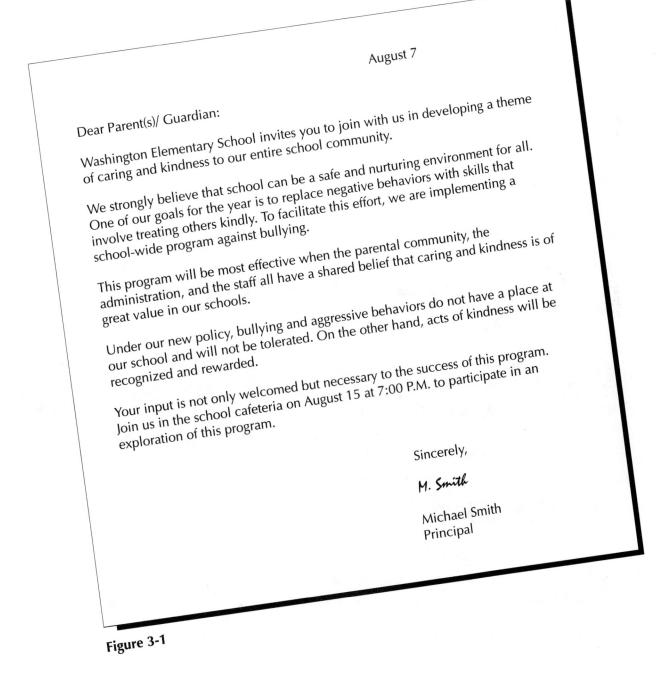

August 7

Dear Parent(s)/ Guardian:

Washington Elementary School invites you to join with us in developing a theme of caring and kindness to our entire school community.

We strongly believe that school can be a safe and nurturing environment for all. One of our goals for the year is to replace negative behaviors with skills that involve treating others kindly. To facilitate this effort, we are implementing a school-wide program against bullying.

This program will be most effective when the parental community, the administration, and the staff all have a shared belief that caring and kindness is of great value in our schools.

Under our new policy, bullying and aggressive behaviors do not have a place at our school and will not be tolerated. On the other hand, acts of kindness will be recognized and rewarded.

Your input is not only welcomed but necessary to the success of this program. Join us in the school cafeteria on August 15 at 7:00 P.M. to participate in an exploration of this program.

Sincerely,

M. Smith

Michael Smith
Principal

Figure 3-1

representatives from the school network should be invited: the administration, the community of parents, the entire school staff. Five main points will be covered in the orientation presentation:

- The "Paradigm Shift" (or power balance shift) will be described.

- The need to develop new rules against bullying behavior will be stressed. (The actual development of these rules will be accomplished by the staff as a whole during the staff training component of this program.)

- The formal school policy regarding bullying will be presented. (The actual training in the skills required by the policy will be reserved for the staff training and student instruction components of this program.)

- The Five Steps to Building a Caring and Safe Climate will be presented.

- The Climate Surveys will be introduced. The Staff and Parent Surveys can be administered at this time.

Following is an outline of an agenda for the orientation presentation. The facilitator should customize the outline to suit his or her own preference and presenting style.

▼ ORIENTATION PRESENTATION AGENDA

I. Introduction

Provide the attendees with information about why a bully-proofing program is necessary. Include information about the scope of the problem, define bullying and why children need help with it, and identify bullies and victims. (See the Overview and Chapters One and Two of this manual for specific points.)

Handout/Transparency 3-2

II. Presentation of New Bullying Policy

Review the Mission Statement and its three components. Emphasize that the program's goal is to utilize the existing strengths of the students and staff.

III. Introduction of the Philosophy of the *Bully-Proofing Your School Program*

Transparency 3-3

A. Introduce the "Paradigm Shift"

To change the balance of power, a school must replace fear with a sense of caring and support for all. Knowing when and how to intervene is what fosters positive power. Shifting the balance of power in the school setting means conceptualizing in a new and different way. Rather than a reactive approach, this program teaches a preventative approach that values diversity, shifts the power balance within the entire school, and emphasizes positive, caring behaviors.

Key elements of the "Paradigm Shift"

◆ The staff members and students must be supported in assuming increased responsibility and allowing the principal to abandon the role of "all-powerful."

◆ The "caring majority" of students can be and will be the backbone of the caring school environment in this program.

◆ There will be an opportunity to customize this program to the specific needs of the student body.

Handout/Transparency 3-4

B. Comprehensive Systems Approach

Most behavioral intervention programs encourage a vertical power structure (i.e., the power to change the bullies lies in the hands of the administration). *Bully-Proofing Your School* is different. It rests on the premise that the power must lie in the attitudes of the students, the staff, and the community, with support rather than power delivered from the administration. Thus, a more horizontal power structure is created.

C. Identification of the Problem

Power is out of balance in many schools because of fear. Fear leaves both the students and the staff believing that they cannot impact the behavior of bullies.

D. The School Network

It is important to understand the relationship between and different roles of the individual components of the school network. Parents have an interest in knowing how to help their children handle bullying behavior and how to defuse bullying situations. Parents can join with the school components of the network in promoting and supporting the development of caring behaviors at home and at school.

E. Individual Staff Differences—Diversity in Beliefs and Feelings

A diversity of conflict resolution styles among the staff is an **asset**. There is strength in recognizing and employing this diversity in beliefs and skills to create a comprehensive program. Consistency does not equal effectiveness. Effectiveness is eroded over time when everyone responds similarly to conflict.

F. Educative Component—Knowledge of Bully-Victim Problems vs. Normal Peer Conflict

There is a great deal of power in knowing the difference between when to intervene and when the conflict is developmentally appropriate and the children involved can solve it on their own.

G. Skill Development

There is also a great deal of power in knowing **how** to intervene.

H. Program Planning

Through discussion, a bully-proofing program can be developed to fit the individual needs of a staff and school.

I. **Tailoring the Curriculum for Individual Students**

Assessing the capabilities of the students in implementing the classroom curriculum in terms of intervening with the bullies and in supporting the victims will occur with this program.

J. **Need Assessment**

What would be different for the staff and community if this program were to be successful (e.g., fewer behavioral referrals or a more positive atmosphere at school)? Identification of Components needing improvement to shift the climate (see Handout 3-5, Climate Chart).

K. **Review of the Five Steps to Building a Caring and Safe Climate.**

L. **Introduction of Climate Surveys and administration of Staff and Parent Surveys.**

IV. **Discussion Period**

Allow for a discussion period in which staff members and parents can openly discuss their feelings and beliefs about intervening with aggressive children.

V. **Conclusion**

Before ending the presentation, be sure to notify the staff members of the time/location of the first staff training session.

LETTER 3-1
Sample Orientation Presentation Notice

_____

Dear _____ :

_____ Elementary School invites you to join with us in developing a theme of caring and kindness to our entire school community.

We strongly believe that school can be a safe and nurturing environment for all. One of our goals for the year is to replace negative behaviors with skills that involve treating others kindly. To facilitate this effort, we are implementing a school-wide program against bullying.

This program will be most effective when the parents, the administration, and the staff all have a shared belief that caring and kindness is of great value in our schools.

Under our new policy, bullying and aggressive behaviors do not have a place at our school and will not be tolerated. On the other hand, acts of kindness will be recognized and rewarded.

Your input is not only welcomed but necessary to the success of this program. Join us _____ on _____ at _____ to participate in an exploration of this program.

Sincerely,

Mission Statement

Our goal is to make the school environment safe for children both physically and psychologically.

1. Stop the behavior—There will be "no-bullying rules" enforced by staff members.

2. What the students will do—The students will help others by speaking out and getting adult help.

3. How students should treat one another—The students will use extra effort to include everyone.

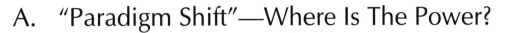

TRANSPARENCY 3-3
Philosophy of the Program

A. "Paradigm Shift"—Where Is The Power?

B. Comprehensive Systems Approach

C. Identification of the Problem

D. The School Network

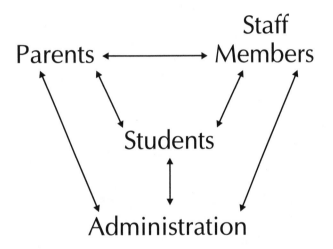

E. Individual Staff Differences—Diversity in Beliefs and Feelings

F. Educative Component—Knowledge of Bully-Victim Problems vs. Normal Peer Conflict

G. Skill Development

H. Program Planning

I. Tailoring Curriculum for Individual Students

J. Need Assessment

Outcome

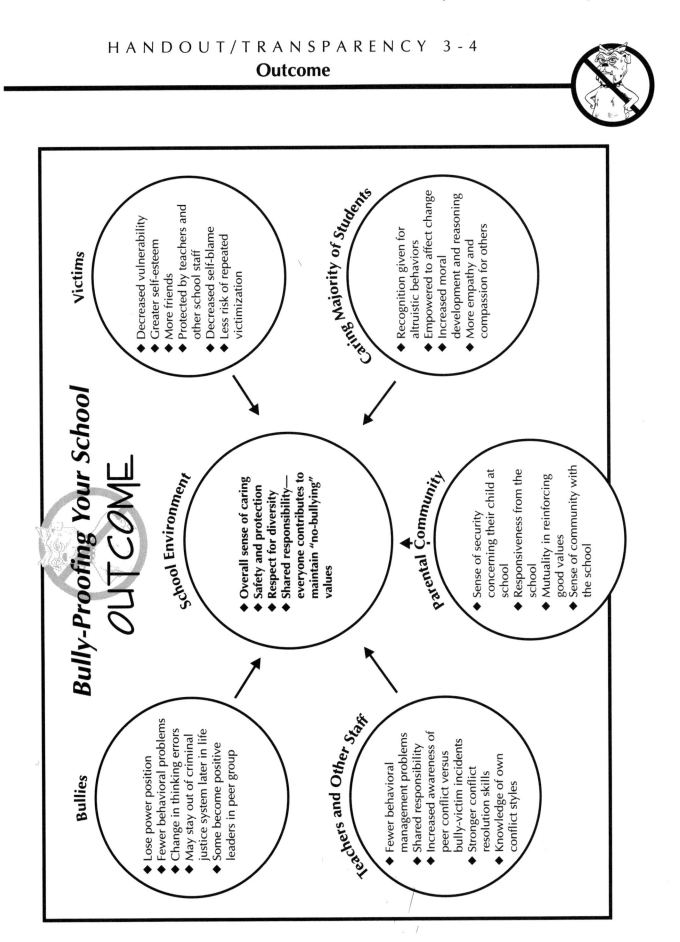

Bully-Proofing Your School
OUTCOME

Victims
- Decreased vulnerability
- Greater self-esteem
- More friends
- Protected by teachers and other school staff
- Decreased self-blame
- Less risk of repeated victimization

Caring Majority of Students
- Recognition given for altruistic behaviors
- Empowered to affect change
- Increased moral development and reasoning
- More empathy and compassion for others

School Environment
- **Overall sense of caring**
- **Safety and protection**
- **Respect for diversity**
- **Shared responsibility— everyone contributes to maintain "no-bullying" values**

Parental Community
- Sense of security concerning their child at school
- Responsiveness from the school
- Mutuality in reinforcing good values
- Sense of community with the school

Bullies
- Lose power position
- Fewer behavioral problems
- Change in thinking errors
- May stay out of criminal justice system later in life
- Some become positive leaders in peer group

Teachers and Other Staff
- Fewer behavioral management problems
- Shared responsibility
- Increased awareness of peer conflict versus bully-victim incidents
- Stronger conflict resolution skills
- Knowledge of own conflict styles

Tools for Planning Your Strategy

The remainder of this chapter contains two parts: a detailed list of the five steps to developing a caring and safe climate and the Colorado School Climate Survey.

The following Climate Development chart provides an overview of what will happen as the environment in the school changes due to adult and student intervention against bullying. Students will feel safer and be more able to learn, teachers will be able to teach, and everyone will be happier in a comfortable, caring climate.

CLIMATE DEVELOPMENT
Stage 1   **Adults Taking Control of Climate** ◆ Evaluation of Problem Areas ◆ General Rules and Expectations ◆ Bully-Proofing Rules ◆ Participation of Parents, Staff, and Students
Stage 2   **Skills Development for Teachers and Students** ◆ Teacher Training/Student Training ◆ Protective Skills (HA HA, SO) ◆ Helping Skills (CARES) ◆ Practicing Skills
Stage 3   **Empowering Teachers and Students to Set the Climate** ◆ Safe, Positive Climate ◆ Learning Climate ◆ Sharing, Supportive Climate

Briefly, the five steps to developing a caring and safe climate in the school provide:

A chart showing the process of developing a caring and safe climate and a list of questions for you to answer which will guide you in how to plan your strategy.

A checklist of areas to evaluate. You can see at a glance which areas are already well established pluses and which ones need attention.

A chance to analyze your current goals, areas of strength, and goals.

A guide to isolating primary areas that need improvement and the opportunity to create a plan for each area identified.

A place to begin and encouragement to start. You know what is needed; you know your strengths and weaknesses; now you can meet the challenge of creating a caring and safe climate.

The Colorado School Climate Survey provides an excellent survey of students, parents, students, and school staff, which can be used to isolate problem areas and provide a better perspective of problem areas from several points of view. You can return to the survey at any time to analyze a particular response or reassess your improvement. You may want to administer the survey again six months or a year later to evaluate your progress or home in on a particular problem.

The Five Steps to Creating a Caring and Safe Climate

Step 1.   Assess the current climate of your school

Data collected from multiple sources will provide the clearest picture with which to plan effective intervention.

This is done formally by assessment with the Colorado School Climate Survey.

The Staff survey can be administered during this session.

This is done informally by observation.

Have a faculty and staff discussion focusing on the following bulleted questions. This can be done during the orientation session or reserved for one of the staff training sessions (see Chapter 4).

- ◆ **How do students treat each other?**

    - ◊ Notice how the students interact with one another. Watch for instances of verbal and physical harassment as well as for social alienation. Where in the school do you see this happen? Most important, what do you see the students currently doing to make an effort to stop these behaviors?

    - ◊ Imagine you are a new student entering the cafeteria. Do you see a table that looks comfortable and accepting to approach?

    - ◊ Watch a classroom where student presentations are taking place. What are the listeners doing? Are they paying attention, smiling, and giving support? Are they chatting during the presentation, doing homework, or even heckling or ridiculing the presenters?

    - ◊ Stand outside as the school buses are loading. Do you see pushing and shoving or is there some sense of orderliness? Look around to see if any child is on crutches, has a leg brace, or is handicapped in some fashion. How are the other students treating this student?

    - ◊ Walk around the playground at recess time. Notice if any boy or girl is standing alone on the sidelines. How many children do you see left out? Watch the activities being played—are they fair and inclusive or is one child being bossy and setting the rules about who can play and who cannot?

◇ Watch students during passing periods.

◆ **How does the staff treat students?**

◇ Stand in the hallways as children are arriving. Do you see staff greeting the children? How many know names?

◇ Watch a P.E. class, music period, or art class. Pay special attention to the children who appear not to fit in because of lack of interest or skill. Do you see any effort being made to include these children?

◇ The cafeteria is a good place to observe. What are the rules regarding seating, throwing away trash, and permission to leave? Do you hear friendly conversation or exclusions, put-downs, and gossiping? Are any efforts made to assure that no child eats alone?

◆ **How does the staff treat each other?**

◇ At the next faculty meeting, notice how discussions are conducted. Does everyone feel free to express an opinion? Do you see cliques amongst the staff? Is diversity of thought respected?

◇ Think back on the last time there was a problem to be handled. Who made the final decision? Was discussion allowed?

◇ Are all members of the staff given the same respect? How do classroom teachers respond to support staff, such as aides in the library or computer room?

◆ **How does the administration treat the staff?**

◇ If a staff member has a suggestion for improvement or a new program worth consideration, how can he or she call it to someone's attention?

◇ What are the channels of communication?

◇ Are decisions made and handed down or is some democratic process involved?

Step 2. Decide what kind of climate you want for your school

Look at the list below. These are the characteristics of a safe and caring climate. Notice that climate is a comprehensive issue. It is the tone set on many levels throughout the school.

Put a check mark by the characteristics that are currently true for your school climate.

◆ **General Policy**
  ❏ Clear policy of behavior expectation
  ❏ Zero tolerance for bullying and harassment

❑ Knowledge of rules and expectations by all students and staff

❑ Understanding of normal conflict versus bully/harassment behavior

❑ Use of names of students and staff for personal connectedness

❑ Staff involvement in policy development, implementation, and assessment

❑ An identified adult mentor for every student to ensure a safe climate

❑ Students have protective skills to decrease their vulnerability for victimization

❑ Music, art, and other activities have a caring community component

❑ P.E. focuses directly on teaching aspects of character

❑ Consistent, predictable, and effective discipline is evident

❑ Efforts of all students are valued and recognized

◆ **Caring Majority of Students Set the Climate by:**
❑ Students supporting one another

❑ Inclusion of all

❑ Acceptance of diversity

❑ Creative problem solving to build a safe environment

❑ Recognition of caring behavior

◆ **Balancing Climate and Control by:**
❑ Understanding issues of power/empowerment around discipline

❑ Redirecting student's need for power into positive climate

❑ Using developmentally appropriate intervention

❑ Giving positive reinforcement for appropriate behavior

❑ Taking a no-nonsense approach with bullies

◆ **Bus Drivers Reinforce a Caring Climate by:**
❑ Knowing student names

❑ Understanding buses as an extension of the school

❑ Being sensitive to the tone the bus experience sets for remainder of day

❑ Rewarding positive bus behavior

❑ Maintaining a caring community on the bus

❑ Encouraging positive behavior at bus stops

◆ **Community Nurtures Students by:**
❑ Supportive tips and articles in local newspapers

❑ Use of local media

❑ Involvement of churches and service clubs

❑ Support of service to community projects

❏ Family education through newsletters, PTO meetings, and general education

❏ Using bully-proofing language.

Step 3. Identify current strengths and weaknesses in the climate

Look at the Climate Chart (Handout 3-5). Remember that a shift in climate is a comprehensive shift. Strengthening one area alone will not allow an effective caring majority to build among the students. Shifting the silent majority to a caring majority is a dynamic process that students must sense is present in all areas of their school.

◆ **Identify goals in each area.**

◆ **Discuss areas of strength.**

Step 4. Create a plan to improve areas of weakness

A caring community feels safe and worry-free. It consists of a student-controlled but staff-supported climate.

Use the list below to develop a plan for each area identified as needing improvement.

◆ **P.E., Music, Art and Other Activities**

◇ Goals of program are to teach skill along with character

◇ No inappropriate language

◇ Sportsmanship is valued and rewarded

◇ Goals reinforce the climate

◇ Participation and inclusion are supported and encouraged

◇ Yearbook or school-wide publications set a tone of pride and inclusion

◇ Student council is not just a popularity contest

◆ **Academics**

◇ School as well as individual accomplishment are recognized

◇ All assignments in class are completed

◇ Students helping students is promoted

◇ Harassment about grades is not tolerated

◆ **Discipline (see Chapter Nine)**

◇ Training of disciplinary personnel

◇ Training of security personnel

◇ Training of school resource officer

◇ Disciplinary personnel participate in developing a compassionate school climate

- **Counseling and Guidance**

  ◇ Teach protective skills to decrease victimization

  ◇ Self-advocacy

  ◇ Teach coping skills to deal with loss and disappointments in life

  ◇ Students are seen as a resource

- **To and From School**

  ◇ Plans in place to stop harassment and intimidation

  ◇ Positive and safe environment for those who walk to and from school

  ◇ Positive and safe buses

- **Parents as Partners**

  ◇ Partnerships have been established with parents

  ◇ Parents are supported and valued

  ◇ Parents are supportive of teachers and staff

- **School Rituals**

  ◇ Plan for connecting all students to school

  ◇ Plan for welcoming new students during year

  ◇ All students have an adult mentor they can go to for help

  ◇ All students take responsibility for making their school safe

- **Recognition**

  ◇ Inclusive—the school is proud

  ◇ Ways to recognize—we all make a difference in others' success

  ◇ Pep rally for school as a whole, not just for individuals and teams

- **Tone Set by the Physical Plant**

  ◇ Murals

  ◇ Art in the hallways

  ◇ Student work displayed from many levels, not just the most talented

  ◇ Pride in school evident

  ◇ Recognition for areas other than academic achievement and athletics

◆ **Community Partners**

　◇ All students are accepted and supported in the community

　◇ Community helps to assure that students are safe going to and from school

Step 5.　Decide when to begin the bully-proofing program which will shift the silent majority to a caring majority

◆ Establish bully-proofing rules throughout the school.

◆ Begin the classroom curriculum.

◆ Develop the protective skills and caring skills.

◆ Establish a plan to develop the caring majority in each classroom and school-wide.

◆ Give recognition for positive caring activities.

◆ Students solve the majority of their own problems.

◆ Speaking up, displaying courage, and helping another are values in the school.

◆ Children are aware that a caring majority is in place. They feel safe and know where support will come from if they are harassed or bullied.

Creating a Caring and Safe Climate

The process of creating a caring and safe climate should involve these steps:

1. The school selects a cadre or committee of staff to explore the issues of school safety and climate.

2. The school identifies the kind of climate they would like to achieve.

3. The school conducts both a formal and an informal assessment to determine what the current climate is from the perspective of the students, parents, and staff.

4. The school identifies current strengths and weaknesses.

5. Strategies are identified and implemented to achieve the climate of choice.

6. The school assesses the effectiveness of the chosen strategies.

HANDOUT 3-5
Climate Chart

List climate goal(s). What strategies are you currently using in the following areas to achieve the climate you want?

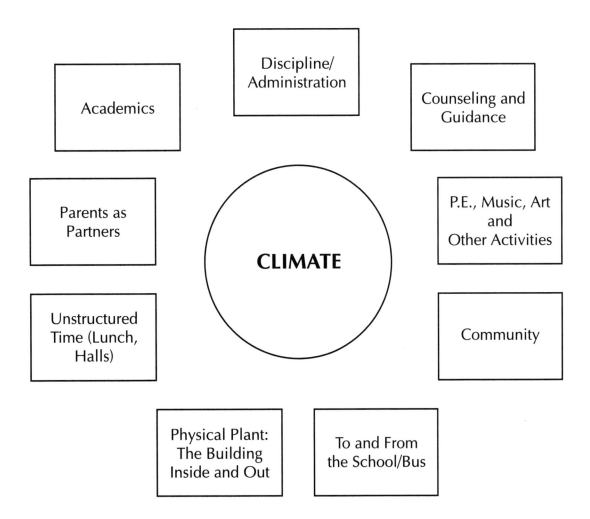

Draw a solid line to areas of significant impact on climate and a dotted line to what the school is doing well.

HANDOUT 3-6
Colorado School Climate Survey

Description

Bullying and harassment in the schools can present students and school staff with significant and far-reaching problems. In order to intervene effectively with these problems, it is important to thoroughly assess the extent and nature of bullying within the school. The **Colorado School Climate Survey (CSCS)** is an instrument that provides comprehensive information about bullying and school climate as perceived by students, parents, and school staff. Separate versions are available for elementary and secondary schools. The **CSCS** provides information across four important domains:

Has This Happened to You?

The **first domain** asks about incidences of bullying personally experienced by the respondent. At the elementary level, this domain assesses verbal, physical, and exclusionary forms of bullying, as well as stealing and threatening. The secondary school version of the **CSCS** includes questions about sexual and ethnic/racial harassment as well.

Have You Seen This Happen?

The **second domain** asks about incidences of bullying observed by the respondent. Respondents answer questions about each of the types of bullying listed in the first domain. Together, these two domains provide a comprehensive evaluation of bullying behaviors in the school.

For each of these first two domains, follow-up questions are asked about perpetrators and locations of the bullying behaviors as well as what students did in response to the incidences (both experienced and observed).

How Safe Do You Feel?

The **third domain** includes questions about how safe respondents believe that students are across several locations in the school.

What Is Your School Like?

The **fourth domain** asks questions about respondents' perceptions of the overall school climate. School climate encompasses the general areas of adult and student helping behavior, sense of inclusion, and enjoyment of school.

Survey results provide each school with a profile that includes information from each of the above domains. This information is helpful both in establishing a baseline measure of the current school climate and in designing effective interventions to achieve the desired school climate. The **CSCS** can also be used to document the progress of identified interventions.

HANDOUT 3-7
Colorado School Climate Survey

Group Administration Instructions for Students

Please read this completely before administering the CSCS.

1. Read through the questions before you read them out loud to the students.

2. You may define words that are not familiar to the students. However, if you are asked to clarify what is meant by a particular item, let the students know that they should answer it as best they can according to whether or not they think the behavior has occurred or the item is true.

3. FYI: for the section that asks about frequency of bullying behaviors, "Less than one time per week" refers to an event that has happened on one or more occasions, but has not occurred on a weekly basis.

4. Hand out the questionnaire.

Say: **This set of questions asks you to tell about your school and things that may or may not have happened to you at school. There are no right or wrong answers. Please answer the questions to show what you think about your school. Please do not write your name anywhere on the questionnaire. This way, your answers will remain private.**

5. Read each question and pause briefly to allow time to respond. Remember to read any instructions (e.g., **check only one box, check all that apply**) that go along with the question. Finally, read the response choices (e.g., never, less than one time per week, one time per week, two to four times per week, five or more times per week) after you have read the first two questions of each of the four domains (Has This Happened to You?, Have You Seen This Happen?, How Safe Do You Feel?, and What Is Your School Like?)

6. Collect questionnaires and return them to the designated person. As you collect the questionnaires, please be sure to check that the students have completed the form properly.

Note: It is important that the questionnaires are read to the students. This is to help ensure that the students, regardless of reading level, understand all the questions. The questionnaire can be administered over multiple sessions. Please administer at least one of the four domains (Has This Happened to You?, Have You Seen This Happen?, How Safe Do You Feel?, and What Is Your School Like?) at a time.

Suggested time for completion is approximately 30 minutes.

Colorado School Climate Survey

School _____   Code _____

Date _____

Elementary School Student Report

This set of questions asks you to tell about your school and things that may or may not have happened to you at school. There are no right or wrong answers. Please answer the questions to show what you think about your school.

Has This Happened to You?

For the following, check only **ONE** box for each item.

During the *past month:*	never	less than 1 time per week	1 time per week	2–4 times per week	5 or more times per week
I was hit, pushed, or kicked by other kids					
Other kids said mean things, teased me, or called me names					
Other kids told stories about me that were not true					
Other kids did not let me join in what they were doing					
Other kids took things that belong to me					
Other kids threatened to hurt me or take things					

If any of these happened to you (**check all that apply**):

What did you do?

I got help from an adult at school	
I got help from another kid	
I hit, kicked, or pushed the kid	
I told the kid to stop	
I told the kid I agreed with what he or she said about me	
I avoided the kid so I would not get hurt or teased again	

I got help from my parents	
I ignored it or walked away	
I said mean things, teased, or called the kid names	
I tried to stop the kid by saying or doing something funny	
I said things to myself to help myself feel better	
I did nothing	

HANDOUT 3-8 (*continued*)

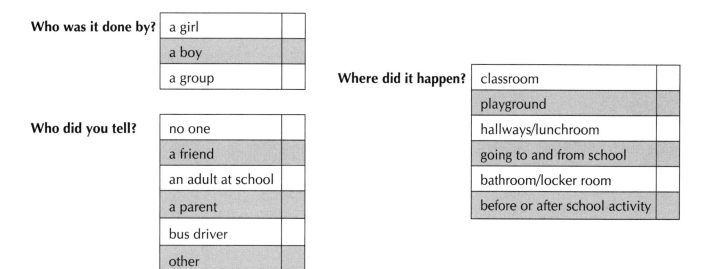

Who was it done by?

a girl	
a boy	
a group	

Where did it happen?

classroom	
playground	
hallways/lunchroom	
going to and from school	
bathroom/locker room	
before or after school activity	

Who did you tell?

no one	
a friend	
an adult at school	
a parent	
bus driver	
other	

Have You Seen This Happen?

For the following, check only **ONE** box for each item.

(Check the box **ONLY** if the item happened to someone else (not to you)).

During the *past month:*	never	less than 1 time per week	1 time per week	2–4 times per week	5 or more times per week
I saw someone get hit, pushed, or kicked by other kids					
I heard kids say mean things, tease, or call someone names					
I heard kids tell stories about someone that were not true					
I saw kids not let someone join in what they were doing					
I saw or heard that kids took things that belong to someone else					
I heard kids threaten to hurt someone or take things					

If you heard or saw any of these things happen (**check all that apply**):

What did you do?

I did nothing	
I asked the kid who was hurt/ teased/left out to play with me	
I helped the kid who was hurt/ teased/left out to get away	
I helped the kid come up with ideas about how to handle the problem	

I got help from an adult at school	
I stood up to the kid who was teasing or hurting the other kid	
I talked to the kid who was hurt/ teased/left out about how he/she felt	

HANDOUT 3-8 (*continued*)

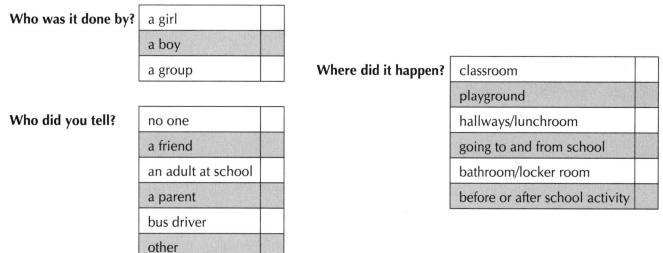

Who was it done by?

a girl	
a boy	
a group	

Who did you tell?

no one	
a friend	
an adult at school	
a parent	
bus driver	
other	

Where did it happen?

classroom	
playground	
hallways/lunchroom	
going to and from school	
bathroom/locker room	
before or after school activity	

How Safe Do You Feel?

During the **past month**, this is how safe I felt in each of these places (check only **ONE** box for each):

	very unsafe & scared	unsafe & scared	kind of unsafe	kind of safe	safe	very safe
In my classroom						
On the playground						
In the hallways and lunchroom						
Going to and from school						
In the bathroom/locker room						
At before or after school activities						

What Is Your School Like?

Check the **ONE** box that best describes you/your school:

	never/hardly ever true	sometimes true	often true	almost always/ always true
The other kids help if they see someone being bullied or picked on				
Kids tell adults at school when other kids are being bullied or being picked on				
If someone is alone at lunch or recess, others will invite him or her to join in				
Kids at this school encourage other kids to do the best they can at their schoolwork				

HANDOUT 3-8 (*continued*)

	never/hardly ever true	sometimes true	often true	almost always/ always true
There are clear rules at our school				
The teachers and staff help if they see someone being bullied or picked on				
Kids who misbehave take a lot of my teacher's time				
Adults at this school care that the students do the best schoolwork they can				
My school tries to make everyone feel included				
I usually play with someone at recess				
When I'm upset, other kids try to comfort me or cheer me up				
I like going to school				
I am afraid to go to school				
Most people at this school are kind				

Grade: _____   **I am a:** Boy ☐   Girl ☐   **I usually go to and from school by:**   (check only one)

walking	
bike	
car	
bus	

I am:

Asian	
African American	
Hispanic	
Native American	
White	

(check all that apply)

Other: _____

HANDOUT 3-9
Colorado School Climate Survey

School _____   Code _____

Date _____

Elementary School Parent Report

This set of questions asks you to tell about your child's school and things that may or may not have happened to him or her at school. There are no right or wrong answers. Please answer the questions to show what you think about your child's school.

Has This Happened to Your Child?

For the following, check only **ONE** box for each item.

During the *past month:*	never	less than 1 time per week	1 time per week	2–4 times per week	5 or more times per week
My child was hit, pushed, or kicked by other kids					
Other kids said mean things, teased, or called my child names					
Stories were told about my child that were not true					
Other kids did not let my child join in what they were doing					
Other kids took things that belong to my child					
Other kids threatened to hurt my child or take things					

If any of these happened to your child (**check all that apply**):

Who was it done by?

a girl	
a boy	
a group	

Who did your child tell?

no one	
a friend	
an adult at school	
a parent	
bus driver	
other	

Where did it happen?

classroom	
playground	
hallways/lunchroom	
going to and from school	
bathroom/locker room	
before or after school activity	

HANDOUT 3-9 (*continued*)

How Safe Is Your Child?

During the **past month**, this is how safe I felt my child was in each of these places (check only **ONE** box for each):

	very unsafe & scared	unsafe & scared	kind of unsafe	kind of safe	safe	very safe
In the classroom						
On the playground						
In the hallways and lunchroom						
Going to and from school						
In the bathroom/locker room						

What Is Your Child's School Like?

Check the **ONE** box that best describes your child's school experience:

	never/ hardly ever true	sometimes true	often true	almost always/ always true
The other kids help if they see someone being bullied or picked on				
Kids tell teachers when other kids are being bullied or picked on				
If someone is alone at lunch or recess, others will invite him or her to join in				
My child's school tries to make everyone feel included				
Kids at this school encourage other kids to do the best they can at their schoolwork				
There is a consistent disciplinary policy at this school				
The teachers and staff help if they see someone being bullied or picked on				
Kids who misbehave take a lot of the teacher's time				
The administrators support teachers in dealing with students				
Adults at this school care that the students do the best schoolwork they can				
Parental involvement is valued by this school				
I like having my child at this school				
Most people at this school are kind				

HANDOUT 3-9 (*continued*)

Grade: _____   **My child is a:** Boy ☐   Girl ☐   **He/she usually goes to and from school by:**

walking	
bike	
car	
bus	

(check only one)

I am:

Asian	
African American	
Hispanic	
Native American	
White	

(check all that apply)

Other: _____

Colorado School Climate Survey

School _____   Code _____

Date _____

Elementary School Staff Report

This set of questions asks you to tell about your school and things that may or may not have happened at this school. There are no right or wrong answers. Please answer the questions to show what you think about your school.

Has This Happened to Your Students?

For the following, check only **ONE** box for each item.

During the *past month:*	never	less than 1 time per week	1 time per week	2–4 times per week	5 or more times per week
Students were hit, pushed, or kicked by other kids					
Students said mean things, teased, or called other children names					
Students told stories about other kids that were not true					
Students did not let other students join in what they were doing					
Students took things that belong to other students					
Students threatened to hurt other students or take things					

If any of these happened to a student (**check all that apply**):

Who was it done by?

a girl	
a boy	
a group	

Who did the child tell?

no one	
a friend	
an adult at school	
a parent	
bus driver	
other	

Where did it happen?

classroom	
playground	
hallways/lunchroom	
going to and from school	
bathroom/locker room	
before or after school activity	

HANDOUT 3-10 (*continued*)

How Safe Are Your Students?

During the **past month**, this is how safe I felt students were in each of these places (check only **ONE** box for each):

	very unsafe & scared	unsafe & scared	kind of unsafe	kind of safe	safe	very safe
In the classroom						
On the playground						
In the hallways and lunchroom						
Going to and from school						
In the bathroom/locker room						

What Is Your School Like?

Check the **ONE** box that best describes this school:

	never/hardly ever true	sometimes true	often true	almost always/ always true
Other kids help if they see someone being bullied or picked on				
Kids tell teachers when other kids are being bullied or picked on				
If students are alone at lunch or recess, others will invite them to join in				
Kids at this school encourage other kids to do the best they can at their schoolwork				
This school tries to make everyone feel included				
There is a consistent disciplinary policy at this school				
The teachers and staff help if they see someone being bullied or picked on				
Students who misbehave take a lot of my time				
The administrators help me in dealing with students				
Teachers respect each other and try to work together				
Adults at this school care that the students do the best schoolwork they can				
Most people at this school are kind				
I like working at this school				
I feel safe at this school				

THE STAFF TRAINING CURRICULUM

The staff training component of this program is organized so that the facilitator can use the information provided to conduct the sessions for the entire staff. Each session includes an outline of all the information to present, ideas about how to organize staff members in the training, where appropriate, and handout and transparency masters to supplement the presentation.

The staff training component is divided into six sessions of approximately 45 minutes each, so it can easily be conducted in a weekly staff meeting format. However, many schools will want to use a larger block of time, if available, and instead have a half-day or full-day workshop, completing many or all of the sessions in that time period. This will allow them to begin implementing the program with the students sooner. This material can be used in either format.

Of course, another option is to use this chapter as a general outline, customizing the training to the specific needs of a particular school, usually when a staff is already very experienced in school-wide intervention techniques. If this is the case, there are still some basic goals to be met by the training. When providing training for this program, it is crucial to assist staff to:

- ◆ Acknowledge the need for and achieve agreement on a comprehensive bully-proofing intervention among the administration, staff members, and the community of parents.

- ◆ Openly discuss feelings and beliefs about intervening with aggressive children.

- Develop skills and strategies for intervening with aggressive children and supporting more passive children.

- Identify staff members who are more comfortable with different aspects of this intervention and how they can support the less knowledgeable and comfortable members.

- Acknowledge that different styles of handling conflict are valuable and the combination of styles creates a strong team.

- Develop a comprehensive plan in regard to the roles of the administration and staff members in intervening with students and parents, including developing classroom rules and assigning consequences.

- Develop support systems for the victimized children.

- Develop effective methods for intervening with bullies.

- Becoming prepared to teach or co-teach the classroom curriculum.

- Specify a plan for regularly evaluating and reviewing the program to maintain staff skills and fine-tune the procedures when necessary.

Before conducting the training sessions, the facilitator should read and review the information in Chapter Three regarding school-wide intervention, Chapter Five regarding the classroom curriculum, and Chapter Six on creating and maintaining the caring majority. The facilitator can then answer questions staff members might have regarding the types of activities included and the amount of time that program implementation will require.

BULLIES AND BULLYING

SESSION 1

GOAL

The first session of staff training should focus on educating the entire staff about bullying behavior, the difference between normal peer conflict and bullying, and the characteristics of bullies. This is a good time to have staff members explore their feelings about bully situations.

HANDOUTS/TRANSPARENCIES

Transparency 4-1: Definition/Nature of Bullying

Handout/Transparency 4-2: Myth or Fact?

Handout/Transparency 4-3: Bullying Behaviors Chart

Introduction

- In the average elementary school classroom, two to three children spend their day afraid.

- Some children avoid the playground, the cafeteria, and the restroom because they fear they will be teased, humiliated, and picked on by bullies.

- Children usually do not tell adults about bullies because they don't expect adults to help and because they fear retaliation.

- Adults often expect children to solve these problems on their own and don't realize that children need help with these situations.

- Adults usually respond to these situations based on their own experiences with bullies.

- To effectively deal with this problem, a school-wide intervention is necessary.

The Definition of Bullying

Transparency 4-1

- Bullying is occurring when a child is the target, over time, of repeated negative actions. It is not bullying when two children of approximately the same age, strength, or developmental level fight or quarrel.

- Bullying means there is an imbalance of power so that the child being victimized has trouble defending himself or herself.

- Bullying is usually characterized by unequal levels of affect.

▼ STAFF VISUALIZATION EXERCISE

Instruct the staff to sit comfortably with eyes open or closed and remember a time they were bullied, bullied someone, or saw someone bullied. Ask the following questions:

1. Where were you?

2. What role were you playing? Bully? Victim? Observer?

3. How were you feeling?

4. What did you do?

5. What do you wish you had done, or wish someone else had done?

Ask for volunteers to share experiences.

Discuss how traumatic bullying is and how adults bullied as children can remember details years later, similar to a post-traumatic stress disorder. This helps staff members begin to understand the need for bully-proofing and their individual feelings and reactions to bullying.

Transparency 4-1

The Serious Nature of Bullying

Children being bullied need and deserve adult intervention and help; the problem is much more serious than they can solve alone. Without intervention, the problem will not go away. Bullies will keep on bullying unless adults do something about it.

Consequences for Victims

- Drop in self-esteem to a self-defeating, fearful attitude;

- Anxiety, fear, sadness, and possible depression;

- Disrupted academic performance, lack of interest in school, and excessive absences;

- Physical symptoms (e.g., stomachaches, headaches, fatigue); and

- Panic and irrational retaliation.

Handout/Transparency 4-2

Who Are the Bullies and Why Do They Bully?

You can use Handout/Transparency 4-2 as a questionnaire to be handed out regarding the staff members' current views. Or use as an overhead and have a show of hands on whether each statement is a myth or fact, then teach the facts. It can also be used with the facilitator supplying the facts (giving the answers) and encouraging discussion of each point.

Facts

1. Both boys and girls bully, but their tactics are usually different. Boys usually bully with physical aggression, girls with social alienation or humiliation.

2. Bullies are not anxious, insecure children, but have positive (often unrealistic) self-images that reflect a strong need to dominate with power and threat.

3. Bullies are not loners, but almost always have a small network of peers who encourage, admire, and model their bullying behavior.

4. Bullies tend to be at least average or only slightly below average academically.

5. Bullies come in all sizes, and bullies can even intimidate victims who are physically larger than they if there's an imbalance of power.

6. Bullies lack compassion for their victims and feel justified in their actions.

7. Bullies value the rewards they achieve from aggression, such as attention, control over someone, or material possessions.

8. Looking different is **one** reason children are victimized, but not the main reason. Isolation and personality type are more often determining factors.

9. Returned aggression is not usually effective, and in fact excites the bully into further attacks. Assertion, rather than aggression, is effective, however.

10. If all the adults within a school are committed to preventing bullying behavior, requesting adult intervention will help in equalizing the power imbalance between the bully and victim.

11. When bullies are confronted with a united front of their peers who support the victims and believe that bullying behavior is not socially acceptable, their power is defused.

12. Some teachers are threatened by conflict-ridden situations and aggressive children. In this program, teachers identify their predominant conflict resolution styles, and identify other staff members with complementary styles they can turn to for support with difficult situations.

13. Bullies can separate home from school, and be taught responsible school behavior even when aggression is modeled and/or reinforced at home.

14. Bullying behavior does not usually change with traditional therapy, but requires specific intervention techniques that increase skill deficits and correct thinking errors. There are some simple, proven intervention tactics, which will be taught in conjunction with this program, that prevent bullying behavior.

15. It is not a good strategy to bring the parent(s) of a bully and the parent(s) of a victim together, and should be avoided at all costs. It is essential to meet with each set of parents individually to provide them the specific assistance they need to help their child.

16. The cycle of victimization can be broken by working at the school and classroom levels, and by working with an individual child who is victimized.

17. The responsibility for the aggression is the bullies'. However, victims of bullying are not randomly targeted but victimized because of characteristics and behaviors that make them easier targets for a bully. These include being physically weak, crying easily, being anxious and insecure, and lacking age-appropriate social skills.

18. Students with special education needs may be at greater risk of being bullied by others due to factors such as their disability or the fact that they may be less well integrated socially. If they have behavior problems and act out aggressively, they can become provocative victims. If they have trouble processing social cues, they may act shy and inhibited and become passive victims. Having a disability is not the **main** reason children get bullied, however.

Handout/Transparency 4-3

Types of Bullying and Differences Between Male and Female Bullies

◆ Bullying can range from mild name calling or shoving to very severe acts of violence and coercion.

◆ Boys frequently use swift and effective physical aggression such as tripping or elbowing another child in the stomach.

◆ Girls tend to use the tactics of social alienation and intimidation, such as gossiping maliciously, writing spiteful notes, or alienating a peer from play.

◆ Girls can use very destructive, insidious techniques that are hard to detect.

◆ Extortion is a common form of bullying used by both boys and girls.

NEXT SESSION

In the next session, staff members will learn about the dynamics of the bully-victim relationship, and why some children are victimized and why others are not.

The Definition of Bullying

◆ Targeting a child for repetitive negative actions

◆ Imbalance of power so victim can't defend himself/herself

◆ Unequal levels of affect

The Serious Nature of Bullying

◆ Children being bullied **need and deserve adult intervention** and help

◆ Problem is too serious for them to solve alone

◆ Without intervention, the **problem will not go away**

◆ Bullies will keep bullying unless adults do something about it

HANDOUT/TRANSPARENCY 4-2
Myth or Fact?

Directions:

Determine whether each of the following statements is a "myth" or a "fact."

1. Bullies are boys. _____

2. Bullies are insecure and have low self-esteem. _____

3. Bullies don't have friends. _____

4. Bullies are usually failing in school. _____

5. Bullies are physically larger than their victims. _____

6. Bullies don't really mean to hurt their victims. _____

7. Bullies usually feel badly about their actions, but they just can't help themselves. _____

8. Looking different is the main reason children get bullied. _____

9. If the victim fights back, the bully will back down. _____

10. Telling on a bully will only make the situation worse for the victim. _____

11. Other children should stay away from the bully-victim situations or they'll get bullied as well. _____

12. All teachers can learn to handle a bully. _____

13. Unless you change the bully's home life, nothing will help. _____

14. Bullies need therapy to stop bullying. _____

15. Bringing the parents of the victim and of the bully together for discussion is a good idea. _____

16. Once a victim, always a victim. _____

17. Victims have usually brought the trouble upon themselves. _____

18. Learning disabled students are at higher risk of being victimized. _____

Bullying Behaviors Chart

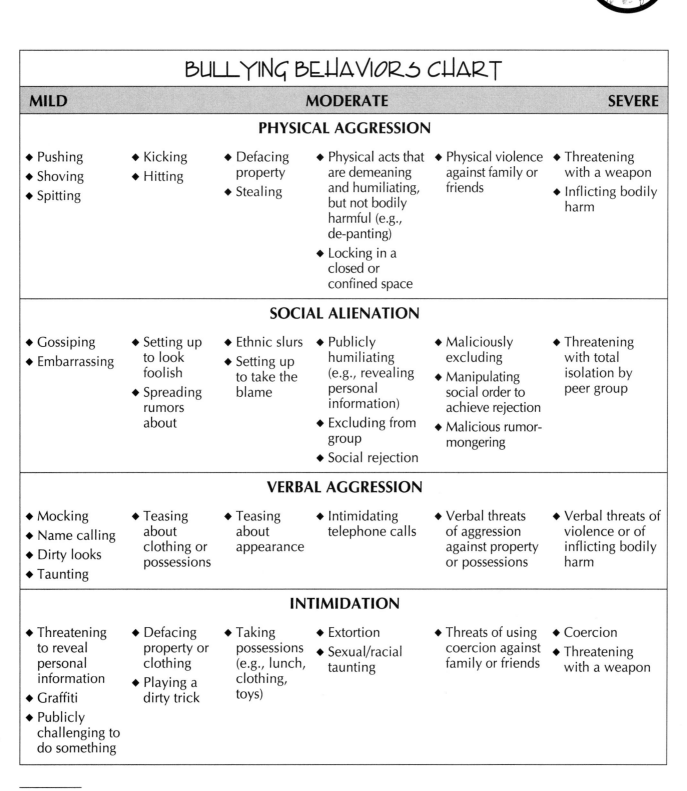

BULLYING BEHAVIORS CHART		
MILD	**MODERATE**	**SEVERE**
PHYSICAL AGGRESSION		
◆ Pushing ◆ Shoving ◆ Spitting ◆ Kicking ◆ Hitting	◆ Defacing property ◆ Stealing ◆ Physical acts that are demeaning and humiliating, but not bodily harmful (e.g., de-panting) ◆ Locking in a closed or confined space ◆ Physical violence against family or friends	◆ Threatening with a weapon ◆ Inflicting bodily harm
SOCIAL ALIENATION		
◆ Gossiping ◆ Embarrassing ◆ Setting up to look foolish ◆ Spreading rumors about	◆ Ethnic slurs ◆ Setting up to take the blame ◆ Publicly humiliating (e.g., revealing personal information) ◆ Excluding from group ◆ Social rejection ◆ Maliciously excluding ◆ Manipulating social order to achieve rejection ◆ Malicious rumor-mongering	◆ Threatening with total isolation by peer group
VERBAL AGGRESSION		
◆ Mocking ◆ Name calling ◆ Dirty looks ◆ Taunting ◆ Teasing about clothing or possessions	◆ Teasing about appearance ◆ Intimidating telephone calls ◆ Verbal threats of aggression against property or possessions	◆ Verbal threats of violence or of inflicting bodily harm
INTIMIDATION		
◆ Threatening to reveal personal information ◆ Graffiti ◆ Publicly challenging to do something ◆ Defacing property or clothing ◆ Playing a dirty trick	◆ Taking possessions (e.g., lunch, clothing, toys) ◆ Extortion ◆ Sexual/racial taunting ◆ Threats of using coercion against family or friends	◆ Coercion ◆ Threatening with a weapon

VICTIMS

SESSION 2

GOAL

To educate staff members on the characteristics of the two types of victims and children who are not victimized, and to review the difference between normal peer conflict and bullying behavior.

HANDOUTS/TRANSPARENCIES

Transparency 4-4: The Two Types of Victims

Characteristics of Victims

- ◆ Children who are the victims of bullying are not randomly targeted.

- ◆ Victims do not appear to be selected because of external deviations or disabilities, but because of personality type.

- ◆ Victims of bullying are anxious, insecure children who lack social skills and the ability to defend themselves.

- ◆ Victims are usually isolated children.

- ◆ Victims may have suffered previous trauma or loss.

- ◆ Victims don't pick up on social cues well (which can be caused by a disability).

Two Types of Victims

Transparency 4-4

Passive Victims:

- ◆ Are the most common type of victim; easy to identify.

- ◆ Lack social skills.

- ◆ Cry easily.

- ◆ Lack the ability to use humor to defuse conflict.

- ◆ May be lonely and depressed.

- ◆ Yield easily to bullying.

- ◆ Are likely to be anxious and insecure.

- ◆ Are unable to defend themselves.

Provocative Victims:

- ♦ Comprise a much smaller group; are often difficult to recognize as victims.

- ♦ Are restless children who irritate and tease others and don't know when to stop.

- ♦ Fight back in bullying situations but end up losing (ineffectual aggressors).

- ♦ Are easily emotionally aroused.

- ♦ Tend to maintain the conflict and lose with frustration and distress.

- ♦ May be diagnosed with Attention Deficit Hyperactive Disorder (ADHD).

- ♦ Tend to make you feel like they deserve it.

Review of Bully-Victim Situations

In a bully-victim situation there is:

- ♦ An imbalance of power.

- ♦ A difference in emotional affect (the victim is typically distressed and upset while the bully is calm and cool).

- ♦ Conflict between two or more children who are not friends and do not usually play together.

- ♦ A lack of compassion for the victim by the bully.

- ♦ An explanation of the problem by the bully that lays blame on the victim.

Characteristics of Children Who Are *Not* Victimized

Children who manage conflict well and do not become the targets of bullies generally have the following characteristics:

- ♦ They do not insist on their own way arbitrarily. They give a reason for disagreeing.

- ♦ They apologize.

- ♦ They compromise or offer a cooperative proposition.

- ♦ They share or offer to share something later.

- ♦ They bargain and/or negotiate.

- ♦ They change the topic.

These children comprise "the caring majority" within a school, the 85% of children who are neither bullies nor victims. These children often ignore the bullying behavior occurring around them, because they fear that it will be directed at them in turn if they get involved. But this does not have to be the case.

Enlisting the aid of the caring majority, teaching them to participate in the intervention as "helpers," will be an integral factor in the success of this program. As part of the classroom curriculum, staff members will teach their students to be supportive of the victims of bullying and to tell an adult when they observe bullying behavior. They will learn the difference between tattling and getting adult help.

 NEXT SESSION

In the next session, staff members will identify their predominant conflict resolution styles and compare their style with those of the other members of the school staff. They will also learn some general guidelines for intervening in bullying situations, taking those styles into consideration.

Passive Victims

◆ The most common type of victim; easy to identify

◆ Lack social skills

◆ Cry easily

◆ Lack the ability to use humor to defuse conflict

◆ May be lonely and depressed

◆ Yield easily to bullying

◆ Likely to be anxious and insecure

◆ Unable to defend themselves

Provocative Victims

◆ A much smaller group; are often difficult to recognize as victims

◆ Restless children who irritate and tease others and don't know when to stop

◆ Fight back in bullying situations but end up losing (ineffectual aggressors)

◆ Easily emotionally aroused

◆ Tend to maintain the conflict and lose with frustration and distress

◆ May be diagnosed with ADHD

◆ Tend to make you feel like they deserve it

STAFF INTERACTION

GOAL

To help staff members identify the predominant manner in which they typically interact with children and conflict on a daily basis and to introduce guidelines for intervention in "bully-proofing" the school. Secondly, to introduce the process of changing a silent majority into a caring majority and ultimately into a caring community. Within this goal, conflicts are viewed as teachable moments or opportunities for both staff members and students to take positive steps.

HANDOUTS/TRANSPARENCIES

Handout 4-5: The Conflict Resolution Questionnaire

Handout/Transparency 4-6: The Conflict Resolution Questionnaire Scoring Key

Handout/Transparency 4-7: Developmental Guide to Conflict Resolution

Small Group Activities

At this point, it would be helpful to divide your staff into teaching staff, playground staff (if different from the teaching staff), and transportation staff. Have these three groups discuss and review the current rules and discipline policies in effect in the areas of the school in which they work and begin to identify any problem areas.

Divide all the staff members into small groups of five to six (see the Facilitator Notes), and have them all complete and score "The Conflict Resolution Questionnaire." After scoring the questionnaire, request the staff members to share their predominant style. This is a good time to discuss issues that have come up within their classrooms or on the playground. Encourage the staff members to begin sharing what they see as their strengths in dealing with bullies and/or the victimized children and identify areas in which they feel they need support from other staff members.

> **Handout 4-5**
> **Handout/Transparency 4-6**

> **RESOURCE GUIDE**
> See "Videotapes and Films for Educators and Parents" for sources of bus and playground tactics.

Facilitator Notes

Assign staff members to groups according to your school's needs and desired outcomes. For instance, if you want a particular teaching team to develop their teaming by understanding each others' strengths and styles, that would make a natural grouping. If your goal is to create understanding across grade levels and to share developmental differences in children, then you would want to create mixed-grade groups.

Another option would be to create small groups by having staff members count off (1 through the number of desired groups) to move beyond familiar pairings and help staff members to share ideas and learn about those on the staff they don't typically interact with due to building layout, teaming, or for other reasons.

Whole Group Activities

After the small group discussions, reconvene the whole group and lead the staff members in sharing their conflict resolution style results with the whole group. This is helpful in discovering the variety or similarity of styles as a whole staff, and identifying staff members with complementary styles to whom others can turn for assistance. Discuss all five of the predominant conflict resolution styles (no-nonsense, problem solving, compromising, smoothing, and ignoring) with the group so that the staff members gain an understanding of styles other than their own.

Emphasize during this discussion that recognizing the individual abilities and feelings of staff members in dealing with aggressive acts is fundamental. Acknowledging the different styles and comfort levels staff members have in dealing with aggression and conflict helps to create an atmosphere of supportive teamwork. Each staff member has his or her own contribution. Some staff members are smoothers, some are problem solvers, and some have a no-nonsense approach to intervening in bullying situations. Acknowledging that all roles are necessary, as opposed to believing that there is only one right role, is essential. Building a team approach of lateral support based on trust is the goal.

Explain that if this program is to succeed, each staff member must feel supported and comfortable in carrying out the policy. Some staff members may feel intimidated by high conflict or aggressive situations. No one will be expected to handle a situation that he or she feels extremely uncomfortable about or unskilled to manage. Some staff may be excellent at comforting a victimized child, but frightened of confronting an aggressive child. Other staff may be authoritarian and no-nonsense in their approach, but lacking in an empathetic response to victimized children. Those with a no-nonsense approach are often excellent at intervening with the bullies. The greatest benefit will be realized if each staff member's individual strengths are identified and a cooperative effort is employed by all in enforcing the school's policy position on bullying.

Handout/Transparency 4-7

Review the "Developmental Guide to Conflict Resolution" with the whole group.

It is essential that staff members take care to examine their relationships with one another within the school. It is important that staff support each other and develop a caring community among themselves.

NEXT SESSION

In the next session, staff members will practice intervening in specific types of bullying situations by designing interventions and discovering strategies that work and do not work. The strategies can be incorporated into the school-wide plan to be developed in Session 6.

HANDOUT 4-5
The Conflict Resolution Questionnaire

Teaching children to solve their own problems with peers is a difficult task. Some children seem to naturally do this better than others. We do know that those children who are not good at this skill can be taught strategies which assist them. There are no absolute right or wrong ways to solve problems, but there are techniques that work better at different ages and developmental levels.

The following questions will identify your primary approach to solving problems within your area of the school.

Directions:

Read the statements below. If a statement describes a response you typically make to conflict, write "3" in the space next to the question. If it is a response you occasionally make, write "2" in the space, and if you rarely or never make that response, write "1."

When there is a conflict, I:

1. Tell the children to stop it. _____
2. Try to make everyone feel at ease. _____
3. Help the children understand each others' point of view. _____
4. Separate the children and keep them away from each other. _____
5. Let the principal handle it. _____
6. Decide who started it. _____
7. Try to find out what the real problem is. _____
8. Try to work out a compromise. _____
9. Turn it into a joke. _____
10. Tell the children to stop making such a fuss. _____
11. Encourage one child to give in and apologize. _____
12. Encourage the children to find an alternative solution. _____
13. Help the children decide what they can compromise on. _____
14. Try to divert attention away from the conflict. _____
15. Let the children solve it, as long as no one is hurt. _____
16. Threaten to send the children to the principal. _____
17. Present some alternatives from which the children can choose. _____
18. Help all the children to feel comfortable. _____
19. Get all the children busy doing something else. _____
20. Tell the children to try to settle it on their own. _____

Adapted with permission from Kreidler, W.J. (1984). Creative conflict resolution. Glenview, IL: Scott Foresman.

HANDOUT/TRANSPARENCY 4-6

The Conflict Resolution Questionnaire Scoring Key

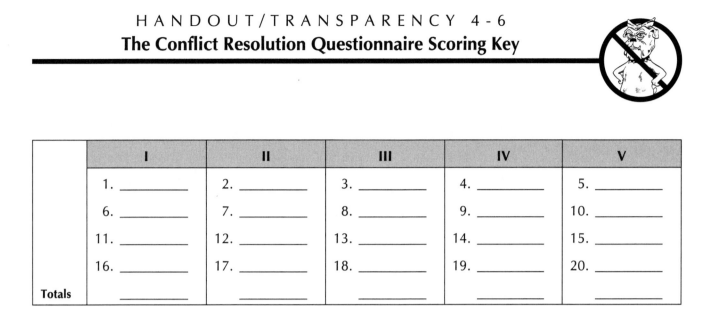

	I	II	III	IV	V
	1. _____	2. _____	3. _____	4. _____	5. _____
	6. _____	7. _____	8. _____	9. _____	10. _____
	11. _____	12. _____	13. _____	14. _____	15. _____
	16. _____	17. _____	18. _____	19. _____	20. _____
Totals	_____	_____	_____	_____	_____

Directions:

Add the numbers in each column, I–V. Each column reflects a particular approach and attitude toward conflict. Find the column with the highest score, and that will correspond to your predominant attitude and manner toward resolving conflict.

I   **The No-Nonsense Approach.** I try to be fair and honest with the children but I believe that they need firm guidance in learning what's acceptable behavior and what isn't. If their behavior is unacceptable, I threaten with consequences or follow through with consequences.

II   **The Problem Solving Approach.** If there's a conflict, I feel there is a problem. Instead of battling with the children, I try to set up a situation in which we can all solve the problem together. This produces creative ideas and stronger relationships.

III   **The Compromising Approach.** I listen to the children and help them to listen to each other. Then I help them give a little. I believe that children need to learn that they can't always have everything they want when they want it.

IV   **The Smoothing Approach.** I prefer that situations stay calm and peaceful whenever possible. Most of the conflicts the children get into are relatively minor, so I just divert their attention to other things.

V   **The Ignoring Approach.** I point out the limits and let the children work things out for themselves. It is good for them to learn the consequences on their own for their behavior.

Adapted with permission from Kreidler, W.J. (1984). *Creative conflict resolution.* Glenview, IL: Scott Foresman.

Developmental Guide to Conflict Resolution

GRADE LEVEL	TYPICAL CONFLICT	PREFERRED STYLES OF RESOLUTION
1	Conflict likely over toys, possessions ("It's mine."), going first	• Action oriented • Separate the children • Change the topic • **No-Nonsense** or **Smoothing**
1 and 2	Selfishness, wanting own way Threatening with tattling or not playing with again ("I'm not inviting you to my birthday.")	• Undo what the offender did • **No-Nonsense** or **Problem Solving**
3, 4, and 5	What's fair and what isn't Teasing, gossiping, feeling superior Putting down, accusing of something not true or distorted	• Beginning stage of understanding others' intentions: mutual negotiation possible with help • Compromise for older grade levels • **Problem Solving** or **Compromising**
5 and 6	Bossiness, tattling, put-downs, showing off, betrayal	• Compromise can be used: empathy possible at this age • Talking things out, even if no compromise is reached • **Ignoring** (only if a minor problem) or **Compromising**

Adapted with permission from Binswanger-Friedman, L. & Ciner, A. (1991, November). Unpublished material presented to Graland School, Denver, Colorado.

SCENARIOS

SESSION 4

GOAL

For staff members to practice intervening in specific types of bullying situations for the purpose of discovering strategies that work and do not work. (Strategies found to be effective can be incorporated into the school-wide plan to be developed in Session 6.)

HANDOUTS/TRANSPARENCIES

Handout 4-8: Scenario 1, First Grade Secret

Handout 4-9: Scenario 2, Second Grade Field Trip

Handout 4-10: Scenario 3, Third Grade Playground Game

Handout 4-11: Scenario 4, A Fourth Grade Fist Fight

Handout 4-12: Scenario 5, Fifth Grade Girls Club

Handout 4-13: Scenario 6, Sixth Grade Frequent Fights

Small Group Activity

Divide the staff members into groups of five to six people and have each group work on one of the six scenarios. Then reconvene the whole group and have one member of each group report on their issues, questions, and interventions designed. You should encourage the staff members to take some brief notes regarding the interventions that the other groups designed for later reference, so that each staff member feels knowledgeable about responding to all six of the scenarios.

Alternate Activity Format

For more in-depth study of a particular scenario or scenarios, you might want to have two (or even all) groups discuss the same scenario and compare their results. The whole group would then reconvene as above.

Facilitator Notes

When forming the groups, consider again your needs as a school in assigning staff members to groups, as discussed in Session 3. You might want to keep the same groups as in Session 3, or divide the staff members differently to meet different needs. The scenarios contained in Handouts 4-8 through 4-13 represent a wide range of both bully-victim situations and normal peer conflict situations. They will assist staff members in:

♦ Identifying the skills and comfort levels of all the staff members in different situations.

♦ Openly discussing feelings and beliefs about intervention with aggressive children.

♦ Developing a plan of action for different types of conflict that can erupt during the school day.

♦ Staying calm and feeling prepared, as bully-victim situations are emotionally intense and require quick and decisive action.

While the handout scenarios provide six very diverse situations for discussion, you may wish to customize or substitute one or all of them, as it is important to identify and discuss the unique needs of your school regarding potentially problematic characteristics. Some examples of these issues include: racial/cultural clashes; socio-economic disparity; frequency of child abuse reporting; influence of gang activities; a frequent incidence of domestic violence, possibly viewed by children at home; and the struggle for acceptance in a homogenous school setting.

NEXT SESSION

In the next session, staff members are presented with the strategies included in the classroom curriculum component of this program and suggestions for consequences and reinforcement.

HANDOUT 4-8
Scenario 1, First Grade Secret

This is your first year teaching at a suburban elementary school of approximately 450 students. Soon after the year begins, you notice that one student in your first grade class, Lauren, is encouraging some of the other girls to perform behavior that makes you uneasy. Specifically, Lauren often makes fun of Tamara, a small, shy girl who has some mild learning difficulties. Lauren will go over to Tamara's desk on Fridays when the spelling tests are handed back and loudly ask Tamara how she did. When Tamara refuses to answer, Lauren says things like, "I bet you got an 'F' again and just don't want to tell." In spite of your reminders that grades are a private matter and that no one has to share his or her grades with another, the pattern persists.

One day later in the fall, you become more alarmed when you have playground duty and observe that Tamara is rejected by the other first grade girls and actively left out of their play. As you walk closer to observe, you overhear Lauren telling three other girls to remember their "secret." After school that day, you ask one of those girls to talk with you about the so called "secret." You learn that Lauren has made a pact with the other girls to "never talk to Tamara." If a girl slips up and talks to Tamara, she is excluded from Lauren's club.

Discussion Questions/Intervention Design

- Design an intervention that details the steps you would take with Lauren to stop her from bullying Tamara and encouraging others to join her in excluding Tamara.

- Would you handle the problem within your classroom alone or involve other members of the school staff to assist you?

- Would you contact Lauren's parent(s) as well as the parents of the other girls and, if so, how would you approach each set of parents?

- Design an intervention that details the steps you would take to protect Tamara from further victimization.

- How would you offer protection to Tamara both on the playground and within the classroom setting?

- What efforts might be needed to restore Tamara's self-esteem and confidence about her academic work as well as her value within the peer group?

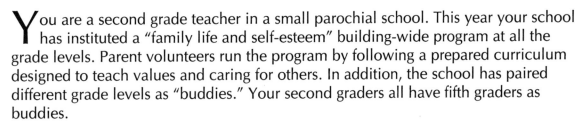

HANDOUT 4-9
Scenario 2, Second Grade Field Trip

You are a second grade teacher in a small parochial school. This year your school has instituted a "family life and self-esteem" building-wide program at all the grade levels. Parent volunteers run the program by following a prepared curriculum designed to teach values and caring for others. In addition, the school has paired different grade levels as "buddies." Your second graders all have fifth graders as buddies.

The older students come into your classroom once every two weeks. Often the time is spent with the students reading together or completing crafts projects. Sometimes a field trip is taken together, with the older students being responsible for the children who are their assigned buddies.

During a field trip to the zoo, you discover that Jerold, one of your second grade students, is missing from the group when everyone meets together for lunch. His fifth grade buddy claims not to know his whereabouts. After a frantic search, Jerold is found hiding in a stall in one of the men's restrooms. He is filthy and visibly upset, trembling and crying, and asking for his mother. It takes much soothing to calm him down and find out what happened.

Eventually the following account is elicited from Jerold. Three of the fifth grade boys began to taunt and tease him when he asked for their help in completing his information sheet about the animals he had observed. They made fun of his drawing and called him a "dummy who doesn't even know how to write." Then one boy reached into the goat pen and picked up some goat excrement. He smeared it on Jerold's arms and cheeks, calling him "Stinky" and "Poop Face." The other two boys laughed and picked up more, and all three rubbed the excrement on Jerold, daring him to go back to the group with "poop on his face."

Discussion Questions/Intervention Design

- How would you respond to the immediate situation of finding a filthy and distraught Jerold in the restroom?

- Design an intervention for the three fifth grade boys involved in humiliating and intimidating Jerold. Would you elect to handle this within the school or would you report this incident to each boy's parent(s)?

- Design an intervention for Jerold that will assist him in reentering your second grade classroom. What would you share and what would you not share with the class as a whole?

- Would you continue the buddy program between your classroom and the fifth grade classroom?

HANDOUT 4-10
Scenario 3, Third Grade Playground Game

You are a third grade teacher in a small, private school of approximately 500 children. Playground time is supervised by different staff members within the school; there are no actual playground aides. One of the physical education teachers comes to you with the following report after supervising your class at recess for the past week.

She reports that the majority of your class is playing a game called "Capture." This game consists of a group of five children, four boys and one girl, who chase the others and capture them. Once captured, a child is taken to a corner area of the playground which is called "The Dungeon." The captured child must perform certain duties as a "slave" before he or she can be released. There is a great deal of belittling and teasing about being "dumb" or "small" as part of the capturing. If a child refuses to perform the duties as ordered, he or she is threatened with physical aggression the next time captured.

Discussion Questions/Intervention Design

- Do you believe that any intervention is called for or is this game of "Capture" a reasonably normal recess activity for third graders?

- If you feel intervention is necessary, what other information would you need to gather before intervening? (Elaborate on the situation by adding this information before planning your intervention.)

- If you feel intervention is necessary, design an intervention that includes a plan for both the leaders of the game and the victims who are captured.

- Since you do not supervise your own class at recess time, what intervention, if any, would you suggest to be used by the staff who are on the playground during your class' recess time?

HANDOUT 4-11
Scenario 4, A Fourth Grade Fist Fight

You are a fourth grade teacher in a suburban public school. Following lunch each day, the children go out on the playground for 20 minutes. Aides supervise that time and you rarely visit the playground. Thus, you are not really aware of how the children interact during this free play period. One day in mid-October, an aide comes to get you, reporting that Brent and Mitchell, two of the boys in your room, have been sent to the office because of a knock-down-drag-out fist fight.

You know that Brent and Mitchell live in the same neighborhood and ride to school together on the bus. Brent is a quiet boy, an excellent student. Mitchell, on the other hand, is mildly hyperactive and often has difficulty completing his work. In spite of their differences, you have seen them together from time to time, before and after school.

You walk down to the office and find both boys in a conference with the principal. Peeking through the window in the door, you observe that both boys are crying as well as talking excitedly and animatedly.

Discussion Questions/Intervention Design

- At this point, would you consider this altercation a bully-victim problem or a normal peer conflict?

- What other information would you need to gather, if any, to determine whether this is a bully-victim situation or a normal peer conflict situation?

- Would you let the principal handle the situation or would you knock on the door and join them?

- Design an intervention that details the steps you would take, if any, when the two boys are returned to your classroom.

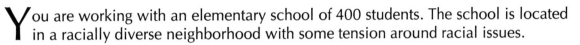

HANDOUT 4-12
Scenario 5, The Fifth Grade Girls Club

You are working with an elementary school of 400 students. The school is located in a racially diverse neighborhood with some tension around racial issues.

The fifth grade teachers have alerted you about a "girls club" consisting of Tonya, Jessica, and Jennifer. These girls have been spreading malicious rumors, frequently using ethnic slurs. They have in particular targeted two students, Leah, who is new to the school, and Stacy, who has a mild learning disability.

The school nurse has noted that she has seen both Leah and Stacy in her office frequently with physical complaints which usually appear to be psychosomatic in nature. She's noted a pattern of the girls visiting her most often in the afternoon after recess.

The fifth grade teachers have never directly observed nor overheard the girls in the club, but have had many complaints from other students in their classes. Stacy has not reported any incidents herself, but recently seems very distracted and anxious.

Discussion Questions/Intervention Design

- ◆ What other information would you need to gather before intervening? (Elaborate on the situation by adding this information before planning your intervention.)

- ◆ Design an intervention, incorporating appropriate options such as building-wide strategies, classroom work, and so forth.

HANDOUT 4-13
Scenario 6, Sixth Grade Frequent Fights

You are working in an elementary school of 600 students. It is a racially diverse neighborhood. During unstructured times (i.e., less teacher supervision) students are involved in frequent fights. Jonathan, a sixth grade student diagnosed with Attention Deficit Disorder (ADD), appears to provoke situations that escalate into aggressive actions. Jonathan is named as the instigator of these fights, but usually ends up getting hurt.

Recently, another sixth grade student, Chris, has been identified by classmates as being involved in a number of fights. Chris is threatening to beat students up after school. Two parents have called to report that their children are fearful about walking home from school.

Yesterday, it was reported that Chris hurt Jonathan. Due to problems escalating overall with the sixth graders, class meetings were held by all of the sixth grade teachers. The students were asked to tell their teachers, via anonymous feedback, which students have been aggressive towards others during the last few months of school. Chris' name appeared twice as many times as Jonathan's name. This was a surprise to the teachers.

Discussion Questions/Intervention Design

◆ What other information would you need to gather before intervening? (Elaborate on the situation by adding this information before planning your intervention.)

◆ Design an intervention, incorporating appropriate options such as building-wide strategies, classroom work, etc.

PROGRAM STRATEGIES, CONSEQUENCES, AND REINFORCEMENT

SESSION 5

GOAL

To present to the staff members the strategies included in the classroom curriculum component of this program, and suggestions for consequences and reinforcement, as background information to be used in Session 6 when planning their own school-wide program.

HANDOUTS/TRANSPARENCIES

Handout/Transparency 4-14: *Bully-Proofing Your School* Strategies

Handout/Transparency 4-15: Ideas for Consequences

Transparency 4-16: "Boys Take Warning Before It Is Too Late"

Handout/Transparency 4-17: Ideas for Reinforcers

Review Chapter Nine: Effective Prosocial Discipline

Program Strategies

Handout/Transparency 4-14

The following strategies are included in the core *Bully-Proofing Your School* program (see Chapter Five: Student Instruction). The adoption of these rules may include or elaborate upon rules already used in the classroom. They work because they define the behavior you want to stop, the behavior you are encouraging, and the outcome you want. Remember, the focus is on the safety of all the students.

- ◆ **Classroom Rules**

  1. We will not bully other students.

  2. We will help others who are being bullied by speaking out and by getting adult help.

  3. We will use extra effort to include **all students** in activities at our school.

  Note: A poster of these rules is provided in Chapter Five. Also point out to the staff members that these rules correspond to the three policy statements comprising the formal school policy regarding bullying.

◆ **"No-Bullying" Posters**

These posters (provided in Chapter Five) are to be hung in the classrooms and around the school building to remind the students about the rules against bullying. Teachers may wish to display no-bullying posters drawn/colored by their students in their classrooms as well as or instead of these posters.

◆ **HA HA, SO**

This is a mnemonic device to help students remember strategies that they can use when they are being bullied. It stands for:

H - Help	**H - Humor**	**S - Self-Talk**
A - Assert Yourself	**A - Avoid**	**O - Own It**

Each of these strategies is detailed for the students in the classroom curriculum (Chapter Five).

◆ **CARES**

This is a mnemonic device to help students remember a set of strategies that they can use when they see someone else being bullied. It stands for:

C - Creative Problem Solving

A - Adult Help

R - Relate and Join

E - Empathy

S - Stand Up and Speak Out

Each of these strategies is detailed for the students in the classroom curriculum (Chapter Five).

◆ **Weekly "I Caught You Caring" Classroom Sessions**

These weekly sessions are designed for reinforcement of caring behavior within the classroom. They occur at the end of the week (e.g., Friday before dismissal), and take approximately five to fifteen minutes.

Each teacher chooses one of his or her students who was "caught" being kind or helpful to another student for this special recognition. The teacher should keep a log of "acts of kindness" that he or she notices during the week, and then pick a good example to reinforce.

During the session, the teacher should announce the "Caring Student of the Week" and describe the caring behavior that he or she performed. The teacher should discuss with the class why the behavior worked/how it complied with the classroom rules, and model the skill(s) for the students. Some brief discussion can then occur about what motivated the caring behavior.

Note: These class discussions can be expanded and enlivened, if you wish, by employing creative discussion techniques. For example, you could read *Finding the Greenstone*, by Alice Walker, to your class, and then allow the children to pass a green marble among themselves as they are "caught caring."

> **RESOURCE GUIDE**
> See "Books for Primary Students" for complete information on Alice Walker's book.

- ◆ **Student Nominations of "Best Caring Behavior" and "CARES Buttons"**

  As the program progresses, and the students become more adept at performing and recognizing caring behavior in the classroom, the students in each class can nominate each other and vote weekly on the best example of caring behavior. The student selected for the "Best Caring Behavior" may wear a special "CARES Button" for the week (provided in Chapter Five).

Consequences

While this program is not a punitive one by nature, as with almost any intervention, some use of consequences will need to be applied. The school staff should discuss and agree on, before the classroom curriculum is begun, what the consequences will be for students who bully. (This planning will occur in Session 6.)

Since "we will not bully other students" becomes a school rule, it is best to have the consequences for breaking this rule consistent with the consequences for breaking other school rules. **Since bullying behavior is antisocial and hurts other children, it works well to assign consequences that involve prosocial behavior and helping other students.** In this way these desired behaviors are practiced and reinforced. Again, please review Chapter Nine: Effective Prosocial Discipline.

It is important to delineate consequences for the first offense and subsequent offenses. It is also important for all staff members to be **consistent** in applying consequences for all bullying incidents by all students.

While the specific consequences assigned will vary from school to school, depending upon each school's unique philosophy regarding discipline, following are some possible consequences for bullying:

Handout/Transparency 4-15

- ◆ Missing recess and instead, helping in the office;
- ◆ Making an "I Caught You Caring" award, button, or poster for use in the school;
- ◆ Staying after school to perform a helpful act;
- ◆ Having to call one's parent(s) to explain one's behavior and have a "caring act" set as a consequence;
- ◆ Teaching a "class" on "thinking errors" at a lower grade level;
- ◆ Cleaning up trash on the playground or in the cafeteria;

- Tutoring another student in a mastered subject;

- Writing a report about an altruistic leader (e.g., Ghandi, Martin Luther King, Mother Theresa);

- Having lunch with or doing something nice for the student one bullied (this requires adult supervision and victim willingness);

- Role playing being the victim of the same behavior with one's teacher;

- Meeting with the counselor or school psychologist to discuss one's aggressive behavior and to process "thinking errors";

- Observing playground time, recording in a journal observed acts of kindness; and

- Observing the playground time of younger students, passing out rewards to children displaying caring, kind behaviors to others.

Transparency 4-16

Of course, there is always the age-old (but not very effective) consequence of **threat**. This method is not recommended!

Reinforcement

Currently in our schools, much of the caring behavior between students goes unnoticed and is not reinforced. If we are lucky, some caring behavior continues anyhow; if we're not, acts of kindness dwindle and die for lack of acknowledgment. Reinforcement is significantly more effective than applying consequences for long-term effects. It is very important for staff members to notice and give rewards for caring, prosocial behaviors observed in their students. (A good general rule is three reinforcements for every correction of a negative behavior to maintain a positive, caring school environment.)

Bullying and misbehavior are pretty easy to spot. (Teachers, parents, playground aides, and bus drivers all seem to have "eyes in the back of their heads" when it comes to misbehavior.) But if they're not accustomed to watching for them, caring behaviors are sometimes elusive to staff members. Following are examples of some typical acts of kindness by elementary school students:

- Asking a new student to eat lunch or play with them;

- Speaking out when one child says something mean to another (e.g., "Calling Billy dumb was mean, and he's not.");

- Including a child who is often excluded in a game, conversation, etc.;

- Noticing another child's distress and asking if he or she is okay (e.g., "You look sad. Did something happen?");

- Easing another child's embarrassment (e.g., "Oh, I lose my place too when I'm reading out loud.");

- Sharing something with a child who has forgotten his or her (e.g., a book, pencil, snack, sports equipment, etc.);

- Noticing and complimenting another child who has shown growth in something that was difficult for him or her (e.g., "You really have gotten good at kickball."); and

- Being patient with another child who is going slower, either mentally or physically (e.g., helping another student who needs more time to complete his or her work or purposefully choosing a game at recess that can be enjoyed by a child who is not as skilled athletically).

Teacher attention and verbal praise are the most powerful reinforcers for elementary age children. But other reinforcers can also be given (either separately, in conjunction with the weekly "I Caught You Caring" sessions, or in addition to the "CARES Buttons"), such as:

Handout/Transparency 4-17

- Being allowed to sit next to the teacher at lunch;

- Helping the teacher with a special project (e.g., hanging holiday decorations in the room, etc.);

- A positive note or special certificate sent home;

- Displaying the child's school photograph and name in the classroom or hallway on a "Caring Student of the Week" poster;

- A "cool" pencil or other school supplies;

- Any small toy or other item coveted by students;

- Gift certificates to a local fast food restaurant or video arcade;

- Any edible treat (candy, popcorn, etc.);

- Being allowed to pick his or her partner for the next project;

- Getting to go first in something;

- Extra free time or recess;

- Etc. Etc. Etc. (The possibilities are almost endless!)

After the students become adept at performing the caring behaviors and following the classroom rules, reinforcement could also be given to entire classrooms in which caring behaviors were exhibited all week. Whole class reinforcement could take the form of:

- A pizza or popcorn party;

- Watching a video or filmstrip in class;

- A field trip; or

- Extra recess time or free time within class.

Whole class reinforcement may be used as a special reward, but it should not replace individual acknowledgment altogether, as this form of reinforcement is much more powerful for most students.

The facilitator should lead the staff members in brainstorming other possible consequences and reinforcers, and sharing strategies that have worked or not worked for them in the past. Encourage the staff members to record these additional ideas on their handouts for future reference.

NEXT SESSION

*In the next session, staff members will plan their **own** school-wide program against bullying!*

Classroom Rules

1. We will not bully other students.

2. We will help others who are being bullied by speaking out and by getting adult help.

3. We will use extra effort to include **all students** in activities at our school.

"No-Bullying" Posters

HA HA, SO

H - Help **H - H**umor **S - S**elf-Talk

A - Assert Yourself **A - A**void **O - O**wn It

CARES

C - Creative Problem Solving

A - Adult Help

R - Relate and Join

E - Empathy

S - Stand Up and Speak Out

HANDOUT/TRANSPARENCY 4-14 (*continued*)

Weekly "I Caught You Caring" Classroom Sessions

◆ Weekly sessions for reinforcement of caring behavior within the classroom

◆ Take place at the end of the week, for about five to fifteen minutes

◆ Teacher chooses a student who was "caught" caring, by logging "acts of kindness" throughout the week

◆ Teacher announces student name and describes caring behavior observed

◆ Teacher models skill(s) and leads brief class discussion

Student Nominations of "Best Caring Behavior" and "CARES Buttons"

◆ Students nominate each other (within classrooms)

◆ Students vote weekly on the best example of caring behavior

◆ Student selected may wear a special "CARES Button" for the week

HANDOUT/TRANSPARENCY 4-15
Ideas for Consequences

- Missing recess and instead, helping in the office

- Making an "I Caught You Caring" award, button, or poster for use in the school

- Staying after school to perform a helpful act

- Having to call one's parent(s) to explain one's behavior and have a "caring act" set as a consequence

- Teaching a "class" on "thinking errors" at a lower grade level

- Cleaning up trash on the playground or in the cafeteria

- Tutoring another student in a mastered subject

- Writing a report about an altruistic leader (e.g., Ghandi, Martin Luther King, Mother Theresa)

- Having lunch with or doing something nice for the student one bullied (this requires adult supervision and victim willingness)

- Role playing the victim of the same behavior with the teacher

- Meeting with the counselor or school psychologist to discuss one's behavior and to process "thinking errors"

- Observing playground time, recording in a journal observed acts of kindness

- Observing the playground time of younger students, passing out rewards to children displaying caring, kind behaviors to others

TRANSPARENCY 4-16
"Boys Take Warning Before It Is Too Late"

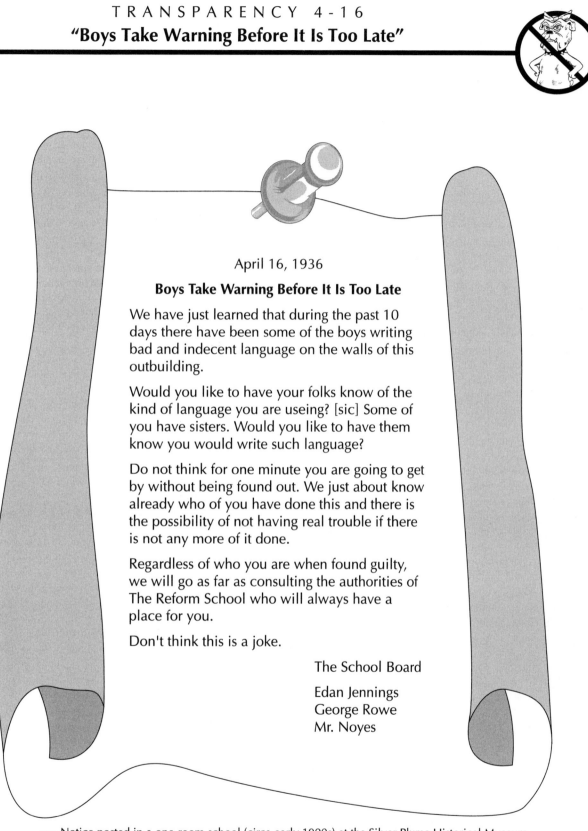

April 16, 1936

Boys Take Warning Before It Is Too Late

We have just learned that during the past 10 days there have been some of the boys writing bad and indecent language on the walls of this outbuilding.

Would you like to have your folks know of the kind of language you are useing? [sic] Some of you have sisters. Would you like to have them know you would write such language?

Do not think for one minute you are going to get by without being found out. We just about know already who of you have done this and there is the possibility of not having real trouble if there is not any more of it done.

Regardless of who you are when found guilty, we will go as far as consulting the authorities of The Reform School who will always have a place for you.

Don't think this is a joke.

The School Board

Edan Jennings
George Rowe
Mr. Noyes

—— Notice posted in a one-room school (circa early 1900s) at the Silver Plume Historical Museum, Silver Plume, Colorado

HANDOUT/TRANSPARENCY 4-17
Ideas for Reinforcers

◆ Sitting next to the teacher at lunch

◆ Helping the teacher with a special project

◆ A note or certificate sent home

◆ Displaying a school photograph/name in the classroom or hallway on a "Caring Student of the Week" poster

◆ A "cool" pencil or other school supplies

◆ Any small toy or other desired item

◆ Gift certificates to a local fast food restaurant or video arcade

◆ Any edible treat (candy, popcorn, etc.)

◆ Picking his or her partner for a project

◆ Going first in something

◆ Extra free time or recess

◆ Etc.!

PLANNING YOUR OWN SCHOOL-WIDE PROGRAM

GOAL

For the school staff to plan, with the assistance of the facilitator, their own school-wide program, taking into account the information and strategies learned in the previous five training sessions. This overall plan will be recorded in writing for future reference and all the participating staff members will be familiar with and in agreement with it before the classroom curriculum (Chapter Five) is begun.

Secondly, to begin the development of a team, cadre, or steering committee to support and direct the program within the school building. Ideally, this would include an administrator, mental health or counseling staff member, and teachers representative of different grade levels and subjects in the building. The planning process is the point at which the facilitator role is expanded into a team to be the culture-carrier and overall problem-solvers.

HANDOUTS/TRANSPARENCIES

Review any handouts or transparencies presented in Sessions 1 through 5 that may assist the staff members in planning their own school-wide program. Those that might be helpful include:

Handout/Transparency 4-3: Bullying Behaviors Chart

Handout/Transparency 4-7: Developmental Guide to Conflict Resolution

Handout/Transparency 4-14: *Bully-Proofing Your School* Strategies

Handout/Transparency 4-15: Ideas for Consequences

Handout/Transparency 4-17: Ideas for Reinforcers

Also, to assist the staff members in planning their own school-wide program, characteristics of an effective policy and a plan outline have been provided in this session. The outline should include most of the main elements of the plan that you will need, but it should be customized, if necessary, to meet the unique needs of your individual school and staff.

Handout/Transparency 4-18: Key Characteristics of an Effective School Policy

Handout/Transparency 4-19: School-Wide Program Planning Outline (photocopy as three double-sided sheets)

It would also be helpful for the facilitator to have on hand a copy of the district policies on discipline, weapons, intervention with students under IEPs, etc.

Facilitator Notes

The process of planning a school-wide program should be an exciting, empowering one. But it can turn into an inordinately lengthy and cumbersome one if not guided efficiently by the facilitator. What should be avoided, at all costs, are lengthy "hair-splitting" discussions (e.g., spending 45 minutes debating the merits of in-class time-out versus staying after school as a consequence of bullying behavior). The facilitator should move the discussion along through the outline provided, obtaining majority consensus and promising to return to minor details as time allows after the framework has been filled in.

Planning the school-wide program can be accomplished in this single session, but may require additional planning session(s) if the school staff is very large or staff members have drastically diverse views on intervention, discipline, and reinforcement. The facilitator should use his or her best judgment in leading and closing the planning session(s). If the staff members appear overwhelmed, frustrated, or rushed, the facilitator may want to end the session and schedule an additional planning session for a later date rather than force the issue. This allows the opportunity for the staff members to digest what's already been discussed, clarify their thoughts about the rest of the plan, and calm any emotional reactions which may have been evoked during the planning session.

An alternate method for school-wide program planning might be to enlist a representative group, comprised of five or six members of the school staff, to draft a plan for the school-wide program which could then be approved by the entire staff. In this case, this first planning session would consist of choosing the representative group, examining the planning outline (Handout/Transparency 4-19), and discussing suggestions for the plan. Then the drafted plan would be presented to and fine tuned by the entire staff in a second planning session. This method of program planning can streamline the process, unless the majority of the staff members have strong feelings about participating in the actual drafting, in which case this method could cause resentment or resistance to the program.

If all the staff members are taking part in the program planning, it is recommended that the staff members be divided into small groups. A natural grouping method would be grade-level groups, as there will be some developmental differences built into the classroom plan, and classroom teachers of the same grade will be able to discuss the unique needs of their students. The other members of the school staff (e.g., playground staff) should also be grouped together appropriately.

The facilitator will lead the plan drafting through the use of the program planning outline (Handout/Transparency 4-19), allowing time for brainstorming, discussion, and recording within the small groups. The facilitator will then attempt to obtain majority consensus on the school-wide plan, so that it will be implemented consistently by all participating staff members. While each staff member may incorporate his or her own unique style and ideas in implementing the program within his or her classroom, general guidelines for the school-wide plan should be agreed upon by all the participating staff members before the plan is implemented across the school.

Note: It is usually a good idea to have an administrator present during appropriate parts or all of the planning session(s) to provide guidelines on appropriate strategies for meeting with parents and similar issues.

When a school-wide plan is agreed upon, the facilitator should type a clean copy of the completed plan and distribute a copy to each participating staff member. The staff members will also want to keep their copies of the plan outlines they have developed and their notes regarding how they will customize the plan for their individual classes. They can then transfer these notes to the completed, clean copy of the plan later if they wish. This plan will be evaluated and updated by the overall steering committee or team as described in the "Goal" section.

Characteristics of Effective Policies

Handout/Transparency 4-18

The *Foundations* program lists the following as key features of effective school-wide policies:

1. An effective policy communicates the vision of a positive and invitational school.

2. An effective policy must be designed by staff.

3. An effective policy is written with involvement from parents and students.

4. An effective policy is centered around a school mission statement.

5. An effective policy describes procedures used by staff to achieve consistency in their day-to-day interactions with students.

6. An effective policy outlines expectations and procedures for consistent staff supervision of school-wide areas.

7. An effective policy, while striving for consistency, should provide flexibility for all classroom teachers to set up and run their own classrooms.

8. An effective policy specifies when to involve administration in behavioral problems and outlines procedures to use when severe misbehavior occurs.

9. An effective policy guides staff development and change.

10. An effective policy is systematically evaluated, revised, and updated each year.

11. An effective policy is user friendly.

12. An effective policy is aligned with school board policy and relevant to state or federal laws.

RESOURCE GUIDE
See "Books for Administrators, School-Based Teams, and Specialists" for complete information on the *Foundations* program.

School-Wide Program Planning

Planning the school-wide program should cover these main areas:

- ◆ The Overall School-Wide Campaign to Bully-Proof the School
  - ◊ The Plan for Informing the Students About the Commencement of the *Bully-Proofing Your School* Program
  - ◊ The Formal School Policy Regarding Bullying
  - ◊ The Individual Classroom Plans (How the Program Will Be Communicated to the Students)
  - ◊ Plans for Other Areas of the School
  - ◊ The Plan for Working With Parents
  - ◊ The Plan for Referring Students for Victim Intervention
  - ◊ The Plan for Referring Students for Bully Intervention

- ◆ Implementation of the School-Wide Program
  - ◊ Time Frames/Human Resource Responsibilities for the Plan for Informing the Students About the Commencement of the *Bully-Proofing Your School* Program
  - ◊ Time Frames/Human Resource Responsibilities for Teaching the Individual Classroom Curricula and Classroom Curriculum Follow-Up Sessions
  - ◊ Time Frames/Human Resource Responsibilities for the Plans for Other Areas of the School
  - ◊ Time Frames/Human Resource Responsibilities for the Plan for Working With Parents
  - ◊ Time Frames/Human Resource Responsibilities for the Plan for Referring Students for Victim Intervention
  - ◊ Time Frames/Human Resource Responsibilities for the Plan for Referring Students for Bully Intervention

- ◆ Ongoing Evaluation/Modification of the Program
  - ◊ The Development of a "Team," "Task Force," "Cadre," or "Committee" to Coordinate, Support, Direct, and Problem-Solve for the School.
  - ◊ The Plan for Evaluating/Modifying the Program
  - ◊ Time Frames/Human Resource Responsibilities for the Plan for Evaluating/Modifying the Program

HANDOUT/TRANSPARENCY 4-18
Key Characteristics of an Effective School Policy

The following are key features to keep in mind when planning a school-wide program against bullying.

An effective policy:

1. Communicates the vision of a positive and invitational school.

2. Must be designed by staff.

3. Is written with involvement from parents and students.

4. Is centered around a school mission statement.

5. Describes procedures used by staff to achieve consistency in their day-to-day interactions with students.

6. Outlines expectations and procedures for consistent staff supervision of school-wide areas.

7. While striving for consistency, should provide flexibility for all classroom teachers to set up and run their own classrooms.

8. Specifies when to involve administration in behavioral problems and outlines procedures to use when severe misbehavior occurs.

9. Guides staff development and change.

10. Is systematically evaluated, revised, and updated each year.

11. Is user friendly.

12. Is aligned with school board policy and relevant to state or federal laws.

Adapted with permission from Sprick, R., Sprick, M., & Garrison, M. (1992). *Foundations: Establishing positive discipline policies.* Longmont, CO: Sopris West.

HANDOUT/TRANSPARENCY 4-19
School-Wide Program Planning Outline

I. OVERALL SCHOOL-WIDE CAMPAIGN TO BULLY-PROOF THE SCHOOL

A. Plan for Informing the Students About the Commencement of the *Bully-Proofing Your School* Program

1. The Classroom Curriculum

2.

3.

(*Suggestions for inclusion:* an announcement by the principal or other administrator; hanging no-bullying posters in the hallways to pique student interest; a special assembly)

B. Formal School Policy Regarding Bullying

▼ MISSION STATEMENT

Our goal is to make the school environment safe for children both physically and psychologically.

1. Stop the behavior—There will be "no-bullying rules" enforced by staff members.

2. What the students will do—The students will help others by speaking out and getting adult help.

3. How students should treat one another—The students will use extra effort to include everyone.

C. The Individual Classroom Plans (How the Program Will Be Communicated to the Students)

1. My Classroom Rules Will Be

   a.

   b.

   c.

(These classroom rules address the mission statement and the three elements of the formal school policy regarding bullying described in Part I-B above.)

HANDOUT/TRANSPARENCY 4-19 (*continued*)

2. Program Strategies I Will Use With My Students

   a. Posting Classroom Rules

   b. Classroom No-Bullying Posters

   c. HA HA, SO

   d. CARES

   e. Weekly "I Caught You Caring" Sessions

   f. Student Nominations of "Best Caring Behavior" and "CARES Buttons"

   (I have crossed out any program strategies that I object to including in my classroom curriculum)

3. Any Other Skills I Will Teach My Students

   a. There is Strength in Numbers

   b. The Difference Between Tattling and Getting Adult Help

   c.

4. How My Students Should Inform Adults of Bullying Situations

   a.

   b.

   c.

5. Reinforcement for Caring Behavior I Will Give My Students

   a. Verbal Praise and Acknowledgment

   b.

   c.

6. Consequences I Will Apply to Bullying Behavior

   a. For a 1st Offense:

   b. For a 2nd Offense:

   c. For a 3rd Offense:

   d. Persistent Bullying Problem:

HANDOUT/TRANSPARENCY 4-19 (*continued*)

7. Any Other Techniques/Strategies I Will Use in My Classroom

  a.

  b.

  c.

D. Plans for Other Areas of the School

  1. Strategies for the Playground/Recess

    a.

    b.

    c.

    (*Suggestions for inclusion:* dealing with conflict; de-escalating dangerous situations; determining the current adequacy/inadequacy of adult to student ratio and ways to increase adult supervision if necessary)

  2. Strategies for the Cafeteria

    a.

    b.

    c.

  3. Strategies for the Bus Area/On the Bus

    a.

    b.

    c.

  4. Strategies for the Hallways/Common Areas

    a.

    b.

    c.

HANDOUT/TRANSPARENCY 4-19 (*continued*)

E. Plan for Working With Parents

1. How Parents Will Be Informed About the Classroom Curriculum and Kept Apprised of Developments With the Program Against Bullying

   a. Orientation Letter Mailed Prior to Orientation Presentation

   b.

   c.

   (*Suggestions for inclusion:* community meetings; newsletters/fliers; PTA involvement; telephone calls/meetings with staff members)

2. How Parents Should Inform the School Staff of a Bullying Situation

   a.

   b.

   c.

   (*Suggestions for inclusion:* Who should the parents contact?)

3. How Parent(s) Will Be Informed of a Bullying Situation Involving Their Child

   a.

   b.

   c.

   (*Suggestions for inclusion:* Who should contact the parent(s)?)

HANDOUT/TRANSPARENCY 4-19 (*continued*)

F. Plan for Referring Students for Victim Intervention

(*Suggestions for inclusion:* classroom teacher referral; parent referral; support personnel referral; assessing the needs of inhibited/shy students; assessing the needs of students who have no friendships; assessing the needs of students who have suffered a loss or trauma; assessing the needs of students new to the school; assessing the needs of physically weak/petite students)

G. Plan for Referring Students for Bully Intervention

(*Suggestions for inclusion:* classroom teacher referral; parent referral; support personnel referral; administrator referral; assessing the needs of students who are aggressive; assessing the needs of students who lack anger management skills; assessing the needs of students who lack empathy; assessing the needs of students who come from violent, abusive homes; assessing the needs of students who have had frequent disciplinary actions or trouble with the law)

II. IMPLEMENTATION OF THE SCHOOL-WIDE PROGRAM

A. Time Frames/Human Resource Responsibilities for the Plan for Informing the Students About the Commencement of the *Bully-Proofing Your School* Program

HANDOUT/TRANSPARENCY 4-19 (*continued*)

B. Time Frames/Human Resource Responsibilities for Teaching the Individual Classroom Curricula and Classroom Curriculum Follow-Up Sessions

(*Suggestions for inclusion:* Will the program be taught in the classrooms grade-by-grade, e.g., all participating first grade classrooms, then all participating second grade classrooms, etc.? Who will teach the individual curricula—the classroom teachers alone or the classroom teachers with the assistance of the facilitator or alternate, appropriate individual? When will the classroom sessions take place? When should the follow-up session be conducted?)

C. Time Frames/Human Resource Responsibilities for the Plans for Other Areas of the School

1. The Playground/Recess Plan

2. The Cafeteria Plan

3. The Bus Area/On the Bus Plan

4. The Hallways/Common Areas Plan

D. Time Frames/Human Resource Responsibilities for the Plan for Working With Parents

1. The Plan to Inform the Parents About the Classroom Curriculum and Keep Them Apprised of Developments With the Program Against Bullying

2. The Plan for How Parents Should Inform the School Staff of a Bullying Situation

3. The Plan for How Parent(s) Will be Informed of a Bullying Situation Involving Their Child

HANDOUT/TRANSPARENCY 4-19 (*continued*)

E. Time Frames/Human Resource Responsibilities for the Plan for Referring Students for Victim Intervention

F. Time Frames/Human Resource Responsibilities for the Plan for Referring Students for Bully Intervention

III. ONGOING EVALUATION/MODIFICATION OF THE PROGRAM

A. Plan for Who Will Be the "Steering Committee," "Team," or "Cadre"

(List of members and how frequently and when they will meet to coordinate, support, direct and problem-solve.)

B. Plan for Evaluating/Modifying the Program

(*Suggestion for inclusion:* setting up an ongoing "Bullying Task Force" to monitor progress, share ideas, and encourage continued staff skill development; annual implementation of the program)

C. Time Frames/Human Resource Responsibilities for the Plan for Evaluating/ Modifying the Program

Conclusion

The training of your staff to prevent bullying is a considerable commitment of time and resources which will greatly benefit your students. Throughout this process, your staff members become more knowledgeable about bullying in general, and learn a great deal about their individual styles in dealing with conflict and aggression.

The development of a school-wide program is a basic step in preventing bully-victim problems. Completing this staff training component empowers your staff members to work cooperatively with each other in the future to meet this goal. The final session in staff training, in which the staff members plan their own unique program to meet the needs of their student body, is the beginning of putting an effective program into place.

During the staff training component, the staff members are given an overview of the classroom curriculum. Once you have taken the steps of informing the community of parents and the student body about the basics of the program, it is time for the staff members to use the student instruction sessions in the next chapter to teach the students principles and skills to use in bully-proofing their school. This will be a rewarding process, as not only will they see growth in their students, but the students will have much to teach all of you.

Bully-proofing your school is important for many reasons, of which the most valuable is providing the children a safe, caring environment where they can apply themselves to learning. However, it will also be of benefit in developing their growth in emotional and moral areas and in leadership skills.

CHAPTER FIVE

STUDENT INSTRUCTION

In the previous chapter of this manual, Chapter Four, staff members planned their own school-wide program against bullying. This chapter presents the classroom curriculum, in which that plan will be put into effect with students.

This classroom curriculum is the core component of the systematic approach to bully-proofing your school, because it provides intervention with those individuals most directly affected by and responsible for bully-victim situations—the children in the school. Keep in mind that while classroom intervention is quite effective for select bully-victim situations where all the children involved are in the same class, this classroom curriculum is most effective when implemented school-wide.

The classroom curriculum educates all participating students about bullying: what it is, what one can do if one is the victim of a bully, and what one can do if one sees another student being bullied. As part of this educative process, the students self-evaluate their involvement in bully-victim situations through an anonymous survey administered in the classroom. This survey also provides the classroom teachers with an accurate assessment of the frequency and severity of bullying situations involving their students. Finally, a set of rules to bully-proof the classroom and strategies to reinforce the rules are presented to the students.

Key points of the underlying philosophy of the program as it pertains to the classroom curriculum follow. The facilitator and classroom teachers conducting the classroom curriculum should refer to these points often, especially when questions or new issues arise. The philosophy of the classroom curriculum is based on the following principles:

- ◆ Adults must be involved in helping children deal with bullies because of the power imbalance which occurs in bullying situations.

- To stop bullying, we must shift the power from the bully or bullying group to the caring majority of students by: (1) setting explicit rules that say bullying is not allowed, and (2) by teaching all the students ways to speak out against bullying.

- It is important for the adults to convey a "can do" attitude. This means that the adults portray confidence in the belief that they can implement their program to prevent bullying and that the children can learn the techniques to prevent bullying.

- It is also important that the adults maintain a nonpunitive attitude. Bullies and victims should never be mentioned by name in the classroom group discussions, unless a student volunteers that information about himself or herself.

- Caring and compassion are valued attributes in children that must be verbally acknowledged and reinforced by the adults.

- Children learn social/emotional concepts best by discussion and modeling rather than by lecture. The more of the ideas that are generated by the children themselves, the better.

- Children learn social skills by trying them out themselves. This practice can best be accomplished by role play, puppet play, and storytelling by children.

SECTION ONE: Elementary Curriculum

Schools which implemented the *Bully-Proofing Your School* program experienced very positive, and sometimes surprising, results with the classroom curriculum. In some of the classrooms, the **bullies became positive leaders** within their peer group. As the rules for how to have power shifted as a result of the classroom curriculum intervention, some of the bullies were able to stay powerful, but by caring and helping other students instead of threatening and intimidating them. It was also found that the classroom curriculum spurred the moral and social development of a set of students who previously went unnoticed, for the most part. These children were not academic or athletic stars, but suddenly they found something that they were good at and an arena where they could receive attention. These children began to shine. They would often spend time thinking up very creative and fair solutions to conflicts and dilemmas in their peer group and classroom. They would proudly share their ideas with the adults involved in the curriculum with as much pride as if they had just performed the leading role in a play or competed in the soccer finals.

The classroom curriculum consists of six weekly sessions (with two additional optional sessions) and a postintervention follow-up session, which is conducted four to eight weeks after the completion of this curriculum. The sessions can be led by the classroom teacher alone in his or her classroom or, ideally, with the assistance of the facilitator. Each session typically lasts 30 to 45 minutes, but the curriculum is meant to be flexible. Sessions that appear to be requiring more time can be extended or divided into multiple sessions, as the needs of individual classes dictate.

Each session includes an outline of the information to present, and handout and other reproducible classroom material masters to supplement the presentation. **The classroom curriculum is not scripted, as each teacher should be presenting the curriculum to his or her class with the exact content and presentation format planned for during staff training** Session 6 (see Chapter Four). For example, some schools will use the rules for bully-proofing in verbatim form, while other schools may want to add qualifiers such as "No racial slurs are allowed," etc.

After introducing the standard classroom curriculum, a three session refresher curriculum to be used in subsequent years of bully-proofing and an adaptation of the curriculum for younger students in kindergarten and first grade are presented (Section Two).

THE CONCEPT OF BULLYING

GOAL

To introduce the concept of bullying to the students (including information about bullying tactics and the types of children likely to be bullies and victims) and to determine the extent of bullying occurring in the classroom.

HANDOUTS/POSTERS/BUTTONS

Handout 3-8: The Colorado School Climate Student Report
Handout 5-1: Recognizing the Difference
Handout 5-2: Optional Sociogram

Introduce the Concept of Bullying to the Students As

- An imbalance of power (psychological, physical, or social);

- Repeated incidences of negative actions, not just one time (unless very severe);

- Done by either a single individual or a group;

- Done to gain attention or popularity;

- Done to get one's way or material things; and

- Between children who are not friends and don't usually play together.

Discuss Why Children Bully Others

- To get power.

- To gain popularity and attention or material things.

- To act out problems at home.

- To copy what another person they may admire does.

Discuss What Types of Children Are Likely to Be Bullies

- A child who likes the rewards that aggression can bring.

- A child who lacks compassion for his or her victim.

- A child who lacks guilt.

- A child who believes that the victim provoked his or her attack and deserved what happened.

- A child who likes to be in charge and to get his or her own way with power.

- A child whose parent(s) (or older brothers and sisters) are bullying him or her.

- A child who misperceives how others treat him or her.

Discuss How Children Bully

- By physical aggression (e.g., spitting, tripping, pushing, shoving, destroying another's things, hitting, threatening with a weapon);

- By social alienation (e.g., gossiping, spreading rumors, ethnic or racial slurs, excluding from a group, publicly humiliating, threatening with total isolation from the peer group);

- By verbal aggression (e.g., mocking, name calling, teasing, intimidating telephone calls, verbal threats of aggression); and

- By intimidation (e.g., graffiti, a public challenge to do something, playing a dirty trick, taking possessions, coercion).

Discuss What Types of Children Are Likely to Be Victims

- A child who is isolated and alone during much of the school day.

- A child who is anxious, insecure, and has trouble making friends.

- A child who is small or weak and therefore unable to defend himself or herself.

- A child who cries easily, gives up when bullied, and is unable to successfully stick up for himself or herself.

- A child who may have suffered past abuse at home.

- A child who may have a learning disability.

Sometimes a victim (even though he or she may not seem like a victim) is:

- A child who is often restless, irritable, and who teases and provokes other children.

- A child who will fight back, but ends up losing.

- A child who tries not to give in to the bully, and gets very upset when he or she does lose.

Handout 5-1

Discuss the Difference Between Normal Peer Conflict and Bullying

Use Handout 5-1 to discuss the differences between normal peer conflict and bullying. Initially, let students brainstorm their ideas about the differences.

It helps children to understand that bullying is different from regular conflict because it involves danger—the danger of someone being physically and/or emotionally hurt. For example, if a child teasingly sits in another's chair, there really is not any danger. This is a normal peer conflict. But if a child is repeatedly called names, this can result in harm to that child's self-esteem, so it is dangerous.

Discuss the Emotional Consequences for the Victim

- ◆ Drop in self-esteem to self-defeating, fearful attitude;

- ◆ Feeling scared, withdrawn, isolated, and/or sad;

- ◆ Physical symptoms (e.g., headache, stomachache, general fatigue);

- ◆ Not liking school; and

- ◆ Panic and irrational retaliation.

Facilitator Notes

Begin each discussion topic by asking the class for their ideas (e.g., "Why do you think children bully others?").

Be sure, when leading these class discussions, to present the material using examples relevant to the students' lives and experiences at school. Never identify any child (whether bully or victim) by name in your examples, and encourage the students to avoid the use of names in their examples as well. Instead, coach them to say: "Someone I know . . . "; "A boy in our grade . . . "; "A girl in this class . . . "; etc.

Administer "The Colorado School Climate Student Report"

Handout 3-6
Handout 3-7
Handout 3-8

Remind the students to not write their names on their surveys as the surveys are meant to be anonymous.

Please read Handouts 3-6 and 3-7 carefully. As teachers and facilitators administering the survey, you will want to be familiar with the instructions your students need to answer the survey questions. The accuracy of the survey depends on how well students understand the questions and how to answer them.

Read through the questions before you read them out loud to the students. You may define words that are not familiar to the students. However, if you are asked to clarify what is meant by a particular item, tell the student to answer it as best he or she can according to whether or not the behavior has occurred. For example: look at the section that asks about frequency of bullying behaviors, "Less than one time per week" refers to an event that has happened on one or more occasions, but has not occurred on a weekly basis.

Note: It is important to read the questionnaires to the students. This is to help ensure that the students, regardless of reading level, understand all the questions. The questionnaire can be administered over multiple sessions (at least one page at a time). As you collect the questionnaires, please be sure to check that the students have provided **one and only one** response for each question.

Handout 5-2

Scoring the Optional Sociogram

Questions A, B and C from "The Social Survey" may be used for a sociogram at each elementary grade level. Begin with a list of all the students at a grade level within your school or in one specific classroom at a grade level. Put a plus sign (+) next to a child's name each time he or she is listed in response to Question A. Put a minus sign (–) next to a child's name each time he or she is listed in response to Question B. Put a zero (0) next to a child's name each time he or she is listed in responses to Question C. Popular children will end up with many plus signs, bullies with a mixture of plus and minus signs, provocative victims with many minus signs and zeros, and passive victims will end up with many zeros.

The sociogram helps teachers assess social interactional patterns within a grade level or classroom. It is an easy way to identify the socially isolated students.

NEXT SESSION

Before the next session, you should compile the scores of "The Colorado School Climate Student Report" and determine the frequency, severity, and most common types of bullying occurring in the classroom. In the next session, the students will be given feedback on their responses to "The Colorado School Climate Student Report," and the classroom rules and "no-bullying" posters will be introduced.

HANDOUT 5-1
Recognizing the Difference

NORMAL PEER CONFLICT	BULLYING
Equal power or friends	Imbalance of power; not friends
Happens occasionally	Repeated negative actions
Accidental	Purposeful
Not serious	Serious with threat of physical or emotional harm
Equal emotional reaction	Strong emotional reaction from victim and little or no emotional reaction from bully
Not seeking power or attention	Seeking power, control, or material things
Not trying to get something	Attempt to gain material things or power
Remorse—will take responsibility	No remorse—blames victim
Effort to solve the problem	No effort to solve problem

Social Survey

A. List the three children in your grade who you most like to do things with:

_____

_____

_____

B. List the three children in your grade who you don't like to spend time with:

_____

_____

_____

C. List the three children in your grade who you think most need a friend:

_____

_____

_____

RULES FOR BULLY-PROOFING THE CLASSROOM

SESSION 2

GOAL

The goal of this session is threefold: (1) to provide feedback about the students' responses to "The Colorado School Climate Student Report"; (2) to introduce some key concepts (e.g., the difference between tattling and getting adult help); and (3) to present the classroom rules about bullying that the students will be expected to abide by.

HANDOUTS/POSTERS/BUTTONS

Handout/Poster 5-3: Classroom Rules (or Teacher Alternate)

Poster 5-4: The Bullydog

Poster 5-5: "Don't Be a Bullydog!" (or Teacher Alternate)

Poster 5-6: "No Bullying Allowed!" (or Teacher Alternate)

Last Session Review

Ask the students to recall the definition of bullying, why someone might bully, and who is likely to be a victim.

Feedback

Give the students feedback about their class' responses to "The Colorado School Climate Student Report" (administered in Session 1).

For primary students (grades 1, 2, and 3):   Feedback may be general rather than specific. For example:

"Bullying is a problem in this classroom."

For intermediate students (grades 4, 5, and 6):   More specific feedback about problem areas may be given. For example:

"In your class, there is a problem with teasing (or getting hurt physically)."

"More girls than boys in your class reported being bullied."

"Many children in your class need a friend."

Facilitator Notes

Remember to never identify by name or insinuation who the bullies are or who the victims are during any of the class discussions. This could embarrass the students, and thus cause resistance to the program.

Present the Goal of This Program

Assure the students that you and they together are going to make the classroom **safe** for all people from now on. Let them know that **no physical or verbal bullying will be allowed**.

Present Key Program Concepts

◆ Introduce the idea of bully-proofing.

The adults in your school have been trained and will help to keep you safe.

◆ Introduce the concept that strength is found in numbers.

If a bully is trying to be popular, then having most of the class saying, "I don't like what you are doing" will stop the bully from achieving that goal. It is difficult for the bully to target a victim if children stick together and no one is left out.

◆ Explain the difference between tattling and getting adult help.

It is not tattling when you help someone who is in danger, who is being hurt physically or emotionally, by speaking out. The goal of telling an adult is to get help, not to get someone in trouble.

It might be helpful to model speaking out about bullying for the students, and to give the students some examples to cement their understanding of the difference between "tattling" and "getting adult help." Two examples to discuss are: "Jimmy took my place in line. Teacher, make him move," and "Susie is calling me 'Four Eyes' again. Teacher, I need help." Have the students vote on whether each example is tattling or getting adult help.

Introduce the Classroom Rules and the "No-Bullying" Posters

Handout/Poster 5-3 (or Teacher Alternate)
Poster 5-4
Poster 5-5 (or Teacher Alternate)
Poster 5-6 (or Teacher Alternate)

Present the following classroom rules about bullying, or your own alternate rules developed during staff training Session 6:

1. We will not bully other students.

2. We will help others who are being bullied by speaking out and by getting adult help.

3. We will use extra effort to include **all students** in activities at our school.

Explain to the students that the goal is for everyone to be physically and emotionally safe. For primary students, you may want to reword rule 3 as

"You can't say, 'You can't play' " (Paley, 1992) and the goal as "We all have the right not to have our bodies or our feelings hurt."

Tell the students that you are going to hang the classroom rules and some posters about bullying around the room to remind them that bullying is no longer allowed in their classroom.

Alternate Activity

Instead of or in addition to hanging up Posters 5-5 and 5-6 provided with this program, you may wish to have the students draw or color their own posters about bullying (both male and female). You could then hang all their posters on a special no-bullying display, or even have a poster contest.

NEXT SESSION

In the next session, the students will learn strategies that they can use when they are being victimized by a bully.

HANDOUT/POSTER 5-3
Classroom Rules

Rules for Bully-Proofing Our Classroom

1. We will not bully other students.

2. We will help others who are being bullied by speaking out and by getting adult help.

3. We will use extra effort to include **all students** in activities at our school.

POSTER 5-4
The Bullydog

Don't Be a

Bullydog!

POSTER 5-6
"No Bullying Allowed!"

TEACHING STRATEGIES FOR THE VICTIMS

SESSION 3

GOAL

To teach the students strategies that they can use when they are being victimized by a bully—"HA HA, SO."

HANDOUTS/POSTERS/BUTTONS

Handout/Poster 5-7: The Difference Between Tattling and Telling

Poster 5-8: HA HA, SO

Handout 5-9: Skills to Disengage

Handout 5-10: "Pushing Your Buttons"

Handout 5-11: HA HA, SO Shield

Last Session Review

Ask the students to recall the classroom rules.

Group Activity

To refamiliarize the students with bullying situations and break the ice, read a story from your school's library or show a video that addresses a bully-victim situation. Be sure to select one that is appropriate to the age group of the children.

Teach and Model for the Students the HA HA, SO Strategies

HA HA, SO

H - **H**elp	**H** - **H**umor	**S** - **S**elf-Talk
A - **A**ssert Yourself	**A** - **A**void	**O** - **O**wn It

- **Help**—Teach the students when and how to seek help from peers and/or an adult.

   This strategy is best used in situations where help is available and willing, like at a "bully-proofed school." A victim can use this strategy during a bullying situation by calling to some other

> **RESOURCE GUIDE**
>
> See "Videotapes and Films for Students," "Books for Primary Students," or "Books for Intermediate Students" for materials that address bullying situations.

Handout/Poster 5-7

children, for example, "Could you help me ask Teddy to stop taking my books away from me?" or by running to an adult, describing what is happening, and saying, "I need help." Refer to Handout/Poster 5-7, Tattling or Telling, and have students brainstorm and discuss the differences between these behaviors.

A victim can also use this strategy when anticipating a bullying situation by asking several other children to stay close. For example, "Susan and her friends have been bullying me at recess. Could you play with me today and help me figure out what to do if they come at me again?" or by informing the teacher and asking for a watchful eye. It can be helpful to have each student think of and name at least one adult and one peer he or she can turn to for help.

- **Assert Yourself**—Teach the students when it would be wise to use assertiveness and when it would not.

This strategy is usually the best strategy for a victim to start with. But it should not be used with severe bullying or when the victim is very scared. To use this strategy, the victim looks the bully in the eye and says, for example, "I don't like how you are gossiping about me and trying to make me have no friends. It is mean and unfair. Stop doing it."

RESOURCE GUIDE

See "Books for Primary Students" or "Books for Intermediate Students" for books which feature the use of humor in bullying situations.

- **Humor**—Teach the students how to use humor to de-escalate a situation.

This strategy is fun for children and can be used in conjunction with the "Help" strategy by asking other children to help dream up humorous ways to deal with a certain bullying situation. Several of the books listed in the Resource Guide illustrate humor as a strategy for dealing with the bully (e.g., in *Loudmouth George and the Sixth Grade Bully,* the victim, with the help of his friend, makes a horrific lunch with pickles in the sandwich and hot chili sauce in the thermos for a bully who has stealing his lunch). The victim could also use this strategy by writing a funny note or poem to the bully.

- **Avoid**—Teach the students how to walk away in order to avoid a bullying situation.

This strategy may be best for situations when the victim is alone. One way for the victim to use the "Avoid" strategy is to avoid a bully physically. The victim can cross the street or can avoid the situation(s) where the bullying is occurring. The victim can also avoid a bully by being with others rather than alone, perhaps by asking to walk home from school with other children. Another way for the victim to use the "Avoid" strategy is to analyze the situation and to stop doing anything that might be provoking the bully. If the bullying is happening when the class lines up and both the victim and the bully want to be at the front of the line, the victim can choose to be at the end of the line in order to avoid a bullying situation.

◆ **Self-Talk**—Teach the students how to use their self-talk to maintain positive self-esteem during a bullying situation.

Remind the students that in Session 1 they learned how victims' self-esteem drops when they are being bullied. The "Self-Talk" strategy is used to keep feeling good about oneself. The strategy involves "putting on a record in one's mind" that says nice things like: "I'm a good kid. I try my best at school and I'm nice to other kids. When Jason calls me dumb, it is not my fault. It is his problem that he is being mean. It is unfair. I don't have to accept his opinion of me. I can have my own opinion about me and I like myself."

◆ **Own It**—Teach the students how to "own" the put-down or belittling comment in order to defuse it.

This strategy can be combined with the "Humor" strategy with responses like, "I agree that this is an ugly dress; my mother made me wear it." It can also be combined with the "Assert Yourself" strategy with responses like, "I do have slanted eyes and that is because I'm Korean. Korea is a really cool country. Do you want to hear some things about it?"

Explain to the students that the first strategy that they try with a bully may not work. In that case, they will have to try another. That is why you are giving them six strategies and an easy way to remember them (HA HA, SO)—so that they will have lots of things to try. After they know the six strategies really well, they will be able to quickly figure out which strategy to try first, second, and so on, in each unique bullying situation.

As an indication of their understanding of these strategies, ask the class to identify the strategy or strategies used by the victim character in the story or video you presented to the class at the beginning of this session. If none of the HA HA, SO strategies were used, ask the students to identify a strategy or strategy that the victim character **should have** used.

To reinforce the memorization of the HA HA, SO mnemonic, you may wish to have the students repeat the strategies in some way, such as singing HA HA, SO to a familiar tune, calling out the strategies as you yell the HA HA, SO "cheer" (i.e., "Give me an H!" "Help!" "Give me an A!" "Assert Yourself!" and so on), or by any other means you can think of that would be fun and memorable for the students.

Hang the poster up in the classroom with the other bullying posters to remind the students about the strategies they can use when they are being bullied.

Poster 5-8

Handouts 5-9, 5-10, and 5-11 can be used to teach students how to disengage from a bully's attempts to push their buttons and how to use HA HA, SO as a protective shield to cover their buttons.

Handout 5-9
Handout 5-10
Handout 5-11

Facilitator Notes

Be sure to present these strategies using examples relevant to the students' lives and experiences at school. This will assist the students in internalizing them.

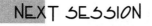 NEXT SESSION

In the next session, the students will have the opportunity to try these strategies themselves, and practice them to a comfort level through role play.

HANDOUT/POSTER 5-7
The Difference Between Tattling and Telling

TATTLING		TELLING
Unimportant	vs.	Important
Harmless	vs.	Harmful or dangerous physically or psychologically
Can handle by self	vs.	Need help from an adult to solve
Purpose is to get someone in trouble	vs.	Purpose is to keep people safe
Behavior is accidental	vs.	Behavior is purposeful

POSTER 5-8
HA HA, SO

What I Can Do If I Am Being Bullied

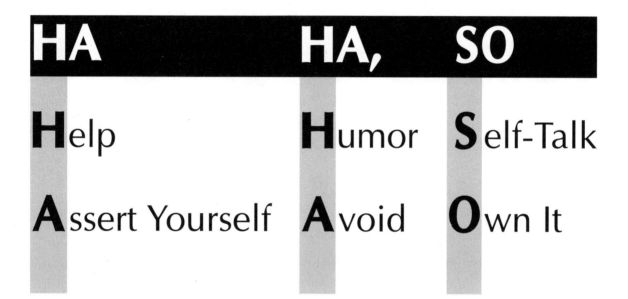

HA	HA,	SO
Help	**H**umor	**S**elf-Talk
Assert Yourself	**A**void	**O**wn It

HANDOUT 5-9
Skills to Disengage

1. Think about what gets to you.

   What are your buttons?

2. When you find someone has pushed one of your buttons, try this

   ◆ Say your multiplication tables in your head

   ◆ Count backward from 30 to 1

   ◆ Think about the last time you were really bored

   ◆ Most of all, do not think about what the other person did or said to you

3. Remember that you are giving control to the other person if you respond. Doing nothing means that you win and they lose because you stayed in control.

Plan for the next time this same person tries to get to you. Remember that there will be a next time. People who like to push the buttons of others usually try again and the second and third time it might be worse. When it happens, remind yourself that

   ◆ It Gets Worse Before It Gets Better

   ◆ Winning Is Not Who Is Best at Put-Downs

   ◆ Winning Is Taking Care of Your Own Emotions

HANDOUT 5-10
"Pushing Your Buttons"

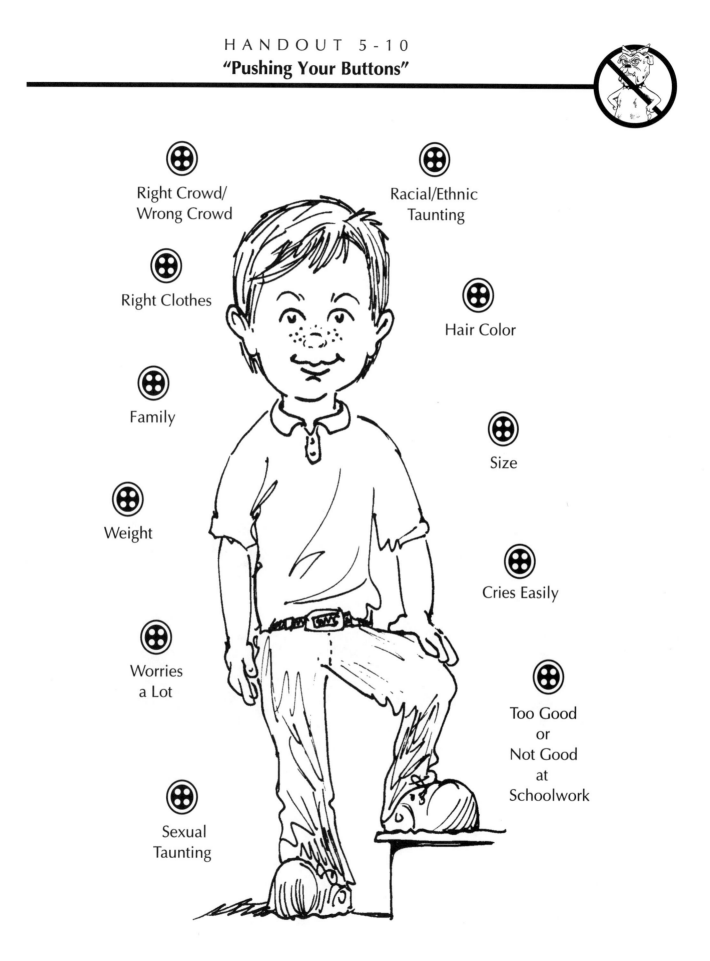

Right Crowd/
Wrong Crowd

Racial/Ethnic
Taunting

Right Clothes

Hair Color

Family

Size

Weight

Cries Easily

Worries
a Lot

Too Good
or
Not Good
at
Schoolwork

Sexual
Taunting

HANDOUT 5-11
HA HA, SO Shield

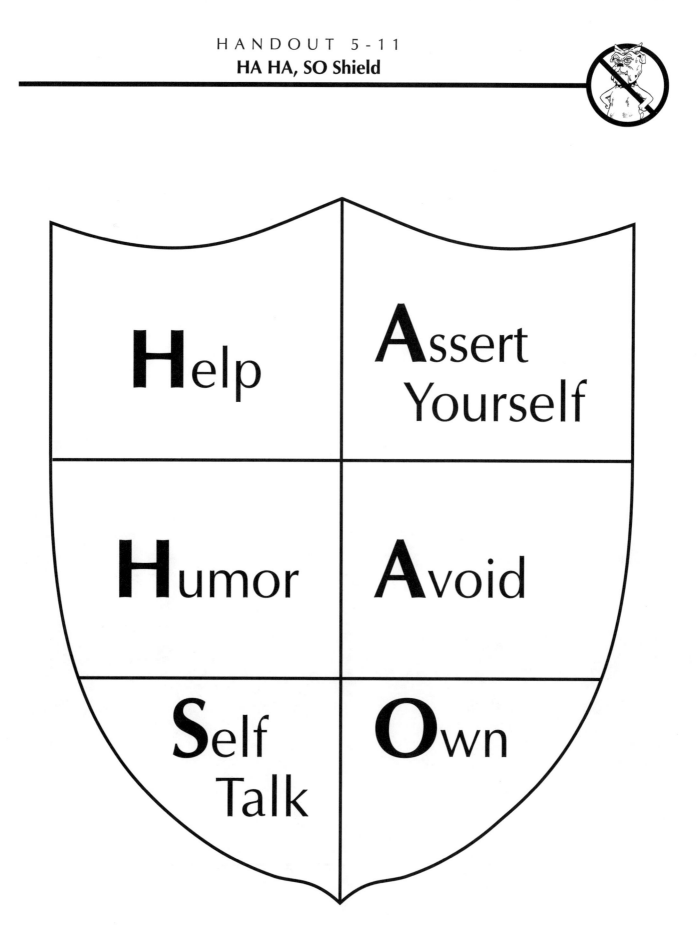

PRACTICING STRATEGIES FOR THE VICTIMS

GOAL

To have the students practice the strategies that they learned to use when they are being victimized by a bully.

HANDOUTS/POSTERS/BUTTONS

Handout 5-12: First/Second Grade Role Play—Female

Handout 5-13: First/Second Grade Role Play—Male

Handout 5-14: Third/Fourth Grade Role Play—Female

Handout 5-15: Third/Fourth Grade Role Play—Male

Handout 5-16: Fifth/Sixth Grade Role Play—Female

Handout 5-17: Fifth/Sixth Grade Role Play—Male

Last Session Review

Ask the students to recall what HA HA, SO stands for.

Role Play

Ask the children to each write one bullying incident that they have either experienced or witnessed on an index card or piece of paper. (If for some reason the children are unable to generate any scenarios, sample role plays are provided—see Handouts 5-12 through 5-17.) Select a few of the children's scenarios to role play that are representative of both typical male and female bullying tactics. Be sure to include at least one example of a provocative victim.

For each role play scenario, ask for student volunteers to play the bully and the victim. As the rest of the class watches quietly, direct the volunteers in performing the role plays appropriately (using one or more of the HA HA, SO strategies). After each role play, have the whole class discuss the role play scenario and identify the strategy or strategies used by the victim.

Facilitator Notes

It is important to allow the students to **volunteer** for performing the role play parts, as students who are actual victims of bullying may find enacting bully-victim incidents before the class too emotionally charged. If the majority of the students appear to find the role playing uncomfortable or intimidating, an alternate method of enacting the bully-victim situations is through puppet play. Using puppets (available in any toy store) sometimes distances the students from the roles they are playing and allows them to more easily "speak through the character."

Sample Role Plays

Handout 5-12

You are a student in first or second grade. A group of girls leaves out one girl and won't let her play. Finally she finds a friend to play with one recess, and the other girls go over to the playmate and say, "Why would you want to play with her?"

Handout 5-13

You are a student in first or second grade. You notice that a couple of boys constantly make fun of another boy who is artistic. They tease him and call him a "sissy." They invite him to play kickball, although they know he doesn't like to play. After they encourage him to play, they leave him out or pick him last for their team.

Handout 5-14

You are a student in third or fourth grade. A new girl has just joined your class. She moved to your town from another state. Although she is pretty, she uses expressions and mannerisms that sound and seem different. A group of girls begin to mimic her way of talking and gesturing. They especially laugh and make fun of her at lunch time, refusing to leave a place for her at the table.

Handout 5-15

You are a student in third or fourth grade. One boy in your class has a learning disability and leaves the classroom each morning to go to a resource class for help with reading. Boys in your class call him "Stupid." Other boys call him at home and ask for "the dumb kid." One day, some boys take his special reading book and toss it back and forth on the playground, saying, "See if you can get anything right now, you dummy."

Handout 5-16

You are a student in fifth or sixth grade. A couple of girls have been picking on one of your classmates. They have been spreading rumors that she has an older boyfriend in high school. They wrote fake notes to her from this boyfriend with things about sex in them. Then they showed these notes to other girls. Now no one wants to be that girl's friend.

Handout 5-17

You are a student in fifth or sixth grade. One boy in your class whose parents are getting a divorce is in an angry mood a lot. He has gotten into some minor physical fights with other boys.

Lately he seems to be going after one particular boy. He trips him in the halls and runs into him at recess. Then he calls him "Clumsy" or says, "Why don't you watch where you are going?"

Optional Activity

Using Handouts 5-9, 5-10, and 5-11, students can discuss which buttons of the victim were being pushed by the bully in each role-play. Furthermore, which HA HA, SO strategies would be most effective can be discussed.

NEXT SESSION

In the next session, strategies for the students to use as "helpers" in the classroom are presented. These are techniques that "the caring majority" of students (the 85% of students who are neither bullies nor victims) can employ to assist the victims and prevent bullying behavior.

HANDOUT 5-12
First/Second Grade Role Play—Female

 You are a student in first or second grade. A group of girls leaves out one girl and won't let her play. Finally she finds a friend to play with one recess, and the other girls go over to the playmate and say, "Why would you want to play with her?"

Discussion Questions

1. How could the victim use each of the following HA HA, SO strategies?
    - Help
    - Assert Yourself
    - Humor
    - Avoid
    - Self-Talk
    - Own It

2. Which is the best strategy to try first?

3. Which is the best strategy to try second?

4. Is there any strategy the victim would be wise not to try?

HANDOUT 5-13
First/Second Grade Role Play—Male

◆ You are a student in first or second grade. You notice that a couple of boys constantly make fun of another boy who is artistic. They tease him and call him a "sissy." They invite him to play kickball, although they know he doesn't like to play. After they encourage him to play, they leave him out or pick him last for their team.

Discussion Questions

1. How could the victim use each of the following HA HA, SO strategies?
   - Help
   - Assert Yourself
   - Humor
   - Avoid
   - Self-Talk
   - Own It

2. Which is the best strategy to try first?

3. Which is the best strategy to try second?

4. Is there any strategy the victim would be wise not to try?

HANDOUT 5-14
Third/Fourth Grade Role Play—Female

◆ You are a student in third or fourth grade. A new girl has just joined your class. She moved to your town from another state. Although she is pretty, she uses expressions and mannerisms that sound and seem different. A group of girls begin to mimic her way of talking and gesturing. They especially laugh and make fun of her at lunch time, refusing to leave a place for her at the table.

Discussion Questions

1. How could the victim use each of the following HA HA, SO strategies?
   - Help
   - Assert Yourself
   - Humor
   - Avoid
   - Self-Talk
   - Own It

2. Which is the best strategy to try first?

3. Which is the best strategy to try second?

4. Is there any strategy the victim would be wise not to try?

HANDOUT 5-15
Third/Fourth Grade Role Play—Male

◆ You are a student in third or fourth grade. One boy in your class has a learning disability and leaves the classroom each morning to go to a resource class for help with reading. Boys in your class call him "Stupid." Other boys call him at home and ask for "the dumb kid." One day, some boys take his special reading book and toss it back and forth on the playground, saying, "See if you can get anything right now, you dummy."

Discussion Questions

1. How could the victim use each of the following HA HA, SO strategies?
   - Help
   - Assert Yourself
   - Humor
   - Avoid
   - Self-Talk
   - Own It

2. Which is the best strategy to try first?

3. Which is the best strategy to try second?

4. Is there any strategy the victim would be wise not to try?

HANDOUT 5-16
Fifth/Sixth Grade Role Play—Female

◆ You are a student in fifth or sixth grade. A couple of girls have been picking on one of your classmates. They have been spreading rumors that she has an older boyfriend in high school. They wrote fake notes to her from this boyfriend with things about sex in them. Then they showed these notes to other girls. Now no one wants to be that girl's friend.

Discussion Questions

1. How could the victim use each of the following HA HA, SO strategies?
   - Help
   - Assert Yourself
   - Humor
   - Avoid
   - Self-Talk
   - Own It

2. Which is the best strategy to try first?

3. Which is the best strategy to try second?

4. Is there any strategy the victim would be wise not to try?

HANDOUT 5-17
Fifth/Sixth Grade Role Play—Male

◆ You are a student in fifth or sixth grade. One boy in your class whose parents are getting a divorce is in an angry mood a lot. He has gotten into some minor physical fights with other boys.

Lately he seems to be going after one particular boy. He trips him in the halls and runs into him at recess. Then he calls him "Clumsy" or says, "Why don't you watch where you are going?"

Discussion Questions

1. How could the victim use each of the following HA HA, SO strategies?
   - ◆ Help
   - ◆ Assert Yourself
   - ◆ Humor
   - ◆ Avoid
   - ◆ Self-Talk
   - ◆ Own It

2. Which is the best strategy to try first?

3. Which is the best strategy to try second?

4. Is there any strategy the victim would be wise not to try?

TEACHING STRATEGIES FOR THE HELPERS

SESSION 5

GOAL

To present strategies for the students to use as "helpers" in the classroom. These "CARES" strategies are techniques that "the caring majority" of students (the 85% of students who are neither bullies nor victims) can employ to assist the victims and prevent bullying behavior.

HANDOUTS/POSTERS/BUTTONS

Poster 5-18: CARES

Handout 5-19: What I Can Do If . . .

Last Session Review

Check that the students still remember what HA HA, SO stands for.

Group Activity

To expand upon the students' understanding of bullying situations and break the ice, read a story from your school's library or show a video that addresses a bully-victim situation that **emphasizes the feelings of the victim**. Be sure to select one that is appropriate to the age group of the children.

After the story or video, lead a class discussion about how the victim character might have been feeling. Have the class brainstorm appropriate "feeling words," and write them on the board. Get them started with words like "scared," "lonely," "sad," "hurt," and "fearful."

Encourage the students to develop compassion for the victim by making pointed statements and asking leading questions, such as:

- ◆ "How many of you have ever had a similar thing happen to you?"
- ◆ "Feeling afraid is not a very nice feeling, is it?"
- ◆ "How does your body feel when you are scared?"
- ◆ "What does it feel like to be sad? Do you ever feel like crying when you are sad?"
- ◆ "Does everyone feel lonely sometimes? Can you remember the last time you felt lonely?"

> **RESOURCE GUIDE**
> See "Videotapes and Films for Students," "Books for Primary Students," or "Books for Intermediate Students" for materials which emphasize the feelings of the victim in bullying situations.

Encourage the students to **think about their answers** to these questions. They will not have to raise their hands or answer out loud, to avoid embarrassment, but they can volunteer answers or feelings if they like.

Teach and Model for the Students the CARES Strategies

Explain to the children that as part of their classroom rules against bullying, they will be expected to (and taught how to) help the victims of bullying.

Poster 5-18

CARES

C - **C**reative Problem Solving
A - **A**dult Help
R - **R**elate and Join
E - **E**mpathy
S - **S**tand Up and Speak Out

Creative Problem Solving   Teach the students how to address a bullying situation through creative problem solving.

A helper can use this strategy by saying, for example, "It looks like you two have a problem and maybe I can help you solve it. Lisa, you've been giving Margaret put-downs so now you could even it out by giving her some build-ups."

Handout/Poster 5-7

Adult Help   Teach the students when and how to seek help from an adult to keep things safe. Remind them about the difference between "tattling" and "telling." See Handout/Poster 5-7. Also remind students of the adult they named in Session 3 that they could get help from.

This strategy should be used when the "Stand Up and Speak Out" and "Creative Problem Solving" strategies are not working and especially when the helper feels scared too. The helper should seek out the teacher or another adult, explain the bullying situation and the strategies that have been tried, and ask for help.

Relate and Join   Teach the students how to join with and support the victim. Remind them that "there is strength in numbers."

This strategy involves helping the victim by clarifying differences. If a learning-disabled student is called "dumb," for example, a helper could say, "We all have things we're good at and things we're not so good at. I'm not so good at being organized." With racial slurs, a helper might say, for example, "Jody is black and I'm glad. Think how boring our class would be if we were all white."

This helping strategy can be illustrated by historical examples of joining, e.g., King of Denmark putting on the Star of David when the Nazis arrived and demanded it of the Jews.

Empathy   Teach the students how to empathize with feelings the victim might be experiencing. This strategy can involve simply telling a victim you felt with them after an observed bullying incident.

This strategy also can involve speaking out against bullying (the "Stand Up and Speak Out" strategy). A helper could say, for example, "Janet, you've been spreading rumors about Amy that aren't true. I don't like it and it is against our school rules. If I were Amy, I'd feel hurt, confused, and mad."

Stand Up and Speak Out   Teach the students how to speak out against bullying.

Handout 5-19

A helper might say, "Juan, making fun of James' baggy sweater isn't nice. I have one almost like it at home and I think I'll wear it tomorrow because old, soft sweaters are so comfortable. You can wear one too if you want to."

Explain to the students that the first strategy that they try when helping a victim may not work. In that case, they will have to try another. That is why you are giving them five strategies and an easy way to remember them (CARES)—so that they will have lots of things to try. After they know the five strategies really well, they will be able to quickly figure out which strategy to try first, second, and so on, in each unique bullying situation.

As an indication of their understanding of these strategies, ask the class to identify the strategy or strategies used by the other characters (other than the bully and victim) in the story or video you presented to the class at the beginning of this session. If none of the CARES strategies were used, ask the students to identify the strategy or strategies that the other characters **should have** used to help the victim.

To reinforce the memorization of the CARES mnemonic, you may wish to have the students repeat the strategies in some way, such as singing CARES to a familiar tune, calling out the strategies as you yell the CARES "cheer" (e.g., "Give me a C!" "Creative Problem Solving!" "Give me an A!" "Adult Help!"), or by any other means you can think of that would be fun and memorable for the students.

Hang the poster up in the classroom with the other bullying posters to remind the students about the strategies they can use to help the victims of bullying.

Poster 5-18

Facilitator Notes

Be sure to present these strategies using examples relevant to the students' lives and experiences at school. This will assist the students in internalizing them.

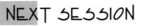

NEXT SESSION

In the next session, the children will have the opportunity to try these strategies themselves, and practice them to a comfort level through role play.

What I Can Do If I See Someone Being Bullied

CARES

C reative Problem Solving

A dult Help

R elate and Join

E mpathy

S tand Up and Speak Out

HANDOUT 5-19
What I Can Do IF . . .

WHAT I CAN DO IF I AM BEING BULLIED	
Help	When someone bullies you, you can ask other students, teachers, brothers and sisters to help you.
Assert Yourself	When someone picks on you, you can say "Please stop that. I don't like it."
Humor	You can try to find a funny way to deal with the bully.
Avoid	Stay away from kids who are mean.
Self-Talk	When someone is mean to you, say to yourself "I'm O.K., this is that kid's problem. I'm a nice kid; being mean isn't right."
Own It	Sometimes you can deflect a put-down by owning it. For example, if someone says "That's an ugly dress," you can say "I don't like it either, but my mom made me wear it."

WHAT I CAN DO IF I SEE SOMEONE BEING BULLIED	
Creative Problem Solving	Come up with helpful ways to deal with bullying.
Adult Help	This is not tattling when it keeps others safe.
Relate and Join	Join with and support the victims. There is safety and strength in numbers
Empathy	Try to understand the feelings of the victim and speak out against bullying.
Stand Up and Speak Out	Say, "Bullying is not allowed."

PRACTICING STRATEGIES FOR THE HELPERS

SESSION 6

GOAL

To have the students practice the strategies that they learned to use to help the victims of bullying, and to introduce a weekly reinforcement program for caring behavior ("I Caught You Caring").

HANDOUTS/POSTERS/BUTTONS

Handout 5-20: First Grade Role Play

Handout 5-21: Second Grade Role Play

Handout 5-22: Third Grade Role Play

Handout 5-23: Fourth Grade Role Play

Handout 5-24: Fifth Grade Role Play

Handout 5-25: Sixth Grade Role Play

Buttons 5-26: CARES Buttons

Last Session Review

Ask the students to recall what CARES stands for.

Role Play

Ask the students to each write one bullying incident that they have witnessed on an index card or piece of paper. (If for some reason the students are unable to generate any scenarios, sample role plays are provided—see Handouts 5-20 through 5-25.) Select a few of the students' scenarios to role play that are representative of both typical male and female bullying tactics. Be sure to include at least one example with a provocative victim.

For each role play scenario, ask for student volunteers to play the bully, the victim, and the "helper." As the rest of the class watches quietly, direct the volunteers in performing the role plays appropriately (using one or more of the CARES strategies). After each role play, have the whole class discuss the role play scenario and identify the strategy or strategies used by the helper.

Facilitator Notes

If the majority of the students appear to find the role playing uncomfortable or intimidating, an alternate method of enacting the bully-victim situations is through puppet play. Using puppets (available in any toy store) sometimes distances the students from the roles they are playing and allows them to more easily "speak through the character."

Sample Role Plays

The following scenarios are the same scenarios that the staff members worked on as part of their staff training to prevent bully-victim incidents. They have been rewritten from the point of view of the child. Besides role plays, these six scenarios can be used in a variety of ways:

- ◆ You could read a scenario aloud and then have the class vote on the different alternatives, followed by some classroom discussion.

- ◆ You could hand these out individually and ask each student to read them alone and to indicate the alternative(s) he or she prefers.

- ◆ You could then collect them and without revealing names, share with the class the different alternatives that the most students voted for.

- ◆ With the intermediate grade levels that have reading and writing skills, you could ask the students to complete them on their own as an assignment and to hand them in for discussion during the next session.

Handout 5-20

One Friday you overhear Lauren, a bossy, know-it-all girl who sits next to you, tell another girl in your class, Tamara, "I bet you got an 'F' again on your spelling test." You notice that Tamara looks like she is about to cry. Tamara often looks sad and you know that she is not a very good student, but she is nice and you like her.

Handout 5-21

You are on a class field trip to the zoo with a fifth grade class. You notice three of the fifth grade boys making fun of Jerold, a boy in your class, because he is having trouble filling out his question and answer sheet about the animals. You look around for a parent or teacher to do something and you can't find any adult to help Jerold.

Later in the morning, your group meets with the rest of the class for lunch. Jerold is missing and does not come for lunch. You feel very worried about him.

Handout 5-22

At recess, a lot of the children like to play a game called "Capture." Sometimes Jane doesn't like to play because running a lot is difficult for her. This particular day Jane decides to play and sure enough, she gets captured right away. The captors call her "slow, slimy snail" and take her to "The Dungeon." They tell her to clean all the crab apples off all the other captured children's shoes before she can be released. You can tell she feels angry and doesn't want to do it. You feel scared and worried for Jane.

Finally the bell rings and recess is over. You feel so relieved and happy to go back into class. All through the afternoon, you keep thinking about what happened and worrying about the next recess. You aren't certain what to do.

You usually play with Brent at recess. In fact, Brent is probably one of your best friends. One day you end up playing soccer with some of the other kids instead of playing with Brent. He doesn't mind because he has other friends too.

During the soccer game, you look over and see Brent in a fist fight with Mitchell. Brent doesn't ever play with Mitchell, but they live in the same neighborhood and ride the bus together so you know they know each other. You've never seen Brent fight before and you are really surprised.

You have known for a long time that there is a secret club of girls in your room. The three girls who run it are bossy and pretty mean. They scare you a lot of the time and you just avoid them. They have never picked on you and you are thankful.

One day you are walking into class when you hear them calling Leah, an African-American girl who is new, a really nasty name. You feel upset and sorry for Leah, who seems pretty nice to you. Plus you know that putting someone down for their skin color is wrong and unfair.

Your school has a new program this year. Every morning a group of eight students meets with a teacher advisor to talk about school issues and feelings. You don't really like these meetings and usually you just keep quiet and listen. One morning about five of the other kids start complaining about a boy named Jonathan. They say that he is always a pest. He stands too close to them, bothers them when they are working, and won't play games by the rules. He gets in fights all the time with Chris and the other kids give the impression that Jonathan is the one who starts the fights.

Because you are quiet and watch others a lot, you know that what they are reporting is not quite how it all happens. You agree that Jonathan is a pest, but you also know that Chris is really a bully and the one who starts the fights. Jonathan is just easy for Chris to pick on because he is always pestering others. In fact, you have seen Chris do some really mean things, like write bad names inside Jonathan's locker and threaten him out of money and things in his lunch. You feel like someone needs to tell the advisor the truth about Chris.

| Handout 5-23 |
| Handout 5-24 |
| Handout 5-25 |

Introduce the "I Caught You Caring" Reinforcement Program

Now that the students are familiar with and comfortable about performing the caring behaviors of a "helper," let them know that the best helper each week will be rewarded.

Explain to the students what will happen in the "I Caught You Caring" sessions each week, when these classroom sessions will take place, and what the special reward will be. You can use the program model for these weekly classroom sessions, or substitute your own developed in staff training Session 6.

I Caught You Caring

These weekly sessions are designed for reinforcement of caring behavior within the classroom. They occur at the end of the week (e.g., Friday before dismissal), and take approximately five to fifteen minutes.

Each teacher chooses one of his or her students who he or she "caught" being kind or helpful to another student for this special recognition. The teacher should keep a log of "acts of kindness" that he or she notices during the week, and then pick a good example to reinforce.

During the session, the teacher should announce the "Caring Student of the Week" and describe the caring behavior that he or she performed. The teacher should discuss with the class why the behavior worked/ how it complied with the classroom rules, and model the skill(s) for the students. Some brief discussion can then occur about what motivated the caring behavior.

Note: These class discussions can be expanded upon and enlivened, if you wish, by employing creative discussion techniques. For example, you could read *Finding the Greenstone,* by Alice Walker, to your class, and then allow the children to pass a green marble among themselves as they are "caught caring."

Also explain to the students that when they have all become very good helpers, who perform the caring behaviors almost all the time, they will be able to nominate and vote for the student with the "Best Caring Behavior" each week. When appropriate, explain that program and the special reward (the "CARES Buttons").

RESOURCE GUIDE

See "Books for Primary Students" for complete information on Alice Walker's book.

Buttons 5-26

NEXT SESSION

In the next session, all the skills presented in the classroom curriculum will be reviewed and reinforced for the students.

H A N D O U T   5 - 2 0
First Grade Role Play

One Friday you overhear Lauren, a bossy, know-it-all girl who sits next to you, tell another girl in your class, Tamara, "I bet you got an 'F' again on your spelling test." You notice that Tamara looks like she is about to cry. Tamara often looks sad and you know that she is not a very good student, but she is nice and you like her.

Would you:

1. Say or do something to help Tamara to feel better? What could you say or do?

2. Not try to make Tamara feel better because you're worried that Lauren might say something mean to you if you are kind to Tamara?

3. Do something other than the two ideas above? What would you do instead?

HANDOUT 5-21
Second Grade Role Play

◆ You are on a class field trip to the zoo with your second grade class and a fifth grade class. You notice three of the fifth grade boys making fun of Jerold, a boy in your class, because he is having trouble filling out his question and answer sheet about the animals. You look around for a parent or teacher to do something and you can't find any adult to help Jerold.

Would you:

1. Go over and say something to the three fifth grade boys?

2. Continue to look for an adult?

3. Decide that it would be best not to interfere so that the boys did not decide to pick on you?

4. Do something other than the three ideas above? What would you do instead?

Later in the morning, your group meets with the rest of the class for lunch. Jerold is missing and does not come for lunch. You feel very worried about him.

Would you:

5. Ask someone where Jerold is?

6. Tell an adult what you observed earlier in the morning?

7. Just keep quiet and wait to see if Jerold was there when you got back to school?

HANDOUT 5-22
Third Grade Role Play

◆ At recess, a lot of the children like to play a game called "Capture." Sometimes Jane doesn't like to play because running a lot is difficult for her. This particular day Jane decides to play and sure enough, she gets captured right away. The captors call her "slow, slimy snail" and take her to "The Dungeon." They tell her to clean all the crab apples off all the other captured children's shoes before she can be released. You can tell she feels angry and doesn't want to do it. You feel scared and worried for Jane.

Finally the bell rings and recess is over. You feel so relieved and happy to go back into class. All through the afternoon, you keep thinking about what happened and worrying about the next recess. You aren't certain what to do.

Would you:

1. Tell your mom and dad tonight and ask them to help you figure out what to do?

2. Tell your teacher and ask her to do something?

3. Help Jane to avoid the game at the next recess?

4. Tell the other children that it is not fair to treat Jane like a slave?

5. Do something other than the four ideas above? What would you do instead?

HANDOUT 5-23
Fourth Grade Role Play

◆ You usually play with Brent at recess. In fact, Brent is probably one of your best friends. One day you end up playing soccer with some of the other kids instead of playing with Brent. He doesn't mind because he has other friends too.

During the soccer game, you look over and see Brent in a fist fight with Mitchell. Brent doesn't ever play with Mitchell, but they live in the same neighborhood and ride the bus together so you know they know each other. You've never seen Brent fight before and you are really surprised.

Would you:

1. Leave the soccer game and go see what the fight is about?

2. Wait and talk to Brent later?

3. Look for a playground aide to help break up the fight?

4. Do something other than the three ideas above? What would you do instead?

H A N D O U T   5 - 2 4
Fifth Grade Role Play

◆ You have known for a long time that there is a secret club of girls in your room. The three girls who run it are bossy and pretty mean. They scare you a lot of the time and you just avoid them. They have never picked on you and you are thankful.

One day you are walking into class when you hear them calling Leah, an African-American girl who is new, a really nasty name. You feel upset and sorry for Leah, who seems pretty nice to you. Plus you know that putting someone down for their skin color is wrong and unfair.

Would you:

1. Find Leah later and tell her about the club and how mean those girls are?

2. Not say anything but try to be nice to Leah and be her friend?

3. Find a teacher or adult to tell?

4. Confront the three girls who run the club and tell them that what they did was unfair?

5. Ask some of your other friends to give you advice and decide together what to do?

6. Do something other than the five ideas above? What would you do instead?

HANDOUT 5-25
Sixth Grade Role Play

◆ Your school has a new program this year. Every morning a group of eight students meets with a teacher advisor to talk about school issues and feelings. You don't really like these meetings and usually you just keep quiet and listen. One morning about five of the other kids start complaining about a boy named Jonathan. They say that he is always a pest. He stands too close to them, bothers them when they are working, and won't play games by the rules. He gets in fights all the time with Chris and the other kids give the impression that Jonathan is the one who starts the fights.

Because you are quiet and watch others a lot, you know that what they are reporting is not quite how it all happens. You agree that Jonathan is a pest, but you also know that Chris is really a bully and the one who starts the fights. Jonathan is just easy for Chris to pick on because he is always pestering others. In fact, you have seen Chris do some really mean things, like write bad names inside Jonathan's locker and threaten him out of money and things in his lunch. You feel like someone needs to tell the advisor the truth about Chris.

Would you:

1. Speak up in the meeting and tell what you know?

2. Wait until later to find your advisor alone and tell then?

3. Write an anonymous note to your advisor telling him the truth?

4. Tell your teacher?

5. Tell your parent(s) about this problem and ask for their ideas?

6. Do nothing, because Chris really scares you?

7. Do something other than the six ideas above? What would you do instead?

BUTTONS 5-26
CARES Buttons

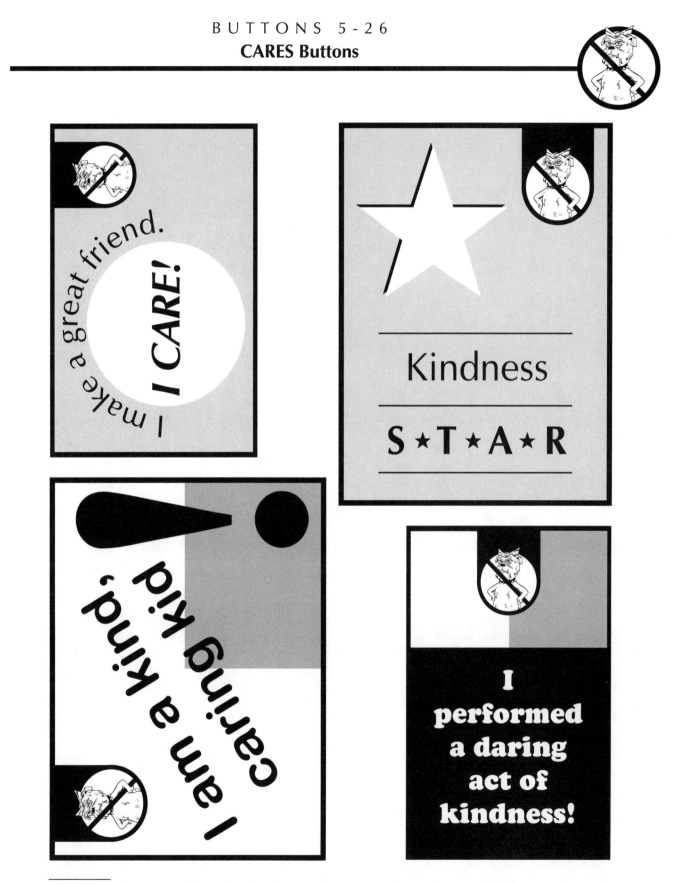

Note: These "buttons" are designed to be photocopied, cut out, and inserted into two popular sizes of pin style name badges (convention size: 4" 3", or 3½" 2¼"), available in most office supply stores.

CONFLICT RESOLUTION
(SKILL BUILDING)

OPTIONAL

GOAL

To teach the students and model for the students some additional prosocial and problem-solving skills which will assist them in preventing and coping with bullying behavior.

The topic of this session should be based on a simple needs assessment for each classroom by consultation with the teacher and playground supervisor as well as by ongoing observation by the facilitator.

Session goals include:

♦ To practice and demonstrate the ability to use effective conflict resolution strategies.

♦ To help students identify what situations cause them conflicts.

♦ To help students demonstrate "Active Listening" skills.

Certain classrooms might also benefit from adding additional sessions on Friendship-Making Skills (see Chapter Seven, Session 2) or Anger Management Skills (see Chapter Eight, Session 4).

HANDOUTS/POSTERS/BUTTONS

Handout 5-27: Getting Along the Best I Can (Primary)
Handout 5-28: Conflict Resolution Steps (Intermediate)
Handout 5-29: Reflective Listening

Conflict Resolution Activities

To help teach some effective conflict resolution alternatives, read a story from your school's library or show a video or movie that addresses effective conflict resolution. Be sure to select one that is appropriate to the age group of the students.

As a follow-up to the story or video, provide time for the students to practice what they have learned with the appropriate handout:

♦ **With primary students** (grades 1, 2, and 3): Use Handout 5-27.

Review the points that help students **avoid conflicts** that are typical for their age. Have each student formulate an individualized plan for getting along better with others (i.e., avoid conflict).

> **RESOURCE GUIDE**
> See "Videotapes and Films for Students," "Books for Primary Students," or "Books for Intermediate Students," for materials that address conflict resolution.

Handout 5-27

It may be helpful to problem solve with students who seem to be having difficulty with the assignment. Help the students identify tough parts of their school day and brainstorm conflict situations that have arisen during the school year.

◆ **With intermediate students** (grades 4, 5, and 6): Use Handout 5-28.

Teach the students the six steps of effective conflict resolution. To personalize the steps for the students, elicit examples of conflict situations that the students have encountered or create an appropriate example to fit their needs.

Reinforce continually to the students that they are not expected to be able to use **all** of these strategies perfectly at this point. These are actually life skills that **adults** even continue to work on.

Reflective Listening

Using Handout 5-29, introduce the skill of "reflective listening." Explain to the students that "reflective listening" is when you repeat back or paraphrase what you think you heard another person saying.

This skill is helpful in letting another person know you are interested in really understanding what he or she is saying. **It can help prevent conflicts or misunderstandings**.

Examples of reflective listening:

◆ "I think I heard you say . . . ."

◆ "So you think . . . ?"

Reflective Listening Activity

After modeling an example or two, have the students pair off to practice this skill, following the instructions on Handout 5-29.

NEXT SESSION (ALSO OPTIONAL)

In the next session, all the skills presented in the classroom curriculum will be reviewed and reinforced for the students.

Getting Along the Best I Can

- ◆ I share my toys.
- ◆ I take turns.
- ◆ I include others.
- ◆ I am kind.
- ◆ I apologize if I make a mistake.
- ◆ I ask for help to solve problems.

_____

_____

How I Plan to Get Along With Others

I will keep on: _____

_____

_____

_____

_____

I will try to get better at: _____

_____

_____

_____

_____

HANDOUT 5-28
Conflict Resolution Steps (Intermediate)

1. **Cool down if you are angry.**

   Ways to cool down:

   A. Count to 10.

   B. Take 10 deep breaths.

   C. Wait an hour.

2. **State your view of the problem. Use "I statements" and avoid those starting with "you."**

   Examples of "I statements":

   A. "**I** think we have a problem because . . . ."

   B. "**I**'m bothered about . . . ."

   C. "**I**'m angry because . . . ."

   D. "**I** want to talk to you about . . . ."

3. **Ask for the other person's viewpoint—use "reflective listening."**

4. **Brainstorm "win-win" solutions.**

5. **Pick a solution and talk about how to put it into action.**

6. **Affirm the resolution with a handshake.**

HANDOUT 5-29
Reflective Listening

 To be a **reflective listener**, you will try to be like a mirror. A mirror reflects back someone's physical image. You will reflect back a person's **thoughts** or **feelings**.

For example, you could say:

- "I think I heard you say . . . ."
- "So you think . . . ?"

Directions:

To practice this, pick a partner and take turns talking about and using reflective listening on these topics:

1. A time that you felt happy

2. A time that you felt scared

3. A time that you felt sad

4. A time that you felt mad

Reflective Listening

REVIEW
(SKILL BUILDING)

OPTIONAL

GOAL

To review and reinforce for the students all the skills presented in the classroom curriculum.

HANDOUTS/POSTERS/BUTTONS

Review any handouts or posters presented in Sessions 1 through 6 and the optional session on Conflict Resolution that may assist in reinforcing for the students the program skills. Those that might be helpful include:

Handout/Poster 5-3: Classroom Rules (or Teacher Alternate)

Poster 5-8: HA HA, SO

Poster 5-18: CARES

Reinforcement and Review

Reinforce and review the skills the students have practiced and learned. Review the classroom rules, strategies for the victims (HA HA, SO), and strategies for the helpers (CARES). Ask the students to give examples of how they have followed the rules and used the strategies.

Remind the students that although this is the last classroom session, the rules against bullying will still stay posted and in effect. **No bullying will be allowed in their classroom**. Tell the students that the weekly "I Caught You Caring" sessions will continue for at least eight more weeks or until the end of the school year, and that you look forward to watching them grow and mature in all the weeks ahead.

At this time, you may also request feedback from the students about how they feel about the no-bullying program, and answer any last questions they may have about what is expected from them.

Handout/Poster 5-3
Poster 5-8
Poster 5-18

NEXT SESSION

The next session is a postintervention session to be conducted in about six weeks. During the postintervention session, the facilitator will: (1) evaluate student progress and determine whether any new bullying problems have surfaced, (2) review and reinforce the student skills to prevent bullying behavior, and (3) provide any additional instruction necessary to ensure the continued success of the no-bullying program.

POSTINTERVENTION SESSION

FOLLOW-UP

GOAL

To revisit the classroom four to six weeks after the classroom curriculum was taught to: (1) evaluate student progress and determine whether any new bullying problems have surfaced; (2) review and reinforce the student skills to prevent bullying behavior; and (3) provide any additional instruction necessary to ensure the continued success of the no-bullying program.

HANDOUTS/POSTERS/BUTTONS

Refer back to:

Handout 3-8: The Colorado School Climate Student Report

Any other handouts/posters from Sessions 1-6 relating to skills to reinforce and review.

Evaluate Student Progress

Before the postintervention session, discuss with the classroom teacher his or her perceptions of student progress, and find out whether any new bullying problems have surfaced in the classroom.

Several days prior to the session, readminister to the students "The Colorado School Climate Student Report." Score the survey (refer back to the instructions found in Session 1 of this chapter) and have the results ready to present to the class.

Handout 3-8

During the session with the students, review and discuss the primary bully-victim problems in that specific classroom, both past and present (refer to the results of the readministered survey and to the guidelines for discussion provided in Session 2 of this chapter).

Reteach Any Skills Specifically Related to Any Problems Identified in the Class Discussion

Based on the results of the readministered survey, reteach all or applicable parts of the sessions addressing deficient skills. Specific skills presented in Chapter Seven: Supporting the Victims or in Chapter Eight: Changing the Bullies could also be drawn from for additional sessions, as appropriate.

Conclude the Session

Summarize for the students that they have learned some important things about bullying: what it is, what they can do if a bully picks on them, and what to do if they see a bully picking on someone else. Remind them that they will have to keep practicing these strategies to get good at them and that their teacher will be available to help them if they have any questions or need help practicing.

Point out to the students that when they grow up, they will still need to use these strategies. That is why it is important for them to learn them well now. To illustrate your point in a fun manner, ask the students: "Do you think your mom or dad needs to deal with bullies? If so, do you ever see them use or hear about them using any of the HA HA, SO strategies?" Also ask the students, "Have you ever seen your mom or dad helping someone who was being bullied? Did they use the CARES strategies?" Point out to the students that for adults, calling the authorities (e.g., the police) is the equivalent of "getting adult help."

KEEP THE MOMENTUM GOING

2ND YEAR REVIEW CURRICULUM

Session 1

- ◆ Review the concept of bullying
  - ◊ What is bullying
  - ◊ Why children bully
  - ◊ Who bullys
  - ◊ Who is victimized/bullied
- ◆ Do the "Colorado School Climate Student Report"
- ◆ Discuss classroom rules and the "No Bullying" posters
  - ◊ We will not bully others
  - ◊ We will help others
  - ◊ We will include ALL students in activities
- ◆ Remember the key concepts
  - ◊ Strength in numbers
  - ◊ Tattling vs. getting needed adult help
  - ◊ Adults have been trained in bully-proofing and will help keep you safe

Session 2

- ◆ Review last session
- ◆ Read a story or see a video about bully-proofing
- ◆ Teach HA HA, SO (use Handout 5-19: What Can I Do If I Am Being Bullied? for review)
- ◆ Have the kids ID strategies used in the story or video, and discuss what strategies the characters COULD have used
- ◆ Teach children to understand the bullying situation and help develop empathy for how the child being bullied feels
- ◆ Teach the C.A.R.E.S. strategies (Use Handout 5-19 for review)

- Discuss examples of when students have used the above strategies
- Try a sample role play in teams, using HA HA, SO and another using CARES

Session 3

- Review the last session
- Have students discuss bullying incidents they have seen (without using names)
- Reintroduce the "I Caught You Caring" program
- Discuss what it means to care and have the children think of examples
- Read a story about caring

Conclusion

Most classroom bully-victim situations can be changed effectively with the staff training and student instruction components of this program. Adult responsiveness and an empowered caring majority of students create the power shift, which stops bullies from continuing their behavior. Chapter Six describes ways to further the development of the caring majority of students.

Occasionally, certain children will need more intensive training and support to cope with bullying behavior. Chapter Seven addresses the special needs of victimized children. Some bullies may continue their antisocial behavior and be resistant to a changed environment. Strategies for intervention with bullies are described in Chapter Eight.

SECTION TWO: Early Elementary Curriculum (K–1)

The eight week student instruction format has been used successfully with the first to fifth grade student population. When a school-wide bully-proofing program has been adopted, it is important to teach the common language of the program and introduce the protective strategies as early as possible. A modified curriculum has been developed to meet the unique needs of the kindergarten and first grade children. (See Chapter One.)

Key points of the underlying philosophy of the bully-proofing program apply to the early elementary curriculum. The approach may be slightly different, but the goal is the same. Providing children with an understanding of what bullying is and how to deal with it appropriately is the focus at this level, as well. An emphasis is placed on understanding FRIENDSHIP. This starting point has proven to be an effective "jumping off" point to teach the language and strategies of bully-proofing.

Children can relate to the need for specific social skills instruction to effectively initiate and maintain friendships after understanding what a positive friendship looks and feels like. The protective strategies (HA HA, SO) are taught and emerge as part of a discussion of what to do if kids are not being friendly. The difference between tattling and telling/reporting supports the CARES strategies—it is important to help OTHERS who are not being treated with kindness and respect. Teaching, modeling, and reinforcing children to perform random acts of kindness is a positive, proactive way to encourage moral development.

The early elementary classroom curriculum (K–1) consists of six weekly sessions and a postintervention follow-up session, which is conducted three to six weeks after the completion of this curriculum. Additional follow-up sessions are suggested as needed. The sessions can be led by the classroom teacher alone in his or her classroom, or ideally, with the assistance of the facilitator. Each session typically lasts 20 to 30 minutes, but the curriculum is meant to be flexible. The age and attention span of younger students will vary. Sessions that appear to require more time can be extended or divided into multiple sessions, as the individual needs of the classes dictate.

WHAT I WANT IN A FRIEND

GOAL

To understand that friendship is positive in nature and involves a number of characteristics.

HANDOUTS/POSTERS/BUTTONS

Handout/Poster 5-30: "What I Want in a Good Friend" (or Teacher Alternate)

Group Activity

Brainstorm ideas about "what makes a good friend" as a lead-in to compiling a list of friendship characteristics.

An enlarged (poster size) version of "What I Want in a Good Friend" (or Teacher Alternate) is an effective format to record the children's ideas. After a few examples are recorded, read a book that describes friendship. Discuss and review the key points of the story emphasizing specific characteristics that help to make friendships positive.

> **RESOURCE GUIDE**
>
> See "Books for Primary Students" for ideas. *Friends* by Helme Heine is recommended.

Art Activity

Handout/Poster 5-30

Provide "What I Want in a Good Friend" handouts for each child. Depending upon skill level, students can either fill in balloons with words or color in the balloons and draw pictures on the back illustrating positive friendship skills.

Facilitator Notes

Key points to reinforce:

- ◆ **FRIENDS . . .**   Share

    CARE about one another

    Fair to each other

    Have fun

    Celebrate differences

    Have similar interests

- ◆ **FRIENDSHIPS . . .**   Should be positive

NEXT SESSION

In the next session, the students will discuss their current friendships as they continue to learn the skills necessary to initiate positive relationships.

HANDOUT/POSTER 5-30
What I Want in a Good Friend

HOW TO MAKE FRIENDS

SESSION 2

 GOAL

To develop the skills necessary to initiate friendships in a positive manner.

HANDOUTS/POSTERS/BUTTONS

Poster/Handout 7-6: Tips for Joining a Group of Kids

Last Session Review

Allow a few students to share their positive friendship experiences. Weave into the discussion a review of the characteristics necessary to help make friendships positive. Emphasize the importance that each and every person deserves to feel safe, have fun, and be treated kindly.

Group Activity

Read a story or show a video that illustrates the do's and don'ts of making friends. A discussion about making friends is enhanced by breaking the ice with feedback from the students. Offer the children a chance to think and talk about what friendship means and why some people have trouble making friends.

Encourage the students to talk about an experience in which they made a new friend. Was it hard? Easy? How did you feel? Ask students if they want to tell about an experience in which they tried but weren't able to make a new friend. What went wrong? How could they have acted differently?

> **RESOURCE GUIDE**
> See "Videotapes and Films for Students" and "Books for Primary Students." The video *Hopscotch* is recommended.

Teach 5 Good Tips for Joining a Group of Kids

Handout 7-6

1. Try to join with kids who are friendly.

2. Look for kids who enjoy the same activities you like.

3. Remember—it is easier to join one person or a group of four or more.

4. Remember—"no" does not mean "never."

5. Observe the activity you want to join first. Imitate, don't change what the other children are playing.

Practice the 5 tips with the children. To structure the role play, teacher and facilitator should participate.

Facilitator Notes

Ask students to practice being a good friend at school, in the neighborhood, at soccer practice, etc. Request that they begin to notice who is being a good friend and report their observations during the next group session.

NEXT SESSION

In the next session, the children will learn the skills necessary to keep friends. The classroom rules and "no bullying" posters will be introduced.

How To Keep Friends

SESSION 3

GOAL

To develop the skills necessary to maintain friendships.

HANDOUTS/POSTERS/BUTTONS

Handout/Poster 5-3: Classroom Rules (or Teacher Alternate)

Poster 5-4: The Bulldog (or Teacher Alternate)

Poster 5-5: "Don't Be A Bulldog!" (or Teacher Alternate)

Poster 5-6: "No Bullying Allowed!" (or Teacher Alternate)

Handout/Poster 5-31: Kids' Kindness Laws (or Teacher Alternate)

Last Session Review

Ask the students to recall and/or demonstrate the steps needed to initiate positive friendships. Ask for feedback regarding their assignment—who did you notice being a good friend this week. Teachers and facilitators may share their observations also.

Facilitator Notes

You may want to set a ground rule for discussions whereby a student's name may only be used if something **positive** is shared.

Group Activity

Choose a book or video that is an appropriate level and describes bullying behavior, as defined in the basic curriculum. Ask the children to first share their definition of "Bullying." It is important to understand the difference between normal peer conflict and bully behavior at a developmental level they can comprehend.

For example, friends have times when they do not get along well, but this is **not** bullying. Bullying usually does not occur between friends. Letting students know that if they feel like they don't have as much power as another child and/or they don't feel "safe" (both with their feelings and bodies), it might be a bully situation.

> **RESOURCE GUIDE**
>
> See "Books for Primary Students" or "Videotapes and Films for Students" which feature the issue of bullying. *The Big Bully* by Lizi Boyd is highly recommended.

Introduce the Classroom Rules and the "No Bullying" Posters

Present the following classroom rules or your alternate rules about bullying:

1. We will not bully other students.

2. We will help others who are being bullied by speaking out and by getting adult help.

3. We will use extra effort to include **all students** in activities at our school.

You may want to reword rule #3 as "You can't say, 'you can't play' " (Paley, 1992) and the goal as "we all have the right not to have our bodies or our feelings hurt." Mount the rules on construction paper and tell the students you are going to hang the rules and some posters around the classroom to remind them of how bullying is no longer allowed!

Alternate Activity

Instead of or in addition to hanging up Posters 5-5 and 5-6 provided with this program, you may wish to have the students draw or color their own posters about bullying. You could then hang their posters on a special "no-bullying" display.

Handout/Poster 5-31

Follow-up Activity: Kindness Laws

After the classroom rules are developed, those students who are capable of writing can fill out Handout 5-31: Kids' Kindness Laws. This would be an excellent activity to stress the importance of treating others with kindness as a critical step to developing and maintaining positive friendships.

NEXT SESSION

In the next session, the students will learn strategies that they can use when they are being victimized by a bully.

Kids' Kindness Laws

Write 5 "Kids' Kindness Laws" that would make this class a happier place for everyone.

1. _____

2. _____

3. _____

4. _____

5. _____

Write 2 things you already do to be kind.

1. _____

2. _____

Write 1 thing you might do today to be kind. Pick something you don't do a lot.

_____

_____

Reprinted with permission from Huggins, P. (1993). *Teaching friendship skills: Primary version.* Longmont, CO: Sopris West.

WHAT TO DO IF KIDS ARE NOT BEING FRIENDLY

GOAL

To teach the students strategies that they can use when they are being victimized by a bully.

HANDOUTS/POSTERS/BUTTONS

Handout/Poster 5-32: Modified HA HA, SO Strategies

Handout 5-10: "Pushing Your Buttons"

Handout 5-11: HA HA, SO Shield

Last Session Review

Ask the students to recall the classroom rules. Provide time on a daily basis to applaud friendly behavior and problem-solve issues as they arise. This discussion works well after recess time. Input from the playground supervisor, where appropriate, can be helpful.

Group Activity

- ◆ To refamiliarize the students with friendly behavior vs. bullying situations and break the ice, read a story or show a video that is suitable to the age group of the children and **emphasizes appropriate responses** to being bullied.

- ◆ Teach and Model for the Students the HA HA, SO Strategies

    See Chapter Five, Session 3: Teaching Strategies for the Victims

- ◆ Modified HA HA, SO Strategies

    Modified Protective Strategies may be more appropriate when working with young children. The language and complexity level is more easily understood.

    ◇ Get Help: Go for help—it's not "tattling" when you feel unsafe.

    ◇ Stand Up for Yourself: Be strong, you are important.

    ◇ Walk Away: Stay away or find another way.

    ◇ Say Good Things to Yourself: Think!! Build yourself up—**NOT** down.

- ◆ HA HA, SO Shield Activity

    See Handouts 5-10 and 5-11.

> **RESOURCE GUIDE**
>
> See "Videotapes and Films for Students" and "Books for Primary Students" for materials suggestions. The video *Standing Up for Yourself* is recommended.

Handout/Poster 5-32

Refer to explanation in Session 3/page 253.

Handouts 5-10 and 5-11 can be used to teach students how to disengage from a bully's attempts to push their buttons and how to use HA HA, SO as a protective shield to cover their buttons.

Facilitator Notes

Be sure to present these strategies using examples relevant to the students' lives and experiences at school. This will assist the students in internalizing them. It is important to practice these strategies daily or at least two to three times before the next group session. The teacher or facilitator should "set up" the scenario in a structured format—playing one of the characters. Some students may not be comfortable with role play activities. They can be members of the audience and still learn when and how to use the strategies. (See Chapter Five, Session 4, for sample role plays **or** design a situation that you have observed in the classroom or on the playground.)

Alternate Activity

If the student(s) appear to find the role playing uncomfortable, an alternative method of practicing protective strategies is through puppet play. Using puppets sometimes distances the students from the roles they are playing and allows them to more easily "speak through the character." The students may even enjoy making puppets for future use in role-playing activities.

NEXT SESSION

In the next session, students will learn the difference between "Tattling and Telling" and will begin to review skills they have been taught to this point.

Bully-Proofing

1. GET HELP

2. STAND UP FOR YOURSELF

3. WALK AWAY

4. SAY GOOD THINGS TO YOURSELF

FRIENDS GET HELP FOR FRIENDS

SESSION 5

GOAL

To understand the difference between "tattling" and "telling."

HANDOUT/POSTERS/BUTTONS

Handout/Poster 5-7: The Difference Between Tattling and Telling

Last Session Review

Check that students still remember protective strategies.

Group Activity

To clarify the difference between "telling" and "tattling," read a story or show a video that addresses this issue. Ask the children to be "Detectives" to see how many protective strategies (HA HA, SO) they can pick out from the story or video. After the story or video, lead a class discussion that promotes an understanding of the differences between "telling/ reporting" and "tattling." If something **dangerous**, **unsafe**, or **important** happens then it is important to "**tell**" an adult. If something **harmless**, **unimportant**, or **irritating** happens and the child does not feel "unsafe" or "powerless"—then it might be considered "tattling" if he or she reports it to an adult.

Examples of "Tattling"

- Someone cuts in front of you in line, but doesn't hurt you in the process

- The teacher asks all students to complete a color, cut, paste activity. You notice a student at your table is playing with a puzzle.

Examples of "Telling"

- You see children fighting on the playground

- A student or adult threatens to hurt you

- Even after you try to walk away or stand up for yourself, a child keeps calling you very cruel names.

> **RESOURCE GUIDE**
>
> See "Books for Primary Students" *Tattlin' Madeline* by Carol Cummings is recommended.

> **Handout/Poster 5-7 in Section One**

Expand upon these examples to include situations that occur in the classroom or on the playground.

Facilitator Notes

This lesson is sometimes presented after Session 1 due to the severity of "tattling" in some classrooms.

It is important for children to feel like they can come to you. Tattling behavior is sometimes the only way a child knows to get **attention**. A response to this behavior by the teacher can be "I'm glad you know the rule," as you guide them in understanding the differences between "tattling" and "telling." In addition, provide the attention they may be seeking and look into possible social skills problems that may be interferring with friendships.

NEXT SESSION

In the next session, the children will be introduced to the "I Caught You Caring" program. You may need badges duplicated and may want to bring candy to be used to teach the concept of a "Random Act of Kindness."

FRIENDS AND CARING ACTS OF KINDNESS

SESSION 6

GOAL

To teach students that each one of them can make a difference. As a group they make up the "Caring Community" where kind and caring acts will be acknowledged and encouraged.

HANDOUTS/POSTERS/BUTTONS

Handout/Poster 5-33: "Caught Caring" Slips

Buttons 5-26: CARES Buttons

Candy (Optional)

Last Session Review

Check that the students still remember the difference between "tattling" and "telling."

Group Activity

Hand out candy. When everyone has received a piece of candy explain that you wanted to do something nice for each of them "just because." Ask the students how they like this surprise. Explain that it feels good to have given them a treat. In other words, it was a "win-win" situation because both parties felt good about the candy surprise. This describes what a Random Act of Kindness is like.

Note: You can also substitute 5 minutes of free time for candy to illustrate a Random Act of Kindness.

Read a few excerpts from *Kids' Random Acts of Kindness* (see "Books for Primary Students" and/or "Books for Intermediate Students") **or** a teacher alternate. After a few examples, the children should be able to share their own experiences of giving and receiving random acts of kindness.

Introduce the "I Caught You Caring" Reinforcement Program

These daily or weekly sessions are designed for reinforcement of caring behavior within the classroom. They can occur at the end of the week for older students, and take five to ten minutes. Younger students may require more frequent recognition, even daily. Each teacher chooses one or more of his or her students, who he or she "caught" being kind or helpful to another student for this special recognition. The teacher should keep a log of "acts of kindness" that he or she notices during the day or week, and then pick a good example—or more—to reinforce.

Buttons 5-26
Handout/Poster 5-33

"I Caught You Caring" Alternative Program Ideas

- ◆ "Caught Caring" slips can be filled out and displayed on class bulletin boards. (See Handouts 5-26 and 5-33.)

- ◆ Budding artists and writers love to "publish" their own books. A sample title: "Random Acts of Kindness in   (Teacher's Name) 's Room."

- ◆ Students can design their own badges. The nomination process works the same way as "I Caught You Caring" program. Teachers can display the badges. Typically badges are worn for one day; students then return them to the teacher.

Facilitator Notes

Remember to stress to children the importance of helping children who are being bullied. Remind them that "kindness is contagious." The teacher should keep things going daily. The classroom "climate" should reflect a safe, positive, inclusive, friendly environment where every individual **deserves** to be treated with respect and kindness. Uncaring, bully behavior will not be tolerated.

NEXT SESSION

The next session is a postintervention session to be conducted in about three to six weeks. During the postintervention session, the facilitator will: (1) evaluate student progress and determine whether any new problems have surfaced, (2) review and reinforce the student skills to prevent bullying and reinforce positive friendship-making skills, and (3) provide any additional instruction necessary to ensure the continued success of the program.

HANDOUT/POSTER 5-33
Caught Caring

CAUGHT CARING

Name _____

How _____

_____

_____

_____

Signature _____

CAUGHT CARING

Name _____

How _____

_____

_____

_____

Signature _____

CAUGHT CARING

Name _____

How _____

_____

_____

_____

Signature _____

CAUGHT CARING

Name _____

How _____

_____

_____

_____

Signature _____

POSTINTERVENTION SESSION

FOLLOW-UP

GOAL

To revisit the classroom three to six weeks after the classroom curriculum was taught to: (1) evaluate student progress and determine whether any new problems have surfaced, (2) review and reinforce the student skills to prevent bullying behavior and reinforce positive friendship-making skills, and (3) provide any additional instruction necessary to ensure the continued success of the program.

HANDOUTS/POSTERS/BUTTONS

Refer back to any handouts/posters from Sessions 1–6 relating to skills to reinforce and review, including:

Poster/Handout 7-6: Tips for Joining a Group of Kids

Handout/Poster 5-32: Modified HA HA, SO Strategies

Handout 5-10: "Pushing Your Buttons"

Handout 5-11: HA HA, SO Shield

Handout/Poster 5-7: The Difference Between Tattling and Telling

Evaluate Student Progress

Before the postintervention session, discuss with the classroom teacher his or her perceptions of student progress. Find out whether any new problems have surfaced in the classroom and/or observations of positive changes. During the session with the students, review and discuss problems and applaud successes in that specific classroom.

Reteach Any Skills Specifically Related to Any Problems Identified in the Class Discussion

Based on the feedback from the classroom teacher, reteach all or applicable parts of the sessions addressing deficient skills. Specific skills presented in Chapter Seven: Supporting the Victims or in Chapter Eight: Changing the Bullies could also be drawn from, modified for younger students, and used for additional sessions, as appropriate.

Conclude the Session

Summarize for the students that they have learned these important things about friendship: (1) what it is, (2) how to make and keep friends, (3) what they can do if a bully picks on them, (4) what to do if they see a bully picking on someone else, and (5) how kind and caring acts can become contagious. Remind them that they will have to keep practicing these strategies to get good at them and that their teacher will be available to help them if they have any questions or need help practicing.

CHAPTER SIX

CREATING AND MAINTAINING THE CARING MAJORITY

The foundation and backbone of bully-proofing is developing the climate of the school into one where everyone sets a tone of caring and carries the message, "Our school will be a safe, respectful, and inclusive environment so teachers can teach and children can learn." The key to creating this climate is shifting the "silent majority" into a "caring majority."

The silent majority consists of the 85% of students who are neither bullies nor victims but who stand helplessly by as their classmates get beaten up emotionally or physically. By doing so, the bystander children are implicitly allowing this to happen. Empowering the silent majority reduces the fear bullies create. Children will report bullying if they know that the staff will intervene effectively. The silent majority know who the bullies and victims are, but they are too frightened to intervene. The children in the younger grades, second and third especially, are eager and willing to lend their support to solving the problem as long as they feel protected. The influence of this silent majority is a powerful resource and a key to the success of the program.

Developing the intervention skills of the silent majority and turning them into a caring majority is crucial in setting a positive tone in a school. These students give strength and support to the victims and defuse the power of the bullies. The caring majority, along with responsive adults, is the most powerful resource in creating a safe and caring school environment.

Developing and Maintaining a Caring Majority

The caring majority is developed by mobilizing the silent majority to join together in shifting the atmosphere of fear and intimidation, which is created by the bullies, to an atmosphere of care and concern. Children remain silent out of fear. They are afraid that no one else feels as frightened as they do, they are afraid that the bullies will retaliate and harm them if they speak up, and they also are afraid that the staff and teachers will not take their side and protect them. Because of these fears, the caring majority cannot be unified until the underlying issues are addressed. The staff must be trained and ready to take action. They must communicate to the students that a "No Bullying" policy is in place and will be enforced. The classroom curriculum sessions need to be completed. These teach the students that they are not alone, what bullying behavior is, and why telling is different from tattling. After these steps have been taken, the students are ready to be mobilized into forming a caring majority in their school environment.

The caring majority must be developed comprehensively at the individual and classroom levels and throughout the school as a whole. This is implemented through the following four guiding principles. These principles are global concepts to be developed by your staff. A variety of effective techniques are described in the following principles. These are ideas for creative thinking among your staff. There are many avenues to developing the caring majority. Use the guiding principles as your goal while developing techniques that fit your school environment.

Guiding Principle One

Clearly Defining Caring Majority Behaviors

Most children fall into the category of bystanders. These children make up the silent majority. They are not targeted nor are they bullies, but they do suffer. Bystander children know the dynamics of the social setting and often report guilt later for not standing up to the bully on behalf of the victim or for joining the bully when they knew the behavior was wrong. They may worry that they will be the next victim if they fail to join in. Developing classroom-wide caring majority groups allows a bystander child the opportunity to not stand alone and to be an important part of changing the climate through a group process.

Techniques

Identifying the Behaviors and Characteristics of a Caring Community
Identifying the Rules and Expectations
Identifying the Necessary Skills
Finding the Courage to Act

Identifying the Behaviors and Characteristics of a Caring Community

This technique is introduced during the classroom sessions described in Chapter Five. Students are encouraged to generate a list of caring majority characteristics. Two sample classroom lists illustrate these characteristics.

A third grade classroom developed this list:

- Caring and kind
- Good student—responsible
- Being nice to everyone
- Sharing and including and inviting
- Knowing when to stop
- Helpful
- Generous
- Funny
- Fair
- Treat others like you would like
- Participate and listen
- Courage

A fourth grade classroom offered this list:

- Friendly to everyone
- Helpful
- Not selfish
- Sense of humor
- Courage
- Honesty
- Consistent
- Popular by liking everyone
- Can think for themselves
- Dependable

Identifying the Rules and Expectations

Once the behaviors and characteristics have been identified, students find it important to know that the adults in their school will be responsive. Clear rules and expectations from the adults are critical. Use the following chart for an overview.

CLEAR RULES AND EXPECTATIONS	
Rules are	**Consequence**
What you **don't want** students to do:	
◆ No fighting	◆ Automatic suspension
◆ No running in hall	◆ You will go back and walk
◆ No abusive language or harassment	◆ In-school suspension
Expectations are	
What you **want** students to do:	
◆ Students will get adult help when needed.	
◆ Students will treat others in a respectful manner.	
◆ Students will include others.	
◆ Students are at school to be learners.	

Identifying the Necessary Skills

Finally, the students need skills. These have been developed during the classroom sessions. Some important skills are outlined below:

SKILLS
How to get adult help
Have students work on these for themselves:
◆ What are the characteristics of adults from whom you would choose to get help?
◆ Who are three adults you can say anything to?
How to join together with others to stand up for what is right
◆ Who can you ask?
◆ How would you support one another?
Feeling empathy for other students
◆ What would help you see others' opinions?
◆ Who has some of the same worries that you have?
How to mediate conflicts with other students
◆ Identify the problem.
◆ Brainstorm the solutions.
◆ Self-regulate, i.e., stop yourself when you are reacting or out of control.
◆ Use self-protective skills so others can't push your buttons. Learn your buttons. Learn HA-HA-SO. Identify what works for you.
◆ Learn to disengage when others are trying to push your buttons.

Finding the Courage to Act

Standing up for another child involves both risk and courage. Risk means the danger a child senses in a given situation. This varies from child to child; what is risky for one child may feel safe for another. Some children will take greater personal risks than others. All children should be encouraged to think about this concept: **"What is the risk for me?"**

Courage is the decision to act. Any level of courage in helping another child is worthwhile. Doing something is better than doing nothing. Sometimes one child may be the first one to stand up for what is fair, and others will then be able to risk joining in. This is part of forming the caring majority. Each child is encouraged to define his or her level of courage: **"How much courage does it take?"** No child should be pushed into an action he or she is not ready to take or to feel comfortable about.

Look at Handout 6-1: The Strategies of Intervention chart. Five different strategies are identified for intervening in bully situations. Each strategy has a level of courage that ranges from low to high. Most of these strategies can be talked about and integrated into the classroom curriculum or presented later at a follow-up session as the school is building a caring community school-wide.

Handout 6-1

For early elementary-aged students, you might present these ideas by using animal metaphors. A giraffe is an animal that sticks its neck "way out" and a turtle is an animal that "hides." Everyone is encouraged to be a giraffe but some may have longer necks than others. Use visual aids to help the children, especially the younger ones, form an internal image of being a giraffe.

"How far can you stick out your neck?" is a question that asks each child to assess the level of risk he or she is ready to take.

For middle and older elementary-aged students, you might present the chart and ideas with the question "How much courage does it take?" Numbers can be assigned from one to ten. Questions can be developed within the classroom to teach this concept. For example:

- How much courage does it take to tell someone his or her shoelace is untied?

- How much courage does it take to ask someone new if he or she would like to sit with you at lunch?

- How much courage does it take to say "hello" to a student in a higher grade?

- How much courage does it take to walk over to someone who is bullying and say, "We don't treat people like that at this school"?

- How much courage does it take to tell the victim that you saw what happened and it was not fair?

Children who have the courage to stand up to the bully, at some level of risk, build their own character in the process of helping someone else. Often they are noticed by other children and adults and admired and recognized for their willingness to do something. This process starts in the classroom and then moves school-wide.

Thus, students are taught that caring majority behaviors exist on a continuum from lower level behaviors, such as picking up a pencil that someone has dropped, to more courageous behaviors such as including a child who has been left out or rejected by other children, at the risk of being rejected as well. While words such as respect, kindness, and caring are important concepts, they are vague and not very useful for teaching children what specific behaviors are expected. Furthermore, the lower-level behaviors are important building blocks for later behaviors, and likely play a more important role in early elementary grades than in the later elementary grades. Caring respectful behaviors must be defined. The following guidelines will help to get you started:

- **Lower Level (courteous behaviors)**
  - ◊ Saying, "Thank You," "Please," and "Excuse Me"
  - ◊ Picking up an item dropped by another person
  - ◊ Standing quietly in line
  - ◊ Waiting one's turn while talking
  - ◊ Apologizing for a mistake
  - ◊ Giving a person a compliment
  - ◊ Doing a favor for someone
  - ◊ Allowing another child to play when he or she asks

- **Middle Level (courageous and caring behaviors)**
  - ◊ Sticking up for a friend
  - ◊ Refusing to join in when someone is being treated badly (e.g., being teased)
  - ◊ Not spreading a rumor that is told to you

- **Higher Level (very courageous and caring behaviors)**
  - ◊ Getting adult assistance during a bully situation
  - ◊ Making an effort to assist a rejected or lonely child (e.g., asking her to play, or helping out in a potentially embarrassing situation)
  - ◊ Stopping the spread of a rumor
  - ◊ Sticking up for a person whom you don't know very well
  - ◊ Saying, "We don't treat people like that at our school."

Guiding Principle Two

Recognizing and Reinforcing Caring Majority Behaviors

Caring majority behaviors need to be reinforced. After the students have developed a classroom list of caring majority behaviors and characteristics, the teacher must immediately start modeling these behaviors. In addition, children who display these characteristics are identified and praised. Practice "I Caught You Caring" as described in the classroom sessions in Chapter Five. The following guidelines will help you in building your own reinforcers.

- ◆ **Verbal praise**

- ◆ **Classroom-wide acknowledgment**

  ◇ Classroom praise

  ◇ Phone call to parents to acknowledge the caring behavior

  ◇ Caring student of the week

  ◇ Caring ticket for an end of the month raffle

- ◆ **Caring Majority Recognition Form** (see Handout 6-2)

  Names of students who receive a caring recognition slip are placed on a bulletin board in a public part of the school. The names are also read over the intercom at the end of each week. A copy of the slip is sent home to parents along with a certificate (see Handout 6-3). Other opportunities for praise can be built-in, such as lunch with a favorite teacher.

> **Handout 6-2**
> **Handout 6-3**

Guiding Principle Three

Developing Classroom and School-Wide Caring Majority Groups

Within each classroom, students create a list of behaviors they would want to see from students in the caring majority. These can be drawn from Guiding Principle One and the students can add to them. Students nominate other students who they think meet these criteria and give a reason for the nomination. Ask for seconds to the nomination. Then the class as a whole votes on whether the student belongs in the caring majority. Sometimes bullies are nominated to be part of the caring majority but usually other students will raise concerns or refrain from voting for the bully. A student needs to be consistently and dependably displaying the caring majority behaviors for the chance to be part of the caring majority community.

Most classrooms hold a caring majority meeting on a predictable basis in which students' behavior is discussed. During the meeting, students are praised for their caring behaviors and respectfully held accountable for inappropriate behaviors. A student in the caring majority may be confronted if he or she has behaved badly (see Chapter Nine for sample letters).

Students are encouraged toward the goal of creating "a safe, respectful, inclusive environment so teachers can teach and students can learn." If a student does not wish to be in the caring majority, that is fine as long as he or she agrees not to disrupt the above stated goal. Once the caring majority is developed, teachers can use this group to solve behavioral problems by asking how they want to resolve a fight at recess or by having a caring majority student mentor another student who is having difficulties.

In some classrooms, the development of the caring majority is combined with themes and art. For example, one teacher experimented with bulletin boards such as the Caring Jungle and added animals with each child's name when he or she was elected to the caring majority. Another teacher created a tree and each student's name was on a leaf. One other teacher created a rainbow across a wall and students worked toward the pot of gold at the end which represented inclusion in the caring majority.

The goal, regardless of the model adopted, is to develop an inclusionary model. Reinforce positive student behavior. Value the children who are displaying the behaviors and characteristics continually and formalize it with weekly classroom meetings. Random reinforcers, rather than competitive ones, are preferred. For example, all the children who receive an "I Caught You Caring" card or nomination have their names placed into a hat at the end of the week. One name is pulled out. This assures that everyone in the caring majority has an equal chance of being the winner. It creates fun rather than competitiveness.

Some suggested ideas for reinforcing caring behavior and recognizing student efforts are listed in the following paragraphs. A special thanks to Dr. Larry Epstein for developing and sharing these ideas: Collateral School-Wide Activities, Focus Board, Projects, and Caring Week.

◆ Collateral School-Wide Activities

In addition to the above classroom caring majority reinforcement programs, collateral activities will help to spread the caring majority into a caring community.

◆ Focus Board

Pictures of every student and their names are placed on a board in the front of the school.

◆ Projects

Classroom special projects are coordinated to reinforce the caring majority concept throughout the school. These might include caring majority posters in art, research projects on historical figures who represented such values, and books on display in the library around such concepts. One classroom created a musical production around these themes and the children selected to perform were chosen by being in the caring majority, not by musical, acting, or dance talents.

◆ **Caring Week**

A week of activities designed to kick off the caring majority project, such as "Ask a New Friend to Lunch Day."

Guiding Principle Four

Using Teachable Moments

Use the opportunities students give through their day-to-day interactions. They will make mistakes. Every time a behavior is displayed that does not reinforce the goal of "a safe, respectful, inclusive environment so teachers can teach and students can learn," talk about the behavior. Most importantly, teach the right behavior. Turn opportunities into teachable moments.

By engaging in activities such as those listed in the first three principles, a caring school environment is built. The goal is for this to carry over into the entire community so that each and every child at the school feels respected, cared for, and special.*

Review

The process of creating a caring and safe climate through the development of the caring majority involves:

1. The school assessing the issues of school safety and climate

2. The school identifying the kind of climate they would like to achieve

3. The school conducting both a formal and an informal assessment to determine what the current climate is from the perspective of students, parents, and staff

4. The school identifying current strengths and weaknesses

5. Strategies being identified and implemented to achieve the climate of choice

6. Adults modeling a clear, no-nonsense approach with consequences for behavior that is in violation of the rules and expectations

7. Reinforcing students who meet the stated goal

8. Efforts put in place to empower students by acknowledging them personally and behaviorally

9. All members of the community—students, parents, colleagues and staff—being treated in a similar fashion

---

* The authors give profound thanks and appreciation to Vicky Temple, Psy.D. and Paul Von Essen, M.S.W. who creatively implemented these caring majority ideas and made them a part of many school communities.

10. Demonstrating expectations and beliefs that students and others can do it. Adults setting the tone and expectation that students can do it

11. The school assessing the effectiveness of the chosen strategies.

A wonderful story appeared in many newspapers a few years ago that exemplified a caring community. A small group of children set the tone for an entire class, eventually for the entire school, and finally for many others across the nation. One boy in a classroom had lost his hair due to chemotherapy. He was being teased and made fun of for something that obviously was tragic. A number of other boys in his class decided to shave their hair off as show of support (joining in). A few days later the rest of the boys did the same. When the teacher saw the courage the students had demonstrated, he joined in as well. Needless to say, the harassment stopped and a great deal of admiration was garnered by the entire class. It was an inspiring experience for the school and modeled "caring" throughout the community.

HANDOUT 6-1
Strategies of Intervention

Strategies of Intervention	LEVELS OF RISK		
	Low ⟵	⟶ High	
Not Joining In	Walk away.	Stay but do not participate.	Declare your non-participation.
Getting Adult Help	Get help anonymously.	Identify who the helpful adults are and get one of them.	Announce loudly your intention to get adult help; then do it.
Mobilizing Peer Group	Identify a peer leader and offer to join in standing up to the bully.	Identify others who are capable of mobilizing peers in defense of the victim and recruit them to the cause.	Be a leader in recruiting others to join in standing up to the bully.
Taking an Individual Stand	Go over to the victim and lead him or her away from the situation.	Say, "Leave him alone."	Say, "We don't treat people like that at our school."
Befriending the Victim	Privately empathize with the victim by saying, "That was unfair or cruel."	Go over and stand with the victim or invite him or her to join you in doing something else.	Stand with the victim and publicly announce the "unfair" behavior of the bully.

From: *Bully-Proofing Your Child: A Parent's Guide* by Garrity, Baris, and Porter.

HANDOUT 6-2
Caring Majority Recognition Form

_____
(Date)

Today, I observed _____ engaging in the
(Name)
following caring behavior:

_____ Sticking up for a child who was being treated unkind

_____ Including a child who had been left out

_____ Stopping the spread of a rumor

_____ Getting adult assistance for a serious bully situation

_____ Displaying empathy

_____ Supporting diversity

_____ Other: _____

Your child typifies the kind of student we value at _____.
(Name of School)

His/her behavior indicates that he/she has gone above and beyond the call of duty in
demonstrating caring for others. His/her name will go on our Caring Majority Board
and will be announced at the end of this week. Please take a few minutes to discuss
this admirable behavior with your child.

_____   _____
Teacher Signature   Principal Signature

_____
Developed by Larry Epstein and Lana Hansen

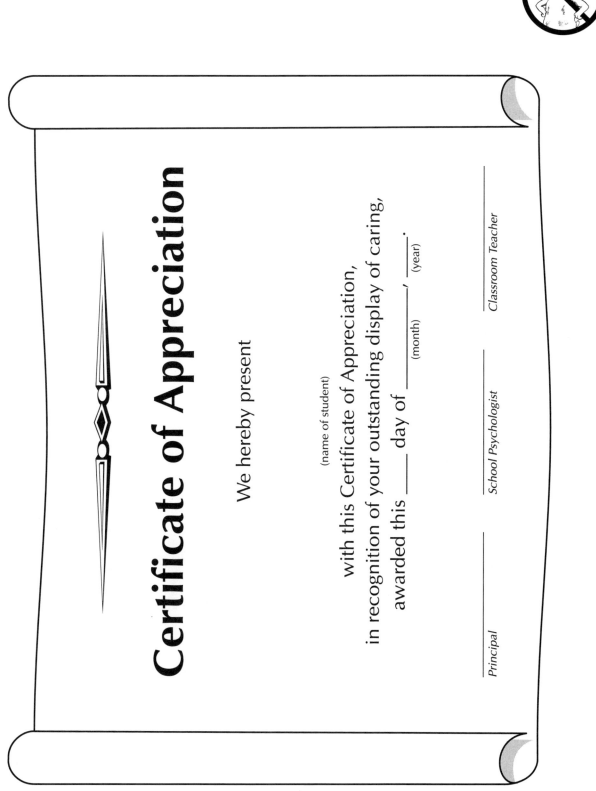

Certificate of Appreciation

We hereby present

_____
(name of student)

with this Certificate of Appreciation,
in recognition of your outstanding display of caring,
awarded this _____ day of _____, _____.
                              (month)   (year)

_____   _____   _____
Principal   School Psychologist   Classroom Teacher

Developed by Larry Epstein, Psy.D.

CHAPTER SEVEN

SUPPORTING THE VICTIMS

The individual/small group curriculum presented in this chapter complements, expands upon, and reinforces the classroom curriculum presented in Chapter Five: Student Instruction. These individual/small group sessions are designed for more intensive intervention with students who are the frequent victims of bullying.

Selecting Students for Intervention

These sessions are suggested for **any** victimized child who could benefit from individualized support. In particular, these sessions should be offered to students who may require special education services or are considered at "high risk" of being victimized.

Effective intervention strategies against bullying used for Special Education Needs (SEN) students should include help with initiating and maintaining relationships as well as with developing coping strategies against teasing and bullying. A study by Jean Hodson (1992) in Sheffield, England found, from interviews and observations, that students with SEN were teased significantly more than mainstream students (non-SEN) and formed fewer friendships. It was also found that mainstream students showed a preference for social interaction with other mainstream peers rather than with students with SEN. Research shows that students who are alone at playtime or do not have many friends or protective peer relationships stand the risk of being victimized.

This study indicates that SEN students may be at greater risk of being bullied by others. There are three factors enhancing the risk of being a victim. Characteristics such as clumsiness or other disabilities may be used as a pretext for bullying. A SEN student in the mainstream or integrated setting may be less well integrated socially and lack the protection against bullying which friendship gives. Lastly, some students with behavioral problems may act in an aggressive way and become provocative victims.

A method for identifying these students and placing them in this curriculum should have been planned for in staff training Session 6. Suggestions for identifying a student who may require intensive training and/or support include:

- Classroom teacher referral.

- Parent referral.

- Support personnel (e.g., special education teacher, counselor, school psychologist or social worker, teacher assistant) referral.

- Assessing the needs of inhibited or shy students.

- Assessing the needs of students who have no friendships.

- Assessing the needs of students who have suffered a loss of significant magnitude or trauma (such as abuse or death of a parent).

- Assessing the needs of students who are new to the school and not making an adequate adjustment after a few months. (These students are of higher risk if they also have another risk factor, such as a learning disability.)

- Assessing the needs of students demonstrating physical weakness or petite size, especially in boys.

All children need help with bullying that is in the moderate to severe range (see Figure 7-1). But some children require help with even mild bullying. These children include:

- Children who are shy or who lack social skills.

- Children who are isolated.

- Children who are learning disabled.

- Children who are repeatedly bullied.

- Children who have experienced a past trauma.

- Children who are using money or toys as bribes to protect themselves.

There are two types of victims who may both need individual intervention: (1) **passive victims**—those who fail to fight back, and (2) a smaller group, **provocative victims**—those who are ineffectual aggressors; who provoke others and try unsuccessfully to fight back against bullies. (More in-depth information about the unique characteristics and special needs of provocative victims is provided in the Working With Provocative Victims section of this chapter.)

BULLYING BEHAVIORS CHART

MILD			MODERATE		SEVERE

PHYSICAL AGGRESSION

MILD			MODERATE		SEVERE
◆ Pushing ◆ Shoving ◆ Spitting	◆ Kicking ◆ Hitting	◆ Defacing property ◆ Stealing	◆ Physical acts that are demeaning and humiliating, but not bodily harmful (e.g., de-panting) ◆ Locking in a closed or confined space	◆ Physical violence against family or friends	◆ Threatening with a weapon ◆ Inflicting bodily harm

SOCIAL ALIENATION

MILD			MODERATE		SEVERE
◆ Gossiping ◆ Embarrassing	◆ Setting up to look foolish ◆ Spreading rumors about	◆ Ethnic slurs ◆ Setting up to take the blame	◆ Publicly humiliating (e.g., revealing personal information) ◆ Excluding from group ◆ Social rejection	◆ Maliciously excluding ◆ Manipulating social order to achieve rejection ◆ Malicious rumor-mongering	◆ Threatening with total isolation by peer group

VERBAL AGGRESSION

MILD			MODERATE		SEVERE
◆ Mocking ◆ Name calling ◆ Dirty looks ◆ Taunting	◆ Teasing about clothing or possessions	◆ Teasing about appearance	◆ Intimidating telephone calls	◆ Verbal threats of aggression against property or possessions	◆ Verbal threats of violence or of inflicting bodily harm

INTIMIDATION

MILD			MODERATE		SEVERE
◆ Threatening to reveal personal information ◆ Graffiti ◆ Publicly challenging to do something	◆ Defacing property or clothing ◆ Playing a dirty trick	◆ Taking possessions (e.g., lunch, clothing, toys)	◆ Extortion ◆ Sexual/racial taunting	◆ Threats of using coercion against family or friends	◆ Coercion ◆ Threatening with a weapon

Figure 7-1   Copyright © 1992 by Garrity & Baris.

In general, characteristics of victims may include:

- ◆ Fragile self-esteem;
- ◆ Poor social skills;
- ◆ Learning disabilities;
- ◆ Social isolation/shyness;

- Anxious/insecure/cry easily;
- Bullied repeatedly;
- Suffered previous trauma;
- Emotional difficulties;
- Behavioral difficulties;
- Attentional problems; and
- Physically weak.

The main goals of these individual/small group sessions are to:

- Increase the self-esteem of the victims;
- Empower the victims;
- Help the victims make friends; and
- Decrease the isolation of the victims.

General Information About Individualized Intervention With Victims

This individual/small group curriculum consists of six weekly sessions. The sessions will be led by a group facilitator. The facilitator can be a special education teacher, school counselor, school psychologist or social worker, or regular classroom teacher familiar with group processes and social skills training.

Each session includes an outline of the information to present, as well as handout and other reproducible material masters to supplement the presentation. The individual/small group curriculum is **not scripted**, as the facilitator should use his or her best judgment in determining the content to emphasize for each student or group of students referred.

Individual/small group sessions can be taught in conjunction with the classroom curriculum (Chapter Five: Student Instruction) or as a reinforcement after the conclusion of the classroom curriculum sessions. Regardless, the skills taught in these individual/small group sessions should be reinforced in the classroom and in less structured times during the day, such as lunch, recess, between classes, and before and after school.

Of important value in this individual/small group curriculum is student advocacy. A child may feel more comfortable in this safe setting sharing bullying events that may require adult attention.

Forming Groups

The group facilitator should work closely with the classroom teachers and/or adults who know the victimized students referred for small group intervention when forming a group. It is advisable to group passive and provocative victims separately because of their unique needs. It is helpful to have a positive role model in the group. The ideal role model would be a student who exhibits emerging skills that simply need refinement and/or more reinforcement than the classroom intervention is able to offer.

An individual approach is suggested for students needing repetition of skills, concrete examples and practice, and/or an approach that meets the individual's unique learning style.

Special considerations when forming groups include:

+ **Number of Students Per Group**

   Small groups should not exceed five students, otherwise the group size becomes too overwhelming and the students will not be receiving the level of individual attention they need.

+ **Number of Small Groups Required**

   There is not as great a need for small group victim intervention when classroom instruction sessions are occurring. It is advisable that no more than two or three groups be ongoing at the same time due to the planning time required to individualize and lead the curriculum on the part of the facilitator.

+ **Generalization of Skills**

   It is advisable to group classmates together so the skills learned in the small group can be practiced outside of the small group environment (i.e., within the classroom). This increases the likelihood that the skills will be generalized.

+ **New Referrals**

   Generally, students referred for a small group victim intervention after the first few sessions have already been presented may be more comfortable waiting for the next cycle. The exceptions to this scheduling method include: (1) if the facilitator has time to review the concepts already taught with the newly referred student, (2) if the group is small enough to absorb a new student comfortably, (3) if the newly referred student feels comfortable with this arrangement, (4) if the group culture can accept a new student in a positive manner, and (5) if no more than one or two sessions have been missed.

School-Home Communication Prior to Intervention

Letter 7-1

The parent(s) of each child chosen for small group victim intervention should be contacted prior to placing him or her in a group. Either the referring teacher or a member of the support staff who knows the child's parent(s) should make the initial call to the home. A follow-up call from the group facilitator is suggested as well. A permission slip for student participation in individual or small group intervention should be sent to the parent(s) after the initial phone contact (see Letter 7-1).

Cycle of Sessions, Time and Location, and Scheduling

◆ **Cycle of Sessions**

These sessions are designed to be conducted for six weeks, but sessions that appear to require more time can be extended or divided into multiple sessions, as the needs of the individual students dictate.

Handout 7-2

It is helpful for the group facilitator to keep notes of each session in order to identify areas that may need to be expanded or areas that should be addressed and haven't yet been taught (see Handout 7-2).

◆ **Time and Location**

The optimum length of group sessions is flexible, according to the needs of the students and their grade level, as follows:

Primary: 30-minute groups

Intermediate: 45-minute groups

It is helpful to conduct groups in a private or semiprivate area in the school to help the students feel comfortable to share. The same location for each session is advised for consistency.

◆ **Scheduling**

A "lunch bunch" approach to small group sessions can work if the referred students are willing. Silent reading time or library time are other possibilities. The key to scheduling is to choose a time that can be consistent from week to week and that includes both the teachers and students in the decision. This involvement increases the likelihood of the classroom teachers supporting small group intervention.

It also helps to know the group meeting time before contacting the parents for initial permission, as this is an often asked question.

Relationship to Special Education

Role of Prereferral for Special Education

Often students referred for small group victim intervention are already staffed into special education. For nonstaffed students referred, valuable information may be gathered **or** this intervention may prove to be the type of support needed to preclude a special education referral.

Use in Special Education Settings

The individual/small group victim intervention curriculum could be adapted by special education teachers for use in special education settings. Research supports that these children are usually at greater risk of being bullied and would probably benefit from skill development to broaden their repertoire of life skills.

Working With Provocative Victims

As described previously, provocative victims are children who are often restless, irritable, and who will tease and provoke others. While these children will fight back against bullies and maintain conflict, they often end up losing, usually with great distress and frustration, and thus are also targets of bullying. Although no scientific studies have been conducted, many clinicians suspect that Attention Deficit Hyperactive Disorder (ADHD) children may be provocative victims. These children will need help with the mildest form of bullying (refer back to Figure 7-1).

Although their actions may not be deliberate, the consequences of the provocative victims' behavior is negative. Typical consequences include being the target of frequent bullying and alienating other peers. Because their provoking behavior is more prevalent in environments with little direct adult supervision, less structured times in the school day tend to present the greatest management challenge for provocative victims. Skills and techniques to be used during these times should be a focus of intervention with provocative victims.

An individual/small group approach to teaching skills is strongly advised for provocative victims. The individualized expectations and consequences taught in the individual/small group victim intervention curriculum will assist provocative victims in managing their own behavior and will help reinforce the newly learned skills from the classroom curriculum.

> **RESOURCE GUIDE**
>
> See "Books for Administrators, School-Based Teams, and Specialists" for sources of information on intervention design, and "Books for Parents" for additional information on the characteristics of provocative victims.

In addition to the strategies provided in the six "Supporting the Victims" sessions following, strategies helpful in assisting provocative victims include:

- **Implementing "Behavior Contracts"** to specify expectations and consequences during structured and unstructured times.

- **Teaching Behavioral-Cognitive Strategies**, such as positive self-talk or self-monitoring skills, in order to reduce impulsive behavior.

- **Modifying High Conflict Situations**

  ◇ Capitalize on student strengths and interests whereby the student performs "school or community service" as an alternative to recess, for example.

  ◇ Task-analyze situations that have previously proven unsuccessful for the student (e.g., transition times, in line, recess, before/after school). Design a plan that maximizes successes.

LETTER 7-1
Sample Consent Form for Individual Victim Intervention

_____
(Date)

Dear Parent(s)/Guardian:

Your child has been invited to participate in a skills group at _____ School. The purpose of this group is to help improve your child's ability to get along with others, solve problems, initiate and maintain friendships, and develop self-esteem.

The group will begin _____ and meet weekly for 30–45 minutes for a minimum of six weeks. A permission slip is attached for you to sign and return so that your child can participate. Please feel free to call me at _____ if you have any questions.

Sincerely,

_____
(Name and title of facilitator)

Return to: _____   by _____

I/we the undersigned give my/our permission for my/our child _____ to participate in a weekly skills group.

_____   _____
Signature of Parent(s) or Guardian   Date

HANDOUT 7-2
Intervention Session Tracking Form

Date of Session: _____ Session Number: _____

Present: _____

_____

Absent: _____

Goal(s): _____

_____

_____

_____

Materials: _____

_____

_____

Agenda:

1. _____

2. _____

3. _____

4. _____

5. _____

Next Session:

1. Complete Agenda Item(s):_____

2. _____

3. _____

Follow-Up:_____

_____

_____

GETTING ACQUAINTED— A FIRST STEP TOWARD FRIENDSHIP

SESSION 1

GOAL

To understand that friendship involves a number of characteristics, but an important first step is getting to know one another.

HANDOUTS/LETTERS

Handout 7-3: Getting to Know You (Primary)

Handout 7-4: Getting-Acquainted Interview (Intermediate)

Handout 7-5: Friendship Is . . .

Introductions

Introduce yourself to the student or students and explain the format and goals of the individual/small group sessions they will be participating in. A review of the regularly scheduled meeting time and place may be helpful.

If this is a small group session, you may want to break the ice with a getting-acquainted activity, such as:

◆ **Getting-Acquainted Interview**

Have the students interview a partner using the appropriate interview form. The group facilitator can interview a student if there is an uneven number of students or if there is a student hesitant to participate. Have the students then introduce their partners and share something they learned about them. Time will dictate how many "facts" can be shared. Shy students sometimes prefer to read from their form—this is fine.

> Handout 7-3
> Handout 7-4

◆ **Spotlight Activity**

Have each student share one or two facts about himself or herself, such as: birthplace, age, favorite activities, places traveled to or places he or she would like to go.

A Basis for Friendship

Emphasize the similarities and differences among the group discovered in the getting-acquainted activity. Both similarities and differences can be qualities that make friendships work. Expand upon the notion of similarities and encourage the students to perceive them as a place to start a friendship. Say, for example, "Did you notice you all have an interest in sports?"

Have the students brainstorm answers to the question: "What does friendship mean to you?" Accept all responses and reinforce their answers if desired.

Handout 7-5

RESOURCE GUIDE

See "Books for Educators" for additional sources of social skills activities.

Introduce the concept of friendship:

- Friendship is positive in nature, it makes children feel good.
- Between friends, there is give and take.
- Friends usually have similar interests.
- Friends share and celebrate their differences.
- Between friends, there is a balance of power.
- Children deserve to be treated well by their friends.

Art Activity

Provide construction paper and markers (and any other art materials you wish to provide) for the students to make and decorate folders. Encourage the students to decorate their folders with words or pictures related to the "friendship" discussion key points. The students can then keep all of their handouts from these sessions in their "Friendship Folders."

Facilitator Notes

Key points for small group instruction:

- Positively reinforce each student's participation to encourage further participation.
- Encourage reluctant students to share, but be aware that they can learn by observing and listening to other group members. Help them feel safe. Shy students may require more time to feel comfortable enough to share.
- Be aware of individual student needs related to learning styles (e.g., reading levels, processing deficits).
- Accommodate the students' learning styles with appropriate teaching styles (e.g., provide adequate time to process verbal information).

NEXT SESSION

In the next session, the students will discuss their current friendships as they continue to explore the concept of friendship and learn the skills necessary to promote positive relationships.

Getting to Know You (Primary)

My Favorite:

Outdoor Activity _____

Dessert _____

Movie _____

Subject at School _____

My Birthday: _____

When I grow up, I would like to: _____

_____

_____

Something else I want you to know about me: _____

_____

_____

HANDOUT 7-4
Getting-Acquainted Interview (Intermediate)

My Name: _____

Partner's Name:_____

Birthplace: _____

Birth Date: _____

Grade:_____

Years at This School:_____

Favorite Subjects at School:_____

Favorite Movie: _____

Favorite TV Show:_____

Interests Outside of School: _____

_____

_____

_____

If you could be anyone in the world, who would it be?_____

_____

_____

What three words best describe you?

1. _____

2. _____

3. _____

Something else you'd like to share about yourself:_____

_____

_____

_____

HANDOUT 7-5
Friendship Is . . .

1. Friendship is positive in nature, it makes children feel good.

2. Between friends, there is give and take.

3. Friends usually have similar interests.

4. Friends share and celebrate their differences.

5. Between friends, there is a balance of power.

6. Children deserve to be treated well by their friends.

Add your own ideas:

7. _____

8. _____

9. _____

10. _____

FRIENDSHIP-MAKING SKILLS— HOW ARE YOU DOING?

SESSION 2

GOAL

To begin to assess the students' current friendships as well as to begin to understand the skills necessary to develop positive friendships. Bullying behaviors, which are introduced in the classroom curriculum (see Chapter Five), will also be reviewed.

HANDOUTS/LETTERS

Handout 7-6: Tips for Joining a Group

Handout 7-7: Friendly Behaviors Checklist

Current Friendships

Discuss the students' current friendships. Listen to the students' perception of their situation. This perception is based upon their ability to cope socially. Remember, when intervening with victimized children, the most helpful techniques are those that focus on examining the students' perceived world instead of the "objective" adult view of the world.

During the discussion, be sure to focus on less supervised times of the day when the students are outside the protection of the teacher—for example, lunch and recess, transition times, and before and after school. (This focus is particularly important when working with provocative victims.)

Questions to initiate this discussion include:

- ◆ Do you look forward to coming to school?

- ◆ Is there at least one student in your class who you would consider a friend?

- ◆ Do you have fun at lunch and recess?

- ◆ Do you sometimes wish there was an adult to help you: (1) join in a group, (2) deal with students who are teasing or threatening you, or (3) deal with students who are actually (physically) hurting you?

Bullying Behavior Review

The previous discussion can lead nicely into a review of bullying behavior, first presented as part of the classroom curriculum. Review the main concepts of bullying:

- There is an imbalance of power.

- There are repeated negative incidences; it doesn't just happen one time.

- The bully can be either a single individual or a bullying group.

Compare these characteristics with the concepts of friendship discussed in Session 1 (refer back to Handout 7-5).

Review why children bully others:

- To gain power.

- To gain popularity and attention.

- To act out problems (from home, generally).

Provide the students with opportunities to talk about being victimized. Encourage them to share bullying situations that they have recently experienced. Enlist their support in agreeing that being victimized is unacceptable. It should be established that every student has the right to be free of fear and intentional humiliation.

Assure the students of this right and encourage them to let adults know if they don't feel safe, as previously discussed in the classroom curriculum. Assure them that the adults in their school are going to make certain of their safety. Ask the students to name an adult at school who they can go to if they do not feel safe.

> **RESOURCE GUIDE**
>
> See "Videotapes and Films for Students" and "Books for Educators" for additional sources of information on friendship-making skills.

The Importance of Friendship

Steer the discussion to one of hope by introducing facts related to bullying and why friendship skills are so critical toward preventing it. Begin by asking questions such as:

- In a bullying situation, what has worked for you?

- What hasn't worked so well?

- Have you ever felt like you wanted to help someone who was being bullied, but you didn't know what to do?

Reinforce the points that the students make by relating them to the importance of friendship in preventing bullying.

Remind the students about the concept that "there is strength in numbers." It is hard for a bully to victimize them if they stick together with other children and avoid being left alone. Learning and practicing friendship-making skills will help ensure that they won't be alone and will have friends that they can depend on.

Skills to Enhance Friendship Making

Present tips for joining a group:

- ◆ Think about which kids are friendly. Try to join those kids.

- ◆ Think about which kids like the same things you like. Try to join those kids.

- ◆ It is easiest to join one person or a group of four or more.

- ◆ Remember "no" does not always mean "never." It could mean "not right now" or "try again later." So try at least three different times to join a group (not always on the same day).

- ◆ Observe the activity you want to join. Try to fit in by imitating what the others are doing. Do not try to change what the other children are playing.

Emphasize that these are tips to remember and practice. Encourage the students to let the group know what is working and what is not working for them so alternatives can be explored.

Friendship Activities

Role Play

The skill of "joining in," as previously described, is an important one for victims in preventing bullying. It allows them to interact with their peers and decrease their isolation. To allow the students the opportunity to practice this skill to a comfort level, have them role play a number of different situations where the skill of "joining in" is required. (If you are working with an individual student instead of a small group, play the other character in the role play situation yourself.)

The role play situations should be tailor-made to student needs. Prepare a large number of index cards, each with a different situation to practice. For example:

- ◆ Join in a soccer game—The student should be able to demonstrate observing the group and either waiting for the best time to join or asking to join.

- ◆ Join a group of girls eating lunch at a table in the cafeteria—The student should be able to demonstrate observing the group and either joining in a natural manner or asking to join.

The student role playing the "joining in" situation should verbalize his or her thought processes while enacting the role play to ensure and demonstrate understanding. For example, a student role playing the soccer situation might say, "I like to play soccer, and I want to join this game. I'm standing on the sideline for a few minutes, watching the players. One of the teams has one less person on it! After a goal is scored, I wave to a boy on that team running back upfield and yell, 'Hey, can I play on your team?' "

Checklist

For goal-setting, review, and assessment purposes, have the students fill out the "Friendly Behaviors Checklist." Reassure the students that they are **not** expected to excel in all the skill areas at this time. These are goals (i.e., pretest) to be worked on in the group and practiced outside of the group.

This checklist will enable the facilitator to adjust upcoming lessons according to the needs of the individual students in the group. This checklist will be readministered in the last session for postmeasurement purposes.

Facilitator Notes

If the student(s) appear to find the role playing uncomfortable or intimidating, an alternate method of enacting the "joining in" situations is through puppet play. Using puppets sometimes distances the students from the roles they are playing and allows them to more easily "speak through the character." The students may even enjoy making puppets for future use in role playing activities.

NEXT SESSION

In the next session, the students will be introduced to the concept of self-esteem. They will be shown that "how we feel about ourselves" plays an important role in forming friendships and handling bullies.

5 Good Tips for Joining a Group of Kids

1. Think about which kids are **friendly**.
Try to join those kids.

2. Think about which kids like the **same things** you like. Try to join those kids.

3. It is easiest to join **one person** or a **group of four** or more.

4. Remember "**no**" does not always mean "never." It could mean "**not right now**" or "**try again later.**" So try at least three different times to join a group of kids (not always on the same day).

5. Observe the activity you want to join. Try to fit in by **imitating** what the others are doing. Do not try to change what the other children are playing.

H A N D O U T 7 - 7
Friendly Behaviors Checklist

Directions:

For each friendly behavior listed below, decide if you are good at it, or if you could use some work on it.

	I'm good at:	I need to work on:
1. Giving compliments		
2. Inviting others to play		
3. Being a good listener (not doing all the talking)		
4. Letting a friend go first		
5. Sharing things		
6. Apologizing if I make a mistake		
7. Doing a favor for a friend		
8. Letting others have their way sometimes		
9. Standing up for a friend		
10. Playing by the rules in games		
11. Being a good sport if I lose		
12. Being honest (not lying)		
13. Offering to help a friend		
14. Encouraging a friend		
15. Noticing if a friend is upset and offering support		
16. Remembering something important in a friend's life and asking about it		

Adapted with permission from Huggins, P. (1993). *Teaching friendship skills: Primary version.* Longmont, CO: Sopris West.

SELF-ESTEEM—HOW IT EFFECTS FRIENDSHIP

SESSION 3

GOAL

To understand that "how we feel about ourselves" plays an important role in forming friendships and handling bullies. Sessions 1 and 2 will also be reviewed (further reinforcing the classroom curriculum).

HANDOUTS/LETTERS

Handout 7-8: Kids Who Have Friendly Behaviors

Handout 7-9: Where We Get a Strong Sense of Self-Esteem (Primary)

Handout 7-10: Where We Get a Strong Sense of Self-Esteem (Intermediate)

Handout 7-11: (Supplementary): Everyone Is a Person of Many Parts

Handout 7-12: (Supplementary): Relax and Say Encouraging Things to Yourself

From Chapter Four (optional):
   Handout/Transparency 4-3: Bullying Behaviors Chart

Session Review Discussion

Provide time for the students to share experiences they have had outside of the group related to the previously learned skills. Then direct the discussion to review the key points covered in Sessions 1 and 2. Suggested questions include:

◆ How are you doing on joining in activities?

◆ Have you included someone at lunch or recess by inviting him or her to join you?

◆ Are you looking at your current friendships to see if there is a balance of power, give and take, you are being treated kindly and with respect, you have fun when playing and feel good afterward, and you are sharing similarities and celebrating differences?

Worksheet Activity

Handout 7-8

Have the students fill out the "Kids Who Have Friendly Behaviors" worksheet. This worksheet provides another opportunity for the facilitator to stress to the students that they deserve to be treated well. It may encourage the children to think about new, more positive relationships.

Due to poor self-esteem, quite often children who are victimized will stay in a negative relationship (which could become bullying) as it supports their negative view of themselves and they fear it is better than no relationship at all. It is important to open the door to new thinking as well as teach the students how to pursue new, more positive friendships.

Handout/Transparency 4-3 (optional)

Classroom Curriculum Review

Children with fragile or weak self-esteem need to be aware of behavior that is not O.K. and be taught that they deserve better treatment. It is helpful to address what to look for in a friend and what to avoid.

Continue to review and reinforce relevant portions of the classroom curriculum. Discuss bullying tactics and the differences that exist for girls and boys. If working with intermediate students, refer to the "Bullying Behaviors Chart" during this discussion. (You can distribute to the students copies of Handout/Transparency 4-3 from the staff training program component if you like.)

Boys Use Primarily:

♦ Physical aggression (e.g., spitting, pushing, shoving, hitting, threatening with a weapon).

Girls Use Primarily:

♦ Social alienation (e.g., gossiping, spreading rumors, ethnic slurs, excluding from group, publicly humiliating, threatening with total isolation from peer group).

Both Boys and Girls Use:

♦ Verbal aggression (e.g., mocking, name calling, teasing, intimidating telephone calls, verbal threats of aggression).

♦ Intimidation (e.g., graffiti, publicly challenging to do something, playing a dirty trick, taking possessions, coercion).

Elicit feedback from the students regarding feelings they might have if they were the target of bullying behaviors. This indirect, less threatening approach can lead to describing **actual** experiences and feelings of being targeted. With the facilitator's guidance, the group can then support one another and reinforce the point that everyone deserves to be treated kindly and with respect.

Discuss the emotional consequences for victims of bullying:

♦ Feeling scared, withdrawn, isolated, and/or sad;

♦ Physical symptoms (headache, stomachache, general fatigue);

♦ Not liking school;

♦ General change in attitude; and/or

♦ Drop in self-esteem.

Use the students' responses to introduce a discussion (including the definition) of self-esteem and how important this can be in forming friendships and handling bullying.

Self-Esteem Activity

Read a story from your school's library or show a video or movie that addresses "self-esteem" in a manner appropriate to the needs of the students. Be sure to select one that is appropriate to the age group of the students.

The Importance of Self-Esteem

After the story or video, lead a discussion that emphasizes how "how we feel about ourselves" plays an important role in forming friendships and handling bullies.

Describe characteristics of self-esteem:

- Self-esteem is learned, therefore it can be taught. It is not something you inherit or are "born with."

- Self-esteem can be changed, regardless of age.

- Self-esteem guides thinking and behavior.

- Self-esteem plays a role in the kinds of friends you choose.

- When you have positive self-esteem, you will value the person you are, no matter what.

- You **can** be your own best friend.

> **RESOURCE GUIDE**
>
> See "Videotapes and Films for Students," "Books for Primary Students," or "Books for Intermediate Students" for materials that address self-esteem.

Session Reinforcement Activities

To emphasize and reinforce material covered in this session, provide the appropriate self-esteem handout for the students to complete.

If additional reinforcement is desired, provide the students with the supplementary handout(s) as well.

> **Handout 7-9**
> **Handout 7-10**

> **Handout 7-11**
> **Handout 7-12**

Facilitator Notes

The exercises provided in this session are not meant to be exhaustive. Since low self-esteem is a common feature of victims, increasing it cannot be over-emphasized in importance. It may be helpful to weave additional self-esteem activities into the remaining sessions. Since victims often see themselves as deserving their fate, fostering children's self-esteem, self-confidence, and independence may help prevent conflicts from escalating into fights and enable children to walk away from fights without experiencing "loss of face." In the following sessions, the students will learn the steps and strategies necessary to deal with difficult bullying situations, but the core issue of "feeling good about yourself" continues to be a critical component to reinforce.

RESOURCE GUIDE

See "Books for Educators," "Books for Primary Students," or "Books for Intermediate Students" for additional materials on self-esteem.

Key points to remember with self-esteem:

♦ Research shows that you can change self-esteem. This change can be either positive or negative.

♦ Change won't be easy—don't expect too much from the students too soon.

♦ Provide as many opportunities for the students to succeed as possible. The more tangible the better.

♦ A positive attitude is contagious. If children hear you consistently say positive things to others, they will begin to verbalize and feel positive feelings, and they'll be passing them on to others.

NEXT SESSION

In the next session, the students will be introduced to effective communication techniques that promote assertive, responsible responses to bullying behavior. These techniques "give the right message" to bullies.

HANDOUT 7-8
Kids Who Have Friendly Behaviors

Ask yourself: "Who has friendly behaviors?"

A Kid Who SHARES

1. _____
2. _____
3. _____

Who will lend you school supplies or share ideas?

A Kid Who Is FAIR

1. _____
2. _____
3. _____

Who is a good sport?

A Kid Who CARES

1. _____
2. _____
3. _____

Who is a good listener?
Who is nice to everyone?

A Kid Who Is FUN

1. _____
2. _____
3. _____

Who enjoys doing things you like, or who does things you want to learn more about?

Adapted with permission from Huggins, P. (1993). *Teaching friendship skills: Primary version.* Longmont, CO: Sopris West.

Where We Get a Strong Sense of Self-Esteem (Primary)

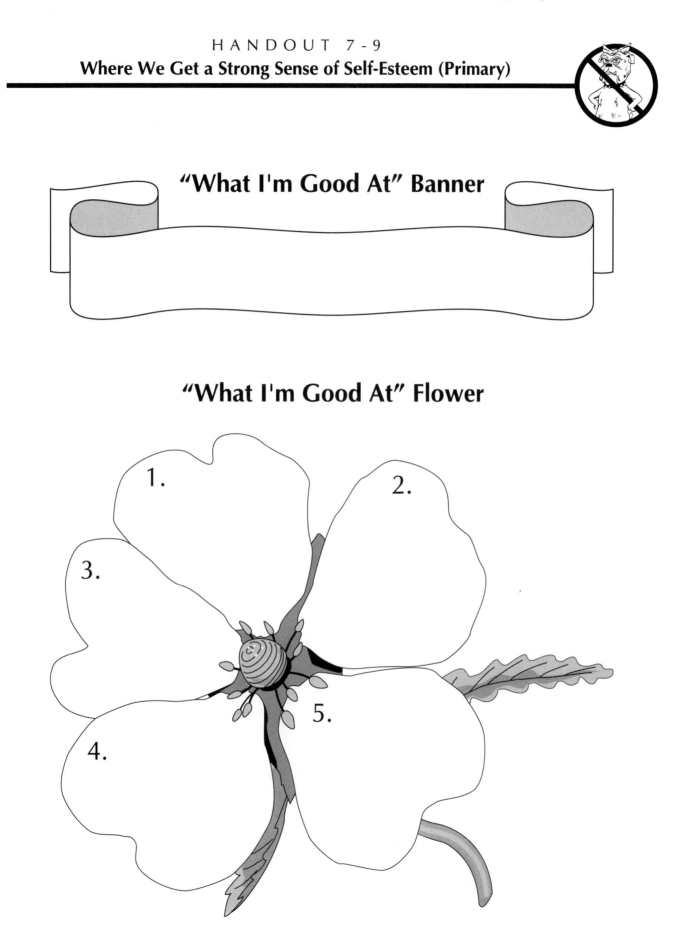

"What I'm Good At" Banner

"What I'm Good At" Flower

HANDOUT 7-10
Where We Get a Strong Sense of Self-Esteem (Intermediate)

People Say or Show You That They Like You

List people who do this in your life:

1. _____   2. _____

3. _____   4. _____

You Do Some Things Well

What are these things?

1. _____   2. _____

3. _____   4. _____

You Try to Do Your Best, Even on Hard Things

What are you working on to improve?

1. _____   2. _____

3. _____   4. _____

You Say or Show Others That You Like Them

Who are they?

1. _____   2. _____

3. _____   4. _____

TO SUM UP

Like Yourself
Forgive Yourself
Be Your Own Best Friend

Question:
How do best friends treat each other?

HANDOUT 7-11 (SUPPLEMENTARY)
Everyone Is a Person of Many Parts

Emily has both good parts and parts that need improvement.

Adapted with permission from Huggins, P. (1994). *Building self-esteem in the classroom: Intermediate version.* Longmont, CO: Sopris West.

HANDOUT 7-11 (SUPPLEMENTARY) (*continued*)

Directions:

Draw a picture of yourself or write your name in the center circle. Then write about parts of you, just like Emily did, in the other circles.

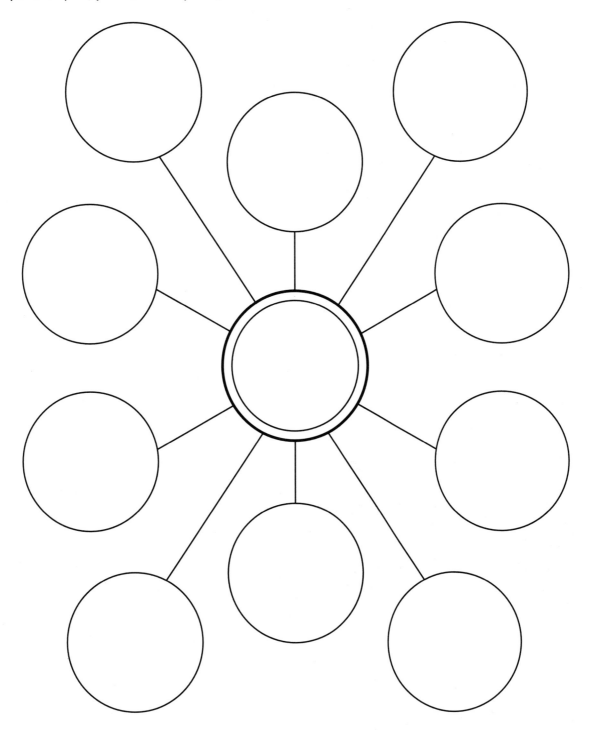

Adapted with permission from Huggins, P. (1994). *Building self-esteem in the classroom: Intermediate version.* Longmont, CO: Sopris West.

Relax and Say Encouraging Things to Yourself

Other things you can say to yourself:

- "I'm fun to play with and people like me. This kid will, too."
- "I like meeting new people and can think of good things to say to them."
- "I feel shy, but I can do it."
- "This kid might be shy and really want a new friend."
- "Maybe it'll work out, maybe it won't—I can handle whatever happens."
- "If this person is not nice to me, he or she is missing out—I'm a neat kid!"
- "If he or she doesn't want to be friends I won't die—I'll just try somebody else."
- _____
- _____

Adapted with permission from Huggins, P. (1993). *Teaching friendship skills: Intermediate version.* Longmont, CO: Sopris West.

GOAL

To become familiar with communication skills that promote responsible, assertive behavior when dealing with bullying.

HANDOUTS/LETTERS

Handout 7-13: Nice Ways to Say Hard Things

Handout 7-14: Rules for Fair Fighting

The Importance of "Giving the Right Message"

Discuss the important impact that assertive, confident, and responsible responses can have in a bullying situation. Emphasize to the students the need to practice these skills so they can become more automatic responses.

Preventing the "Victim Stance"

A confident, assertive demeanor will prevent the "victim stance" and help prevent bullying:

- Stand up straight.

- Use good eye contact.

- Use a strong, clear voice.

- Try not to cry. (This is a payoff for the bully and will increase the likelihood of repeated taunts. If you can't control your crying, walk away.)

- Use strong come-back statements.

Come-Back Statements Activity

Model for the students and have them role play and rehearse the use of strong come-back statements. Stress that these statements should not be put-downs or sound threatening. For example:

- "Don't do that." (**Attack the problem/behavior, not the person.**)

- "I don't like that." (**Use an "I statement."**)

- "Stop it." (**Keep it short.**)

Handout 7-13

When the students appear to understand the criteria of effective come-back statements, direct them to complete the handout. Then discuss it as a group.

Handout 7-14

Introduce and Discuss the "Rules for Fair Fighting"

You want the children to understand that defending themselves verbally is **always** a better alternative to arguing or fighting.

Introduce "I Statements" and Explain Their Importance

"I statements" get to the root of the feeling without blaming. For example:

- ◆ "I want . . . ."
- ◆ "I feel . . . ."
- ◆ "I need . . . ."
- ◆ "I'm glad I could tell you . . . ."

RESOURCE GUIDE
See "Videotapes and Films for Students," "Books for Primary Students," or "Books for Intermediate Students" for materials that highlight appropriate communication skills.

Activities for Reinforcing Effective Communication Skills

Story/Video

To reinforce the effective communication skills taught in this session, read a story from your school's library or show a video that addresses communication skills which are particularly weak in the student(s) in the group. Be sure to select one that is appropriate to the age group of the students.

Role Play

To have the students then practice the effective communication skills, use a role play format. Encourage the students to provide suggestions for role play scenarios featuring "real life" bullying situations they may have been involved in. (If you are working with an individual student instead of a small group, play the other character in the role play situation yourself.)

When conducting the role plays, one of two methods of encouraging feedback could be employed:

- ◆ By videotaping the role play situations and playing back for the student(s) appropriate sequences; or
- ◆ By using a "stop action" technique—interrupting the role play to coach the student(s).

The feedback from both the facilitator and other students (if a small group session) should include identifying the effective communication skills being used (e.g., use of nonverbal cues, a strong come-back statement, or an "I statement") in the role play.

If any student was unable to successfully demonstrate effective communication skills in the role play situation, model for the student use of a skill that would be helpful in preventing bullying in the particular role play situation, and then have the student try the role play again, practicing the skill to a comfort level.

Journals

Suggest that journals be kept as a step toward expressing feelings. When it's too difficult for students to communicate feelings surrounding bullying incidents directly, it helps them to understand what they are feeling and then communicate those feelings effectively if they write them down first.

Facilitator Notes

If the student(s) appear to find the role playing uncomfortable or intimidating, an alternate method of enacting the communication skills situations is through puppet play. Using puppets (available in any toy store) sometimes distances the students from the roles they are playing and allows them to more easily "speak through the character." However, after the students have reached a comfort level with the puppets, if this method is used, they should be encouraged to demonstrate the effective communication skills without the assistance of puppets to ensure that they will be able to employ them with their peers outside of the group.

Remember, vulnerability attracts aggressors. Helping the students work for small gains that nurture their confidence and strength will be beneficial. Additional activities that teach body orientation, body control, posture, and appropriate eye contact may hold promise for some victimized children in the group as well.

NEXT SESSION

In the next session, the students will be introduced to effective communication techniques that assist students in "getting the right message" when interpreting bullying situations.

HANDOUT 7-13
Nice Ways to Say Hard Things

Directions:

Read each sentence, and check whether it is a "nice" or "not nice" way to say a hard thing. If you decide a sentence is "not nice," write in a nice way of saying the same thing below it.

	Nice	Not Nice

1. "I don't want to play now, maybe later."

2. "Quit bugging me!"

3. "That bothers me. Please stop doing it."

4. "I can do it myself—I'm not a baby."

5. "I'm sorry I can't come to your party. I'm already busy on Saturday."

6. "Thanks for offering to share, but I don't like . . . ."

7. "Don't pick **him**. He'll make our team lose."

8. "You're too sloppy. Let me spread the glue."

9. "I can't let you copy my paper. I don't want to get in trouble."

10. "Can't you do anything right?"

HANDOUT 7-14
Rules for Fair Fighting

◆ Attack the problem/behavior, not the person

◆ Keep it short

◆ Get to the root of the conflict with "I statements"
>   "I want . . . ."
>   "I feel . . . ."
>   "I need . . . ."

◆ Be ready to change your own thinking or behavior

◆ Treat the other person as an equal

◆ Stay in the present moment—don't bring up old issues

◆ Show that you are listening to the other person

◆ Look for different options, not just one solution

◆ **Do Not:**
>   — Name Call
>   — Blame
>   — Threaten
>   — Hit
>   — Use Sarcasm
>   — Remain Silent
>   — Generalize ("You always . . .")
>   — Change the Topic

EFFECTIVE COMMUNICATION SKILLS—GETTING THE RIGHT MESSAGE

SESSION 5

GOAL

To become familiar with interpreting a bullying situation accurately and to review and reinforce the strategies that the students can use when they are being victimized by a bully—HA HA, SO.

HANDOUTS/LETTERS

Handout 7-15: HA HA, SO Practice

Introduction

Remind the students that each bully-victim situation is different, and not every strategy will work with every bullying situation. Emphasize the importance of interpreting each situation before responding. Taking these few seconds to evaluate a bullying situation will most likely result in a successful defusion of the bullying situation.

Introduce Nonverbal Communication

Understanding nonverbal cues/body language is important in "reading" a person. Paying attention to the way a person looks (e.g., posture and facial expression) can give you information in addition to what the person says (and how he or she says it) and does.

Note: Also help the students understand that the "language" of their nonverbal cues is important in dealing with victimization issues. (Remind the students that bullies are more likely to target children who appear unable to defend themselves and who cry easily.)

Interpreting Cues Activities*

Hearing Feelings

Ask a student to briefly talk about something that has happened to him or her. The rest of the students are to listen and guess what feelings the speaker is expressing. The students can demonstrate "reflective listening"

---

*Adapted with permission from Huggins, P. (1993). *Teaching friendship skills: Intermediate version.* Longmont, CO: Sopris West.

by saying: "It sounds like you're feeling . . . ." Topic ideas may include: (1) a fight with a brother/sister, (2) the first/last day of school, (3) a time they were surprised, or (4) a vacation they'll never forget.

This activity could also be done with partners.

Getting the Meaning Without Words

Have the students pair up, with their backs to each other. Have one partner select a "feeling" word from a list the students have brainstormed, with facilitator assistance. Have that student use only nonsense syllables (e.g., nee, woo, beep, etc.) to express the feeling. The other partner guesses what feeling is being expressed by just listening to the inflection and tone of the nonsense syllables.

Reading Body Language Pantomimes

Create two sets of note cards. On one set list a physical activity on each card, such as walk, sing, jump, stamp foot. On the second set list a feeling on each card, such as angry, scared, disappointed, strong, happy. Have each student draw a card from each deck and combine the physical activity with the feeling in a pantomime. Have the rest of the class take turns guessing the activity and the feeling.

Feeling Posters

Have the students generate a list of feeling words to be displayed on posters. Then have the students add pictures of people expressing those feelings (cut from magazines, photographs, drawings). This activity reinforces the notion of paying attention to facial expressions as a way to recognize another's feelings.

Review of the HA HA, SO Strategies

Model for the students and have them rehearse the strategies to cope with bullying behavior previously taught in the classroom curriculum: HA HA, SO. Provide examples that are relevant to these students' real life experiences at school (elicit further input from the students if necessary) for rehearsal purposes.

HA HA, SO

H - Help	**H** - Humor	**S** - Self-Talk
A - Assert Yourself	**A** - Avoid	**O** - Own It

- ◆ **Help**—When and how to seek help from peers and/or an adult.

  This strategy is best used in situations where help is available and willing, like at a "bully-proofed school." A victim can use this strategy during a bullying situation by calling to some other children, for example, "Could you help me ask Teddy to stop taking my books away from me?" or by running to an adult, describing what is happening, and saying, "I need help." A victim can also use this strategy when anticipating a bullying situation by asking several other children to stay close. For example, "Susan and her friends have been bullying me at recess. Could you play with me today and help me figure out what to do if they come at me again?" or by informing the teacher and asking for a watchful eye.

◆ **Assert Yourself**—When it would be wise to use assertiveness and when it would not.

This strategy is usually the best strategy for a victim to start with. But it should not be used with severe bullying or when the victim is very scared. To use this strategy, the victim looks the bully in the eye and says, for example, "I don't like how you are gossiping about me and trying to make me have no friends. It is mean and unfair. Stop doing it."

◆ **Humor**—How to use humor to de-escalate a situation.

This strategy is fun for children and can be used in conjunction with the "Help" strategy by asking other children to help dream up humorous ways to deal with a certain bullying situation. Several of the books listed in the Resource Guide illustrate humor as a strategy for dealing with the bully (e.g., in *Loudmouth George and the Sixth Grade Bully*, the victim, with the help of his friend, makes a horrific lunch with pickles in the sandwich and hot sauce in the thermos for a bully who was stealing his lunch). The victim could use this strategy by writing a funny note or poem to the bully.

◆ **Avoid**—How to walk away in order to avoid a bullying situation.

This strategy may be best for situations when the victim is alone. One way for the victim to use the "Avoid" strategy is to avoid a bully physically. The victim can cross the street or can avoid the situation(s) where the bullying is occurring. The victim can also avoid a bully by being with others rather than alone, perhaps by asking to walk home from school with other children. Another way for the victim to use the "Avoid" strategy is to analyze the situation and to stop doing anything that might be provoking the bully. If the bullying happens when the class lines up and both the victim and the bully want to be at the front of the line, the victim can choose to be at the end of the line instead to avoid a bullying situation.

◆ **Self-Talk**—How to use their self-talk to maintain positive self-esteem during a bullying situation.

Remind the students that in Session 3 they learned how victims' self-esteem drops when they are being bullied. The "Self-Talk" strategy is used to keep feeling good about oneself. The strategy involves "putting on a record in one's mind" that says nice things to oneself like: "I'm a good kid. I try my best at school and I'm nice to other kids. When Jason calls me dumb, it is not my fault. It is his problem that he is being mean. It is unfair. I don't have to accept his opinion of me. I can have my own opinion about me and like myself."

> **RESOURCE GUIDE**
> See "Books for Primary Students" or "Books for Intermediate Students" for books which feature the use of humor in bullying situations.

◆ **Own It**—How to "own" the put-down or belittling comment in order to defuse it.

This strategy can be combined with the "Humor" strategy with responses like, "I agree that this is an ugly dress; my mother made me wear it." It can also be combined with the "Assert Yourself" strategy with responses like, "I do have slanted eyes and that is because I'm Korean. Korea is a really cool country. Do you want to hear some things about it?"

Reinforcement Activities

Verbal Review

As in the classroom curriculum, to further reinforce the memorization of the HA HA, SO mnemonic, you may wish to have the students repeat the strategies in some way, such as singing HA HA, SO to a familiar tune or rap, calling out the strategies as you yell the HA HA, SO "cheer" (i.e., "Give me an H!" "Help!" "Give me an A!" "Assert Yourself!", and so on.), or by eliciting other ideas from the individual student or group.

Story/Video

Read a story from your school's library or show a video that addresses a bully-victim situation. Be sure to select one that is appropriate to the age group of the children.

Prior to reading the story or showing the video, ask the students to "listen for" (if a story) or "look for" (if a video) the strategy or strategies the victim character uses. (Depending upon the age or ability level of the individual student or group, it may be helpful to stop the video or stop reading periodically to illustrate the point of identifying strategies.) After the story or video, have the students share the strategy or strategies they heard or observed. If none of the HA HA, SO strategies were used, ask the students to identify a strategy or strategies that the victim character should have used.

Handout

Using Handout 7-15: HA HA, SO Practice, have the students draw or write about an example of when to use a HA HA, SO strategy.

Teachers and Facilitators are referred to page 183, Handout 5-9 Chapter Five: "Skills to Disengage." These skills can be used as additional strategies for victimized children to deal with bullying.

> **RESOURCE GUIDE**
> See "Videotapes and Films for Students," or "Books for Intermediate Students" for materials that address bullying situations.

Handout 7-15

Handout 5-9

NEXT SESSION

In the next session, the students will review the skills learned in the previous five sessions and address any unfinished business. (Let the students know if the next week is the last weekly session together.)

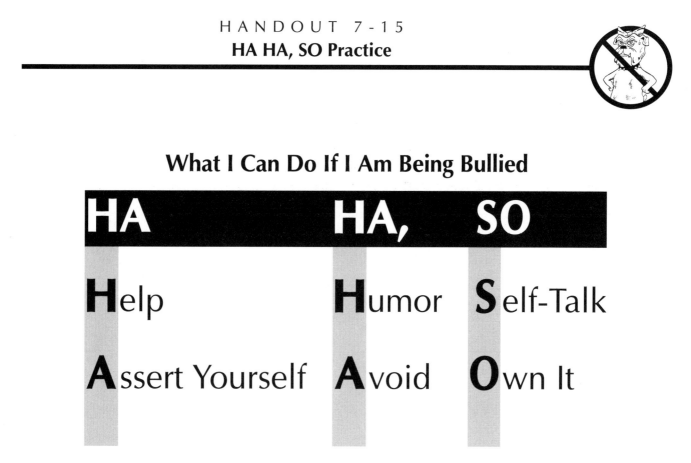

What I Can Do If I Am Being Bullied

HA   **HA,**   **SO**

Help   **H**umor   **S**elf-Talk

Assert Yourself   **A**void   **O**wn It

Directions:

Draw or write about a good time to use a HA HA, SO strategy in the box below.

SKILL REVIEW

GOAL

To review the skills learned in the previous five sessions and recognize the students' growth.

HANDOUTS/LETTERS

Handout 7-16: First/Second Grade Role Plays

Handout 7-17: Third/Fourth Grade Role Plays

Handout 7-18: Fifth/Sixth Grade Role Plays

Handout 7-19: Success Certificate

Letter 7-20: Sample Student Success Follow-Up Letter

For review, from Session 2:
   Handout 7-7: Friendly Behaviors Checklist

Facilitator Notes

Remind the students that this is your last weekly group session, if applicable. Remember that these students may require more than a six-week intervention. Continue to assess their needs via observation and consultation with their teachers, parents, and other school support personnel.

The majority of this session will present opportunities for the students to review and practice the strategies they have learned to use when they are being victimized.

Friendship Goals Evaluation

Handout 7-7

Readminister the "Friendly Behaviors Checklist." Remind the students that they had set friendship goals in the second session. After you re-evaluate their progress with the checklist, give them the opportunity to share how they are doing today with friendship skills, the best defense against victimization by bullies.

Role Play and Discussion for Review

Handout 7-16
Handout 7-17
Handout 7-18

Ask the students to each write one bullying incident that they have experienced on an index card or piece of paper. (If for some reason the children are unable to generate any scenarios, sample role plays are provided—see Handouts 7-16 through 7-18.) Select a few of the children's scenarios to role play that are representative of both typical male and female bullying tactics. Be sure to include at least one example of a provocative victim.

For each role play scenario, ask for student volunteers to play the bully and the victim (or play the bully yourself if working with an individual student). As the rest of the group watches quietly, direct the volunteers in performing the role plays appropriately (using one or more of the HA HA, SO strategies). After each role play, have the whole group discuss the role play scenario and identify the strategy or strategies used by the victim.

Growth Acknowledgment

Handout 7-19

In addition to skill review, a major goal of this session is to celebrate the students' successes and applaud new skills learned. Presenting certificates that are personalized to each student's main area of growth may encourage future success. For each student in the group, think of a behavior that should be reinforced (e.g., being a great friend, demonstrating improved self-esteem, etc.) to acknowledge specifically.

Handout 7-20

Following up with each of the student's teachers and/or parent(s) is suggested. Share the students' gains made and identify areas of future need and what can be done to facilitate their continued growth and success.

Supplemental Classroom Curriculum Review

If additional time is available or if you feel it would be valuable to the group, review an additional area of the classroom curriculum that could be helpful (Chapter Five, Session 5, "Teaching Strategies for the Helpers"). Many victimized students have low self-esteem, and one way to boost their self-esteem is to put these students in the "coaching" or "helper" position. Since Session 5 of the classroom curriculum presents skills for life-long learning such as empathy and assertive behavior, it may be an **excellent** idea to either review these skill areas now or to schedule a future time to reinforce these skill areas.

Session Conclusion

Let your group members know that you sincerely want them to let the adults in their life know if things aren't going well with friends or if they have encountered a situation with a bully that can't be handled on their own. Ask each student to again tell you who that adult at school would be. If the students can't name a trusted adult to help them, tell the students that you will help them identify an appropriate adult.

Finally, let the students know that you will follow up with them in two to three weeks either individually or as a small group to discuss their progress and see how things are going. Again, emphasize that they can talk to the "trusted adult" previously identified.

First/Second Grade Role Plays

Female

◆ You are a student in first or second grade. You notice that a couple of girls constantly make fun of another girl who is athletic. They tease her and call her a "tomboy." They invite her to play dolls with them, although they know she doesn't like to play. After they encourage her to play, they leave her out or ignore her.

Male

◆ You are a student in first or second grade. A group of boys playing soccer leaves out one boy and won't let him play. Finally he finds a friend to play with one recess, and the other boys go over to the playmate and say, "Would you like to play soccer with us?"

Third/Fourth Grade Role Plays

Female

◆ You are a student in third or fourth grade. A new girl has just joined your class. Although she seems shy and nice, she dresses in clothes that are older in style. A group of girls begin to tease her about her clothes. They especially laugh and make fun of her at recess, refusing to include her in conversations.

Male

◆ You are a student in third or fourth grade. One boy in your class has difficulty speaking clearly and leaves the classroom each morning to go to a resource class for help with his speech. Boys in your class call him "Retard." Other boys call him at home and ask for "the dummy." One day, some boys take his backpack and toss it back and forth in the halls before school, saying, "Come get it, you dummy," imitating his speech.

Fifth/Sixth Grade Role Plays

Female

◆ You are a student in fifth or sixth grade. A couple of girls have been picking on one of your classmates. They have been spreading rumors that she has a reading disability. They wrote a fake note to her inviting her to a party that didn't exist. She got very upset and cried when she tried to go to the "fictitious" party. No one wants to be that girl's friend. They think she is immature in every way.

Male

◆ You are a student in fifth or sixth grade. One boy in your class whose parents are talking about getting a divorce and moving is in an angry mood lately. He has gotten into some minor physical fights with other boys but seems to be aggravating one tough kid in particular.

He tries to trip him in the halls and runs into him at recess. Then he says, "Why don't you watch where you are going?" or tries to take his football. He only succeeds in getting hurt whenever he bothers this kid, but he continues anyway.

HANDOUT 7-19
Success Certificate

Success Certificate

Student's Name

Improvement in

Administrator's/Teacher's Signature

Group Facilitator's Signature

HANDOUT 7-20
Sample Student Success Follow-Up Letter

_____
(Date)

Dear _____:

_____ has completed the skills group where we practiced getting along with others, initiating and maintaining friendships, solving problems, and understanding and developing self-esteem.

_____ has shown growth in the following areas:

I recommend additional support and skill building in the following areas:

I will continue to follow-up with _____ to assess progress, and I invite you to contact me to share successes and/or needs that may arise. I have enjoyed working with _____ and appreciate your support.

Sincerely,

_____
(Name and title of facilitator)

_____
(Phone number of facilitator)

Conclusion

The individual/small group victim intervention is a helpful component of the bully-proofing curriculum when there are children who need more intensive training and support than the classroom curriculum can offer. These children are the frequent victims of bullies (passive victims) or the ineffectual aggressors (provocative victims). Quite often these children are receiving special education services and/or are considered at "high risk" of being victimized due to a variety of characteristics such as fragile self-esteem, poor social skills, and attentional problems.

Skill development can be tailored to meet the individualized needs of children more easily in a small group setting. Very often children who are being victimized need a small, safe environment to share their experiences and feelings regarding this aspect of school life. With support, guidance, and specialized social skills training, children can broaden their repertoire of skills necessary for success today as well as in the future.

Others who may benefit from individual/small group instruction are those students who currently bully others or are at risk of becoming chronic bullies. Chapter Eight: Changing the Bullies supplements the classroom curriculum by addressing the special needs of this group.

CHAPTER EIGHT

CHANGING THE BULLIES

Initially, *Bully-Proofing Your School* was designed without a specific intervention component for the bullies. Strong "no-bullying allowed" messages from all the adults combined with an empowered caring majority of the children have been found to be the most effective factors in stopping bullying behaviors.

There are two approaches to changing the bullies. First, this chapter presents an additional intervention component for changing the behavior of students who currently bully others or who are at risk of becoming chronic bullies. This intervention program uses a specialized six session individual or small group counseling format. The curriculum is to be used as a supplement to (preferably as preparation for) the classroom curriculum presented in Chapter Five: Student Instruction.

Second, Chapter Nine: Effective Prosocial Discipline presents ways to make a school's current discipline plan more effective in changing students who bully. Many schools cannot afford an extra intervention program for bullies in terms of personnel time and may prefer to rely on Chapter Nine.

Bullying Behavior Research Findings

Bullies were described in Chapter One as children who are aggressive and like power. They value the rewards that aggression can bring, lack empathy for their victims, and like to control and dominate others. They are identifiable by their antisocial personality style, which they develop early in life and tend to maintain if intervention is not delivered. Research findings from longitudinal studies are frightening. In a study in Norway, Olweus (1991) found that of boys identified as bullies in second grade, 60% were convicted of a felony by age 24. Eron (1987) studied American children and found that aggressive behavior rarely changed over the course of his 22-year study. The more aggressive a boy was at age eight, the greater the likelihood he would be in trouble with the law as an adult and the less likely he was to have finished college or to have found and held a job. Girl bullies, he found, were more likely as mothers to use aggressive means of punishing their own children and, as a result, their children were more likely to become bullies as well. Aggression appears to perpetuate from generation to generation and as Dr. Eron noted, "It is harder and harder for kids to change once the pattern is set and time goes on. Early intervention with bullies is crucial" (p. 14).

Dr. Stan Samenow's (1984, 1989) work on antisocial personality development emphasizes the thinking errors of antisocial youth. He stresses that intervention should not focus on feelings, but on changing these thinking errors. He delineates these thinking errors as follows:

- "Life is a one-way street—my way."; "If I want to do it, it is right, but if you want to do it, it is wrong."; entitled; unfair

- Disregard of injury to others; failure to empathize or make amends

- Unrealistic expectations and pretensions; "I should be number one overnight."; winning is everything; "If someone disagrees with me, they are putting me down."

- Taking the easy way; using shortcuts; quitting if not immediately successful; doing as little work as one can get away with

- Lying as a way of life; secretive; withholding information gives a sense of power; no concept of trust

- "It's not my fault."; refusing to be held accountable; always has an excuse; blaming others

- An island unto oneself; feeling superior to peers; appearing sociable, but in actuality using others; not a team player; not loyal; no sense of mutuality in relationships

Dr. Samenow stresses that parents (and school staff) must understand this pattern of errored thinking in order to challenge it rather than collude with it. Teachers and parents can help stop these thinking errors in children who bully by knowing: (1) how to recognize them, and (2) what corrective thinking to replace these thinking errors with. Handout 8-6 presented in Session 1 illustrates the correct social thinking for school staff to teach when they encounter these thinking errors in bullying students.

The first three sessions of this intervention curriculum for bullies focus on these thinking errors and employ thinking logs as Samenow (1984) has done with antisocial adults.

Goldstein and Glick (1987) have designed aggression replacement training with three main components: prosocial skills training, anger control strategies, and moral reasoning principles. George Spirack and Myrna Shure (1976, 1978) have developed methods for teaching social problem-solving skills to children and shown that these skills are positively correlated with psychological adjustment. In addition to thinking logs, the intervention with bullies program component also includes instruction on anger management, moral reasoning, and social problem solving.

The goals of individual/small group intervention with bullies are to:

 ◆ Decrease bullying and aggressive behaviors;

 ◆ Replace thinking errors with correct thinking;

 ◆ Develop more realistic self-concepts;

 ◆ Increase empathy skills;

 ◆ Improve moral reasoning abilities;

 ◆ Encourage more appropriate anger expression; and

 ◆ Improve social problem-solving skills.

Selecting Students for Intervention

Several other theorists and researchers have represented the deficits of aggressive children in somewhat different ways than Samenow's thinking errors, described previously. Lewis (1992) found that three main personality features ultimately determine which children become overly aggressive. **Children who are impulsive, hypersensitive, and prone to cognitive processing errors are at the highest risk**. The early warning signs that both teachers and parents need to look for in identifying these children are:

 ◆ Irritability, impatience, and mood instability from an early age.

 ◆ Misperceptions and a tendency to attribute hostile intent to the actions of others.

 ◆ A tendency to retaliate for genuine or imagined threats.

 ◆ Trouble putting feelings into words and instead using actions.

 ◆ Trouble recognizing one's own pain as well as the pain of others.

 ◆ An abusive or neglectful environment.

Given these descriptions of the thinking errors and cognitive-behavioral deficits in children who bully, suggestions for identifying students who might benefit from the individual/small group bully intervention presented in this chapter include:

 ◆ Students who receive frequent disciplinary action for aggression.

 ◆ Students who have an established pattern of antisocial thinking errors.

 ◆ Students who lack empathy and who show little emotion about peer conflicts.

- Students who frequently lie, steal, or cheat.

- Students who don't take responsibility for their behavior and tend to blame others.

- Students who frequently misinterpret social cues as hostile and have trouble expressing their anger appropriately.

A method for identifying these students and placing them in this curriculum should have been planned for in staff training Session 6. Suggestions for identifying a student who may require intensive training and/or support include:

- Classroom teacher referral.

- Parent referral.

- Support personnel (e.g., special education teacher, counselor, school psychologist or social worker, teacher assistant) referral.

- Administrator referral.

- Assessing the needs of students who are aggressive.

- Assessing the needs of students who lack anger management skills.

- Assessing the needs of students who lack empathy.

- Assessing the needs of students who come from violent, abusive homes.

- Assessing the needs of students who have had frequent disciplinary actions or trouble with the law.

General Information About Individualized Intervention With Bullies

This individual/small group curriculum consists of six weekly sessions. The sessions will be led by a group facilitator. The facilitator could be a special education teacher, school counselor, school psychologist or social worker, or a regular classroom teacher familiar with group processes and social skills training.

Each session includes an outline of the information to present, as well as handout and other reproducible student material masters to supplement the presentation. The individual/small group curriculum is **not scripted**, as the facilitator should use his or her best judgment in determining the content to emphasize for each student or group of students referred.

The individual/small group sessions for bullies can be conducted at the same time as the classroom curriculum or as preparation for the classroom work by preceding it in time. The latter is preferable since some work on thinking errors will be necessary for these students to be open to the ideas presented in the classroom curriculum and because of their oversensitivity to criticism.

The group facilitator for intervention with bullies must understand that the interactional approach recommended here is very different from the supportive approach recommended with victims. Refer to Handout 8-1: Strategies to Use With Victims and Handout 8-2: Strategies to Use With Bullies to review recommended intervention styles. Bullies need a firm, calm, confronting, "no-nonsense" style. Adults can impact these children only if they understand their characteristic ways of thinking and behaving and do not collude or further reinforce them. As noted in Chapter Four on staff training, some teachers will naturally have a style that is effective with bullies and will be more comfortable intervening with them. These teachers can provide support and coaching for teachers who are less comfortable using this style.

Handout 8-1
Handout 8-2

It is important for the facilitator to work closely with classroom teachers and parents to educate them about antisocial thinking errors so that all the adults are consistent in confronting and providing consequences for these bullying children. Examples of helpful confrontations include:

- "Jason, I saw you hit Robert first so I don't buy your story that you were just defending yourself. The consequence for hitting is 15 minutes in the principal's office. I will also expect you to apologize and do something nice for Robert, and I'll follow up with you tomorrow to find out what you did."

- " Susan, the comment you just made to Laura and the way you said it hurt Laura's feelings. I could see it in her facial expression. How would you feel if she said that to you? So it is not fair to treat her that way."

- "You can't win every time. The world just doesn't work that way."

- "You chose not to turn in your homework. It really isn't your mother's fault for letting you watch television."

It is also important for the adults at home and at school to be role models of correct thinking and to share their ways of thinking aloud. Teachers should try to catch positive behaviors of these students and reinforce them. Don't overdo this reinforcement, however, because students who bully may think they have pulled the wool over your eyes and that they don't need to change anymore (the immediate success thinking error). Make verbal reinforcement specific and remind the student that there is still a lot of hard work ahead.

Forming Groups

There are several advantages to using a small group format rather than working with an individual student. Groups are more efficient in terms of time and there is potential for more learning experiences when several students are sharing their Thinking Logs. Since bullies are good at blaming others and seeing errors that others make, they can be good at confronting each other within the group.

A disadvantage of using small groups is that negative group processes can develop fairly easily amongst antisocial children. The structured format proposed limits disruptive behavior, but the facilitator should be aware of this possibility and be prepared to switch a more difficult student to an individual format, if necessary.

Other special considerations when forming groups include:

◆ **Number of Students Per Group**

Small groups should not exceed five students, otherwise the group size becomes too overwhelming and the students will not be receiving the level of individual attention they need.

◆ **Number of Small Groups Required**

There is not as great a need for small group bully intervention when classroom instruction sessions are occurring. It is advisable that no more than two or three groups be ongoing at the same time due to the planning time required to individualize and lead the curriculum on the part of the facilitator.

◆ **Generalization of Skills**

It is advisable to group classmates together so the skills learned in the small group can be practiced outside of the small group environment (i.e., within the classroom). This increases the likelihood that the skills will be generalized.

◆ **New Referrals**

Generally, students referred for a small group bully intervention after the first few sessions have already been presented may be more comfortable waiting for the next cycle. The exceptions to this scheduling method include: (1) if the facilitator has time to review the concepts already taught with the newly referred student, (2) if the group is small enough to absorb a new student comfortably, (3) if the newly referred student feels comfortable with this arrangement, (4) if the group culture can accept a new student in a positive manner, and (5) if no more than one or two sessions have been missed.

School-Home Communication Prior to Intervention

Communication with the parents of the bullies is particularly important before intervention. Since parents of bullies may model antisocial thinking errors or may collude with their child's thinking errors in their attempts to be a "good parent," it is important to educate them about correct thinking. It is also important to have open, clear communication between the school and home because bullies are very adept at convincing people that they are victims. One alliance building strategy is the "I won't believe everything your child tells me about you, if you won't believe everything he or she tells you about me."

The parent(s) of each child chosen for small group bully intervention should be contacted prior to placing him or her in a group. Either the referring teacher or a member of the support staff who knows the child's parent(s) should make the initial call to the home. A follow-up call from the group facilitator is suggested as well. A permission slip for student participation in individual or small group intervention should be sent to the parent(s) after the initial phone contact (see Letter 8-3).

Letter 8-3

Cycle of Sessions, Time and Location, and Scheduling

◆ **Cycle of Sessions**

These sessions are designed to be conducted for six weeks, but sessions that appear to require more time can be extended or divided into multiple sessions, as the needs of the individual students dictate.

It is helpful for the group facilitator to keep notes of each session in order to identify areas that may need to be expanded upon or areas that should be addressed and haven't yet been taught (see Handout 8-4).

Handout 8-4

◆ **Time and Location**

The optimum length of group sessions is flexible, according to the needs of the students and their grade level, as follows:

◇ Primary—30-minute groups

◇ Intermediate—45-minute groups

It is helpful to conduct groups in a private or semiprivate area in the school to help the students feel comfortable to learn and grow. The same location for each session is advised for consistency.

◆ **Scheduling**

A "lunch bunch" approach to small group sessions can work, and silent reading time or library time are other possibilities. The key to scheduling is to choose a time that can be consistent from week to week and that includes the teachers in the decision. This involvement increases the likelihood of the classroom teachers supporting small group intervention.

It also helps to know the group meeting time before contacting the parents for initial permission, as this is an often asked question.

Strategies to Use With Victims

◆ Use a supportive/fear-reducing style

◆ Reduce self-blame by clear identification of cruel behavior

◆ Demonstrate compassion and empathy

◆ Connect victim to helpful peers

◆ Mobilize caring majority in the classroom

◆ Remind of HA HA, SO strategies

◆ Consider individualized help with friendship skills

Strategies to Use With Bullies

◆ Use a no-nonsense style

◆ Use prosocial consequences

◆ Give brief clear description of unacceptable behavior and consequence

◆ Do not have a long discussion of the situation

◆ Correct the bully's thinking errors

◆ Identify the victim's emotions

◆ Build empathy for the victim

◆ Re-channel power—do not try to suppress

◆ Set the culture for your school through the caring majority

LETTER　8 - 3
Sample Consent Form for Individual Bully Intervention

_____
(Date)

Dear Parent(s)/Guardian:

Your child has been invited to participate in a skills group at _____ School. The purpose of this group is to help improve your child's ability to focus on fair and realistic thinking, express anger appropriately, and use social problem-solving skills. Your child will also bring home handouts on concepts we are teaching and will be keeping a "Thinking Log" notebook.

The group will begin _____ and meet weekly for 30–45 minutes for a minimum of six weeks. A permission slip is attached for you to sign and return so that your child can participate. Please feel free to call me at _____ if you have any questions.

Sincerely,

_____
(Name and title of facilitator)

Return to: _____ by _____

I/we the undersigned give my/our permission for my/our child _____ to participate in a weekly skills group.

_____ 　 _____
Signature of Parent(s) or Guardian 　 Date

HANDOUT 8-4
Intervention Session Tracking Form

Date of Session: _____ Session Number:_____

Present: _____

Absent: _____

Goal(s): _____

_____

_____

_____

_____

Materials: _____

_____

_____

Agenda:

1. _____

2. _____

3. _____

4. _____

5. _____

Next Session:

1. Complete Agenda Item(s): _____

2. _____

3. _____

Follow-Up: _____

_____

_____

GETTING YOUR THINKING STRAIGHT—OVERVIEW

GOAL

To introduce the concept of thinking errors and "Thinking Logs."

HANDOUTS/FACILITATOR KEYS/LETTERS

Handout 8-5: Thinking Style Rating

Handout 8-6: Correct Social Thinking

Handout 8-7: Thinking Log Page (Primary)

Handout 8-8: Thinking Log Page (Intermediate)

Introduction

Introduce yourself to the students and explain that they were selected for the group because they have some things in common about how they think and act. Explain the format and goals of the group, and the time and location of the weekly sessions. Explain to the students that the first three sessions will focus on getting their thinking straight and the next two sessions will focus on solving social problems. Let the students know that in the final session they will be designing a board game to teach others what they've learned and to be thinking about this during the group meetings.

Facilitator Notes

Before this session, the facilitator should have each participating student's classroom teacher, parent (if possible), and a classmate rate the student on his or her thinking style using Handout 8-5. These ratings will be used for comparison with the students' during the session.

Rating Thinking Errors

Handout 8-5

Give the students the "Thinking Style Rating" handout and have them complete it about themselves. Have each student compare his or her rating to a composite rating by the classmate, teacher, and parent (keep anonymous who the raters were). These ratings can be used to challenge the students' self-ratings, which may be inaccurate. If the facilitator knows the students, their past interactions can be used to challenge inaccurate ratings as well.

Handout 8-6

Using Handout 8-6, explain to the students crooked versus straight thinking. Have the students give examples of situations where a person might use each type of crooked thinking and then each type of straight thinking. Ask the students to take this handout home and share it with their families for further discussion.

Introduce "Thinking Logs"

Handout 8-7
Handout 8-8

Introduce the appropriate Thinking Log page (Handout 8-7 or Handout 8-8). Explain that over the next few weeks, you want each of the students to try to catch themselves thinking crooked. Each time they do, they should record it in their Thinking Log notebook. If introducing the primary page, explain to the students that not every occurrence of crooked thinking will involve two people, in which case they should cross out or leave blank the second animal shown on the page when recording the occurrence.

The Thinking Log pages can be put in a notebook for each student or simply stapled together with a blank white page as the cover. Have each student illustrate the cover of his or her Thinking Log. Remind the students to bring their Thinking Logs to the group meetings each week.

Have each student fill out a sample Thinking Log entry based on an example generated in the prior discussion.

Extra Practice With Thinking Logs

If there is extra time, have the students practice using their Thinking Log pages by reviewing their daily activities like waking up in the morning, getting ready to go to school, being in a class at school that they least like, doing chores, doing homework, playing with friends, and having dinner with their family. Then as a group, help the students decide if the thoughts they have entered are crooked or straight using Handout 8-6 for reference.

NEXT SESSION

In the next session, the students will review their Thinking Logs and will focus particularly on thinking errors about themselves.

HANDOUT 8-5
Thinking Style Rating

Student Directions:

For each question, check the box by the thought that represents how you usually think.

Directions for Others:

Rate how _____ thinks. For each question, check the box by the thought that represents how this person usually thinks. Your ratings will remain anonymous.

---

1. ❑ Everything should always go my way. | ❑ To be fair, things should go my way half the time and the other person's way the other half of the time.

---

2. ❑ I don't care if I hurt other people. | ❑ I feel bad if I hurt other people because I know how it feels to be hurt.

---

3. ❑ Success should come easy and quickly or I'll quit. | ❑ I know that success takes hard work and a lot of time.

---

4. ❑ I shouldn't have to follow rules or do boring things. | ❑ I have to follow the rules and do my chores like everyone else.

---

5. ❑ Lying can keep you out of trouble. | ❑ Lying is a wrong thing to do.

---

6. ❑ I never make mistakes and things are never my fault. | ❑ Everyone makes mistakes and things are probably my fault about half the time.

---

7. ❑ Most kids my age are boring and always pleasing adults. | ❑ I have a lot in common with kids my age.

HANDOUT 8-6
Correct Social Thinking

CROOKED (INCORRECT) THINKING	STRAIGHT (CORRECT) THINKING
1. If something goes wrong, it is not my fault. Someone else makes me act badly.	I am responsible for my behavior.
2. When I don't want to do something, I say, "I can't."	"I can't" really means "I won't," and that is a choice which has consequences.
3. I don't hurt other people. They exaggerate being upset to get me in trouble.	My behavior can hurt others, including their feelings.
4. I don't care how other people feel or if I hurt them.	I don't want to hurt others because I don't like feeling hurt.
5. I hate having to work hard or do boring tasks, so I try to avoid them.	Life is not all fun and games; sometimes you have to do boring or difficult tasks.
6. I hate obligations, rules, and "must dos," and refuse or ignore them.	Everyone should play by the rules and fulfill their obligations.
7. I watch out for myself and always try to get my own way.	An attitude of fairness and a give and take balance must exist in good relationships.
8. I don't trust other people and they don't trust me.	Trust must be earned and developed over time.
9. I can always be successful at everything.	Success comes from hard work, planning, learning from mistakes, and being a good person.
10. I make decisions quickly and based on how I feel at that moment.	Good decisions are thought out and based on facts.
11. I am proud that I never make mistakes.	Everyone makes mistakes, and mistakes help you learn.
12. I do what I want and figure that the future will take care of itself.	Things work out better if I think about and plan for the future.
13. I am good at things quickly and without even trying.	Success takes hard work and comes in stages.
14. I get really upset if someone says something negative to me or puts me down.	Constructive criticism can help me learn. I want my friends to be honest with me.
15. I'm never afraid of anything.	Everyone feels fear sometimes and others can help me when I am afraid.
16. I get angry when I don't get my way and sometimes use my anger to get my way.	I am responsible for my feelings and have choices about how I express them.
17. I like having power because then I can win and get my own way.	Power is earned and should never be used to hurt others.

Based upon the work of Dr. Stan Samenow's research on antisocial personality development.

HANDOUT 8-7
Thinking Log Page (Primary)

Date_____

What happened?
_____

Date_____

What happened?
_____

Date_____

What happened?
_____

What happened?
_____

Date_____

H A N D O U T   8 - 8
Thinking Log Page (Intermediate)

Date:

Situation (who, what happened, where, when):

My thoughts:

Was my thinking straight or crooked? Why? How could I make it straight?

Date:

Situation (who, what happened, where, when):

My thoughts:

Was my thinking straight or crooked? Why? How could I make it straight?

Date:

Situation (who, what happened, where, when):

My thoughts:

Was my thinking straight or crooked? Why? How could I make it straight?

Date:

Situation (who, what happened, where, when):

My thoughts:

Was my thinking straight or crooked? Why? How could I make it straight?

GETTING YOUR THINKING STRAIGHT ABOUT YOURSELF

GOAL

To develop more realistic opinions of themselves and their capabilities.

HANDOUTS/FACILITATOR KEYS/LETTERS

Handout 8-9: Mad Math

Handout 8-10: Mad Letters

Facilitator Key: Handouts 8-9, 8-10

Handout 8-11: Mad Physical Activities

From Session 1:
  Handout 8-6: Correct Social Thinking

Thinking Logs Review

Have each student pick one entry from his or her Thinking Log to share with the group. In this discussion, the facilitator should model realistic thinking and use positive reinforcement (e.g., "Sam, I like how you noticed your own thinking error and recorded it in your log. This will be a good chance for you to learn.").

Using Handout 8-6 for reference, explain to the students that some of the crooked thoughts are about oneself and some are about the other person in an interaction. Today the focus will be on the students learning to think straight about themselves. Have the students try to notice their own occurrences of crooked thoughts 9, 11, 12, and 13 in particular.

Handout 8-6

Facilitator Notes

Don't be surprised if most of the students "forget" to bring their Thinking Logs or bring them with no entries completed. Make a group snack (or other reinforcer) contingent upon bringing back a completed Thinking Log in future sessions to encourage participation.

Seeing Oneself Realistically

Using the handouts, the students will make estimates of what they can do and are like cognitively, physically, and socially and then compare these estimates with their real performances. All the students will most likely overestimate their abilities because of their characteristic

Handout 8-9
Handout 8-10
Facilitator Key
Handout 8-11

thinking patterns which include expectations of quick, easy success and unrealistic perceptions of their own abilities.

For Handouts 8-9 and 8-10, have the students complete the exercises as you time them for one-minute intervals (with a stopwatch or second hand of a clock). Although the emphasis should be placed upon discrepancies between their estimated and actual performances, an answer key is provided in case the students would like to check the correctness of their work. Handout 8-11 requires access to gym and playground equipment, but should be used if at all possible (as a "homework assignment," alternately) since there is a strong emphasis on physical performance and achievement among elementary-age students. Most of the students should find these activities fun, which will encourage participation and learning.

When the handouts are completed, have a group discussion about which of the mad activities produced the biggest difference between their estimated and the real performance measures. Have the students think of ways to keep working on straight thinking about themselves in daily life.

NEXT SESSION

In the next session, the students will continue to use their Thinking Logs and will focus on thinking errors they make about others.

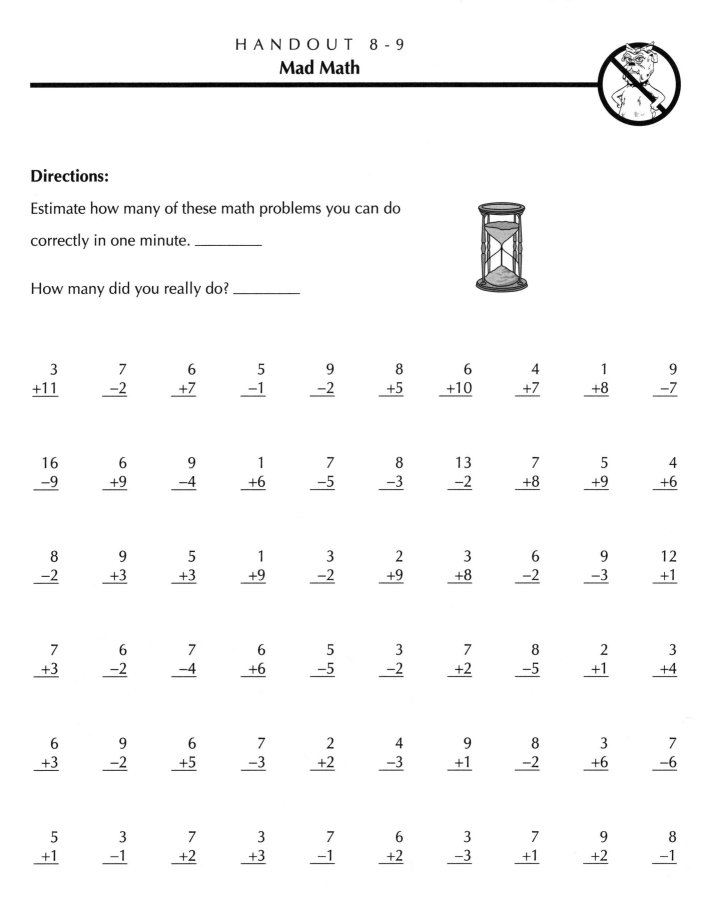

H A N D O U T   8 - 9
Mad Math

Directions:

Estimate how many of these math problems you can do

correctly in one minute. _____

How many did you really do? _____

3 +11	7 −2	6 +7	5 −1	9 −2	8 +5	6 +10	4 +7	1 +8	9 −7
16 −9	6 +9	9 −4	1 +6	7 −5	8 −3	13 −2	7 +8	5 +9	4 +6
8 −2	9 +3	5 +3	1 +9	3 −2	2 +9	3 +8	6 −2	9 −3	12 +1
7 +3	6 −2	7 −4	6 +6	5 −5	3 −2	7 +2	8 −5	2 +1	3 +4
6 +3	9 −2	6 +5	7 −3	2 +2	4 −3	9 +1	8 −2	3 +6	7 −6
5 +1	3 −1	7 +2	3 +3	7 −1	6 +2	3 −3	7 +1	9 +2	8 −1

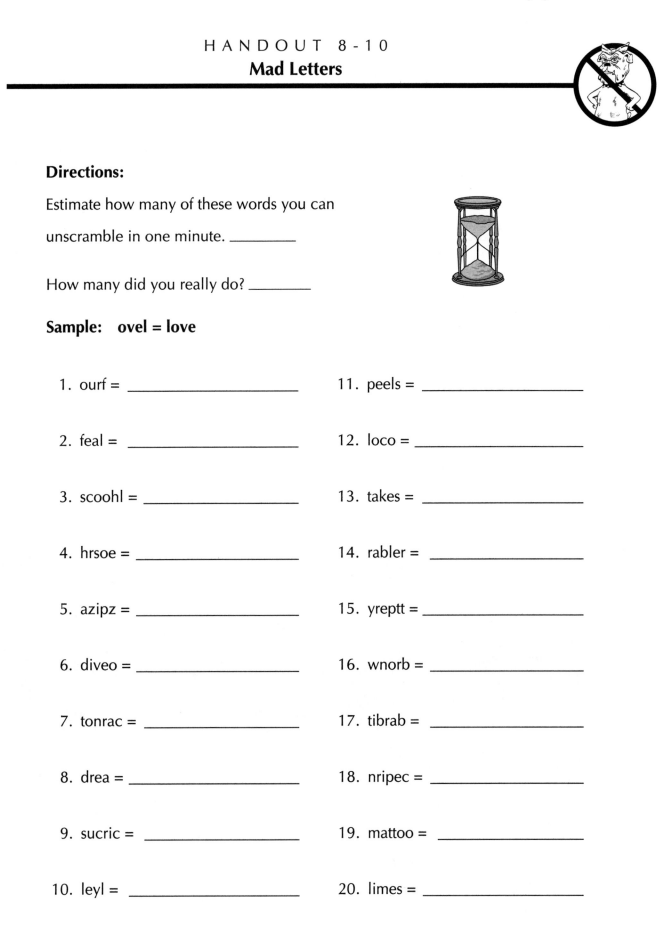

H A N D O U T   8 - 1 0
Mad Letters

Directions:

Estimate how many of these words you can

unscramble in one minute. _____

How many did you really do? _____

Sample: ovel = love

1. ourf = _____

2. feal = _____

3. scoohl = _____

4. hrsoe = _____

5. azipz = _____

6. diveo = _____

7. tonrac = _____

8. drea = _____

9. sucric = _____

10. leyl = _____

11. peels = _____

12. loco = _____

13. takes = _____

14. rabler = _____

15. yreptt = _____

16. wnorb = _____

17. tibrab = _____

18. nripec = _____

19. mattoo = _____

20. limes = _____

Mad Math

14,   5,   13,   4,   7,   13,   16,   11,   9,   2

7,   15,   5,   7,   2,   5,   11,   15,   14,   10

6,   12,   8,   10,   1,   11,   11,   4,   6,   13

10,   4,   3,   12,   0,   1,   9,   3,   3,   7

9,   7,   11,   4,   4,   1,   10,   6,   9,   1

6,   2,   9,   6,   6,   8,   0,   8,   11,   7

Mad Letters

1. four
2. leaf
3. school
4. horse
5. pizza
6. video
7. carton
8. read or dear
9. circus
10. yell
11. sleep
12. cool
13. skate or stake
14. barrel
15. pretty
16. brown
17. rabbit
18. prince
19. tomato
20. smile

HANDOUT 8-11
Mad Physical Activities

Directions:

How long would it take you to do the following activities? Write your estimate (best guess) in the first column. Try the activity and have someone time you. Write the actual time in the second column. Compare your results.

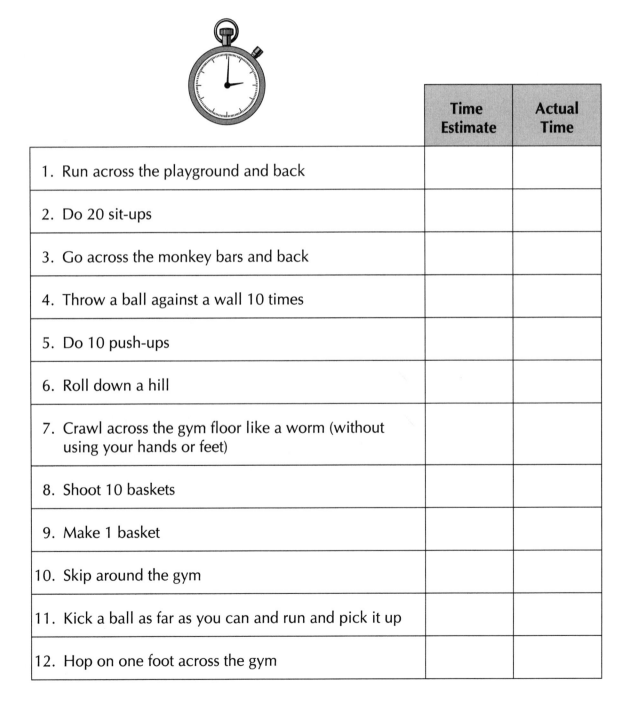

	Time Estimate	Actual Time
1. Run across the playground and back		
2. Do 20 sit-ups		
3. Go across the monkey bars and back		
4. Throw a ball against a wall 10 times		
5. Do 10 push-ups		
6. Roll down a hill		
7. Crawl across the gym floor like a worm (without using your hands or feet)		
8. Shoot 10 baskets		
9. Make 1 basket		
10. Skip around the gym		
11. Kick a ball as far as you can and run and pick it up		
12. Hop on one foot across the gym		

GETTING YOUR THINKING STRAIGHT ABOUT OTHERS

SESSION 3

GOAL

To develop empathy and to improve reasoning about fairness.

HANDOUTS/FACILITATOR KEYS/LETTERS

Handout 8-12: Scenarios for Thinking About Others

From Session 1:
    Handout 8-6: Correct Social Thinking

Thinking Logs Review

Handout 8-6

Have each student select an entry from his or her Thinking Log from the prior week to share with the group. In the group discussion, figure out whether each of these thoughts from the students' logs are straight or crooked. Review Handout 8-6 again and explain that this session will focus on getting their thinking straight about others, especially working on crooked thoughts 3 and 4.

Facilitator Notes

Again, have the group snack or other reinforcer contingent upon bringing a Thinking Log with completed entries. Be prepared to help those students who are still forgetting their logs to come up with strategies to complete and bring their logs so they, too, can enjoy the group snack.

Improving Sensitivity to How Others Think and Feel

Handout 8-12

Using Handout 8-12 and the Thinking Log pages, have each student write down appropriate thoughts for Person A and Person B in each of the scenarios. Then lead a group discussion in which they share their responses. The facilitator may have to model empathy with the characters during this discussion, if the students do not do so.

Additionally, you may wish to have the students read the scenarios again, substituting "you" for person A, and write down appropriate thoughts reflecting this change. Then have them repeat this procedure substituting "you" for Person B. Assist the students in noticing any changes in the thoughts identified when they put themselves in the place of one of the characters. Lead a group discussion in which they share what they noticed.

NEXT SESSION

In the next session, the group will focus on anger management strategies.

HANDOUT 8-12
Scenarios for Thinking About Others

Scenario 1:

Jordan (Person A) told Robert (Person B) that he would sit with him at lunch and now that they are getting in line to go to lunch, Jordan says he changed his mind.

Scenario 2:

Laurie (Person A) and Angela (Person B) have been best friends all year. A new girl moved to their neighborhood and now Laurie wants to spend a lot of time with her.

Scenario 3:

A class has been assigned a science project involving cooperative learning groups. Blair (Person A) is assigned the role of Group Recorder. Her responsibilities include reporting back to the teacher on progress and plans. Sam (Person B) has always wanted this responsibility and feels it is unfair that he hasn't been chosen. He finds the group boring and refuses to participate and instead he wanders around the classroom and bothers other groups.

Scenario 4:

James (Person A) likes to play rough at recess. Bobby (Person B) usually avoids him but today they are both in a soccer game. Bobby gets tripped by James when no one is looking. Bobby falls and tears his new jacket.

Scenario 5:

Toby (Person A) works really hard at school and gets really good grades. His teacher selects one of his stories to enter in a contest. Judy (Person B) wrote her story at the last minute before she came to school and is mad that she didn't get picked.

Scenario 6:

Charles (Person A) wrote some bad words on the wall of the school bathroom. His teacher suspected him and when she talked to him about it, he said he had seen Blake (Person B) do it. Blake starts crying when the teacher talks to him about it.

SOLVING SOCIAL PROBLEMS— MANAGING YOUR ANGER

GOAL

To gain a better understanding of anger and how to manage it effectively.

HANDOUTS/FACILITATOR KEYS/LETTERS

Handout 8-13: Benefits and Problems of Expressing Anger (Primary)

Handout 8-14: Benefits and Problems of Expressing Anger (Intermediate)

Handout 8-15: Things That Make Most Kids Angry

Handout 8-16: Anger Evaluation

Handout 8-17: Anger Situations Worksheet

Handout 8-18: Anger Contract

From Session 1:
   Handout 8-6: Correct Social Thinking

Thinking Logs Review

Have each student select an entry from his or her Thinking Log from the prior week to share with the group. Help the students discuss whether their thoughts were straight or crooked. Review Handout 8-6 and explain that this session is about anger and crooked thoughts 1, 6, 14, and 16.

Handout 8-6

Facilitator Notes

Anger management skill development is an important component of problem solving. It appears to be a widely held misconception that **simply expressing** angry feelings is good and helpful. However, simple expression of angry feelings is rarely adequate for problem resolution. Angry conflicts in the absence of constructive problem solving will often lead to further difficulties. The key concept to understand is that of constructive expression of feelings combined with efforts directed at problem solving. Appropriate anger management means the successful resolution of both the situation that led to the angry feelings and the appropriate expression of the feelings themselves.

RESOURCE GUIDE

See "Videotapes and Films for Students" and "Books for Educators" for additional sources of information on anger management and appropriate assertive behavior.

Handout 8-13
Handout 8-14

Expressing Anger Discussion

Discuss the benefits and potential problems that can result from expressing anger. Use examples which relate to the students' lives. Have the students fill out the appropriate "Benefits and Problems of Expressing Anger" handout during the discussion.

Expressing Anger Role Plays (Optional)

Present expressing anger situations to be role played by the students. Following are two role play examples and follow-up discussion questions:

- ◆ **Role Play 1:** Joe's good friend Tom calls him a name on the playground. Tom is trying to impress a group of popular boys by being unkind to Joe. Joe is angry at Tom for the way he has been treated.

  Role play a way for Joe to express his anger to Tom appropriately.

- ◆ **Role Play 2:** The teacher reprimands Sally for cheating on a spelling test. Sally feels angry at her teacher because she was not cheating. Sally was only responding to a question Mary had asked her regarding recess time.

  Role play a way for Sally to express her anger to her teacher appropriately.

- ◆ **Discussion Questions:**

  ◇ How did Joe/Sally feel?

  ◇ Why was Joe/Sally angry?

  ◇ Do you think it was O.K. for Joe/Sally to be angry?

  ◇ How did Tom/the teacher feel about Joe's/Sally's anger?

  ◇ Did Joe's/Sally's anger help him/her solve the problem?

  ◇ What problems could have resulted from Joe's/Sally's anger?

  ◇ What good came from Joe's/Sally's anger?

Anger Evaluation Activities

Through these activities, the students will gain an understanding of situations that make them angry.

Handout 8-15

Use Handout 8-15 to discuss things that make most children angry.

Anger Questions

Label four large pieces of poster board with the headings: (1) "Where," (2) "What," (3) "Who," and (4) "How."

Have the students generate a list on each board by answering these respective questions:

1. Where do I find myself getting angry most often?

2. What kinds of things make me angry?

3. Who do I get angry with most often?

4. How do I deal with my anger?

After the students have finished compiling the four lists, ask the following discussion questions (for each list) to help them evaluate their anger:

♦ What are the similarities among your responses?

♦ What are the differences among your responses?

♦ Is there any one response that is seen most frequently?

Worksheet

Have the students complete the anger evaluation handout. Alternately, primary students may draw a picture of a problem situation and then answer the questions verbally.

| Handout 8-16 |

Anger Situation Activities

Think-Feel Discussion

To help the students understand that anger is a result of problem situations and thoughts, present and discuss the following ideas:

♦ **First** we think, **then** we feel.

For example: Lisa asks to play with a group of girls. They tease her and refuse to let her join their game. Lisa **thinks**, "nobody likes me." Lisa **feels** sad and lonely.

♦ **What** we **think** affects how we **feel**.

The following thoughts, for example, can have a strong affect on how we feel in a situation:

◊ She's always bothering me.

◊ Nobody likes me.

◊ That's not fair.

◊ He's out to get me.

◊ I'm not very smart.

Worksheet

| Handout 8-17 |

Have the students complete the "Anger Situations Worksheet." Before they begin, discuss with the students the difference between "thoughts" and "feelings." Instead of writing their answers, primary students may draw pictures and then answer the questions verbally.

When the students have completed their worksheets, allow them to share their responses with the following discussion questions:

♦ Why are your feelings in Situations 1 and 2 different?

♦ In Situation 1, how did what you think affect how you feel?

♦ In Situation 2, how did what you think affect how you feel?

Anger Control Activities

Anger Control Strategies

With the students, generate a list of anger control strategies (and explain each fully). Include:

- ◆ Positive thoughts;
- ◆ Time-out;
- ◆ Counting to 10;
- ◆ Listening to music;
- ◆ Exercising;
- ◆ Relaxation;
- ◆ Problem solving;
- ◆ Accepting consequences; and
- ◆ Assertive behavior.

Review all the skills taught in this session so far and point out how they will help the students in everyday situations. As a part of this wrap-up discussion, also highlight other previously learned skills that will support the new anger management strategies they have learned (they are all related).

Handout 8-18
Handout 8-15

Contract Activity

Have each student complete the "Anger Contract." The students are to select three strategies which they can use when angry. If the students need help with identifying what makes them angry before filling out the contract, have them refer to Handout 8-15 for ideas.

NEXT SESSION

In the next session, the students will continue working on social problem solving by reviewing strategies for building empathy and understanding another's feelings and point of view.

Benefits (What's Good)

Expressing anger can:

1. Teach you to solve problems

2. Make you feel calmer

3. Lead to stronger behavior

4. _____

5. _____

Problems (What's Not So Good)

Expressing anger can:

1. Make another person mad

2. Result in a "lose-lose" situation

3. Be hurtful

4. _____

5. _____

HANDOUT 8-14
Benefits and Problems of Expressing Anger (Intermediate)

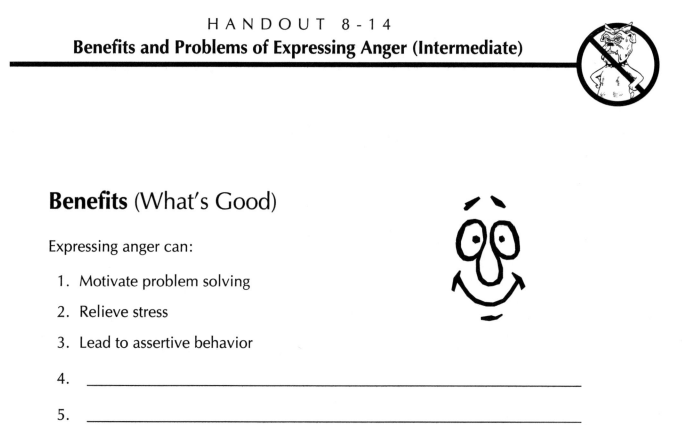

Benefits (What's Good)

Expressing anger can:

1. Motivate problem solving

2. Relieve stress

3. Lead to assertive behavior

4. _____

5. _____

Problems (What's Not So Good)

Expressing anger can:

1. Escalate another person's behavior

2. Result in a stand-off

3. Be hurtful

4. _____

5. _____

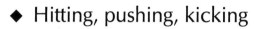

HANDOUT 8-15
Things That Make Most Kids Angry

- ◆ Hitting, pushing, kicking

- ◆ Lying

- ◆ Bragging, acting stuck-up

- ◆ Not playing fair, cheating

- ◆ Name calling, put-downs

- ◆ Spreading rumors, gossiping

- ◆ Tattling

- ◆ Being bossy

- ◆ Being fickle (friendly only when they want something)

- ◆ Hogging attention, talking too much

- ◆ Breaking agreements

- ◆ Laughing at others' mistakes

- ◆ Staying mad, not forgiving

- ◆ Not sharing

- ◆ Copying

- ◆ Being wrongly blamed for something

H A N D O U T 8 - 1 6
Anger Evaluation

Directions:

Think of a time during the week when you were angry. Answer the questions below.

1. Where were you when you got angry?

   _____

   _____

   _____

2. What made you angry?

   _____

   _____

   _____

3. Who or what were you angry with?

   _____

   _____

   _____

4. How did you deal with your anger?

   _____

   _____

   _____

5. What did you do to work out the problem?

   _____

   _____

   _____

H A N D O U T 8 - 1 7
Anger Situations Worksheet

Situation 1:

You are standing in line at the movie theater. It feels like someone kicks you from behind. You turn around and it is a child about your age who sticks his or her tongue out at you then hides behind his or her parent.

What would you think?

_____

_____

_____

What would you feel?

_____

_____

_____

Situation 2:

You are standing in line at the movie theater. It feels like someone kicks you from behind. You turn around and see an elderly woman. She had stumbled on the sidewalk as she moved to get on line for a ticket.

What would you think?

_____

_____

_____

What would you feel?

_____

_____

_____

HANDOUT 8-18
Anger Contract

I, _____ (name), agree to work to improve the
way I express my anger. I will use the following strategies to help me better control
my behavior when I feel angry:

1. _____

_____

2. _____

_____

3. _____

_____

_____
(student)

_____
(facilitator)

_____
(student witness)

Strategies:
- Positive thoughts
- Time-out
- Counting to 10
- Listening to music
- Exercising
- Relaxation
- Problem solving
- Accepting consequences
- Assertive behavior

SOLVING SOCIAL PROBLEMS— WHERE IS THE OTHER KID REALLY COMING FROM?

SESSION 5

GOAL

To improve social problem-solving skills by using cues to define a situation, generate alternative solutions, and think about consequences of behavior.

HANDOUTS/FACILITATOR KEYS/LETTERS

Handout 8-19: Steps for Solving Social Problems

Facilitator Key: Problem Cards for the Problem-Solving Game

Handout 8-20: Answering and Scoring Sheet for the Problem-Solving Game

From Session 4:
    Handout 8-18: Anger Contract

From Session 1:
    Handout 8-6: Correct Social Thinking

Thinking Logs Review

Review with the students' entries in their Thinking Logs as in prior sessions. Also review the "Anger Contract" handouts completed by all of the students in the last session. Discuss anger situations that came up for the students in the prior week and how the students chose to handle them.

Handout 8-18

Facilitator Notes

Review with the students Handout 8-6, and explain that this session will focus on how to use cues, generate alternative solutions, and think about consequences in solving social problems. Crooked thoughts 5, 8, 10, and 14 are related to this session. Aggressive children tend to misperceive others as hostile because they rely on limited cues, especially recent and sensational cues. They also generate only a limited number of alternative responses to problem situations and fail to consider the consequences of their behavior. This session aims to change these patterns in children who bully.

Handout 8-6

Handout 8-19

Steps for Solving Social Problems

Using Handout 8-19, teach the students the five effective steps for solving problems using the acronym SOLVE. Using examples from their Thinking Logs, help the students discuss how to apply these steps to a social problem. After discussing the steps, have the students turn their handouts face down and then try to remember the five strategies associated with the acronym letters S, O, L, V, and E.

Problem-Solving Game

Divide the group members into two or three teams to play the game and have a desired reward (like extra snacks or "cool" pencils) selected for the winning team. If working with an individual student, the facilitator can be the "other team" or the student could compete against a standard (e.g., receiving a reward if his or her score is 30 or more of the 40 total points).

**Facilitator Key
Handout 8-20**

Have the problem cards provided (Facilitator Key), or your own substitutes, cut apart and laying face down. Hand out an answering sheet (Handout 8-20) for each of the four problem cards to each team and explain the procedures and the scoring (described in the next paragraph). Then draw the first problem card and read it aloud to the teams. Each team should, as a group, check the appropriate card number at the top of the handout and generate answers to the problem read, writing them on their answering sheet on the appropriate lines.

The game can be played with either a five-minute time limit or without a time limit. Score one point for each different response. Have another team or the facilitator check for duplicate or bogus responses. Aggressive responses count in response to question 2, but they must have realistic consequences to match in question 3 in order to earn points.

NEXT SESSION

The next session will be a skill review in which the students create a board game to demonstrate what they have learned.

HANDOUT 8-19
Steps for Solving Social Problems

S O L V E

S

Stop and go **slow**.

O

Observe cues to figure out where someone is coming from:
- ◆ Verbal, nonverbal.
- ◆ Has the behavior changed over time?
- ◆ How many times has this behavior happened?
- ◆ Don't just count dramatic behavior.

L

Generate **lots of alternatives**—lots of ways you could try to solve the problem.

V

View the consequences for each of the alternatives:
- ◆ What will happen if I do this?
- ◆ Will anybody be hurt?
- ◆ Short-term and long-run consequences.

E

Choose a solution, try it out, and **evaluate** how it works.

FACILITATOR KEY
Problem Cards for the Problem-Solving Game

PROBLEM CARD

1. Jim cuts in line to go to lunch right in front of you.

PROBLEM CARD

2. You and your best friend usually play together at recess. But for the last four days your best friend has been playing with another group of kids.

PROBLEM CARD

3. During a group project in class, Leslie starts arguing with you about how to spell a certain word.

PROBLEM CARD

4. You and several other kids from your class are playing a board game during free time. Jeff cheats and takes an extra turn.

HANDOUT 8-20

Answering and Scoring Sheet for the Problem-Solving Game

Problem Card Number   ☐ **1**   ☐ **2**   ☐ **3**   ☐ **4**

1. What cues should you observe to figure out where the person is coming from? Write as many different cues as you can.

    1. _____

    2. _____

    3. _____

    4. _____

    5. _____

    6. _____

    7. _____

    8. _____

    9. _____

    10. _____

2. What are some solutions to this problem? Write as many different solutions as you can.

    1. _____

    2. _____

    3. _____

    4. _____

    5. _____

    6. _____

    7. _____

    8. _____

    9. _____

    10. _____

HANDOUT 8-20 (*continued*)

3. What are two likely consequences that you should view for each of the solutions
    you wrote down?

1a. _____

1b. _____

2a. _____

2b. _____

3a. _____

3b. _____

4a. _____

4b. _____

5a. _____

5b. _____

6a. _____

6b. _____

7a. _____

7b. _____

8a. _____

8b. _____

9a. _____

9b. _____

10a. _____

10b. _____

SKILL REVIEW

GOAL

To review the skills learned in the previous five sessions and have fun integrating them in creating a board game, and to acknowledge the students' growth.

HANDOUTS/FACILITATOR KEYS/LETTERS

Handout 8-21: Success Certificate

Letter 8-22: Sample Student Success Follow-Up Letter

From Session 5:
   Handout 8-19: Steps for Solving Social Problems

Thinking Logs Review

Handout 8-19

Review with the students entries in their Thinking Logs as in prior sessions. Review the SOLVE steps from the last session, as well.

Facilitator Notes

You should gather together the following supplies to be used to make the game in this session: tag board for the game board, blank index cards to be cut in half for the learning cards, and markers and old magazines to illustrate the board with.

Creating a Board Game

Explain to the group that this is the final group meeting and their task is to cooperatively create a board game which would teach other kids what they've learned about straight thinking and solving social problems just by playing it.

The board game should have some kind of track or road with 50 to 100 squares leading to a goal (the end). They should create learning cards that demonstrate what they've learned (e.g., "You just lost your temper—go back three spaces."). The students can refer to all their handouts from the prior sessions to stimulate ideas. Encourage the students to be creative in naming their game and in picking a theme for the board (e.g., racetrack, mountain bike journey, space adventure).

When completed, give the students positive and realistic feedback about the game they have created. Encourage them to take turns trying it out with their friends.

Alternate Activity

An alternate way to conduct the skill review is through student self-assessment using handouts from prior sessions: Handouts 8-6, 8-9, 8-10, 8-11, 8-16, and 8-17 specifically. Have the students complete some or all of these handouts and compare the results to when they initially completed them.

Handout 8-21

Growth Acknowledgment

In addition to skill review, a major goal of this session is to celebrate the students' successes and applaud new skills learned. Presenting certificates that are personalized to each student's main area of growth may encourage future success. For each student in the group, think of a behavior that should be reinforced (e.g., demonstrating improved anger control, etc.) to acknowledge specifically.

Letter 8-22

Following up with each of the student's teachers and/or parent(s) is suggested to share his or her gains made and identify areas of future need and what can be done to facilitate the student's continued growth and success.

Session Conclusion

Let the students know that you will follow up with them in two to three weeks either individually or as a small group to discuss their progress and see how things are going.

HANDOUT 8-21
Success Certificate

Success Certificate

Student's Name

Congratulations on your improvement in learning straight thinking and solving social problems.

Group Facilitator's Signature

Administrator's/Teacher's Signature

LETTER 8-22
Sample Student Success Follow-Up Letter

_____
(Date)

Dear _____:

_____ has completed the skills group where we
practiced straight thinking about oneself and others, solving social problems, and
anger management.

_____ has shown growth in the following areas:

I recommend additional support and skill building in the following areas:

I will continue to follow-up with _____ to assess
progress, and I invite you to contact me to share successes and/or needs that may
arise. I have enjoyed working with _____ and
appreciate your support.

Sincerely,

_____
(Name and title of facilitator)

_____
(Phone number of facilitator)

Conclusion

The individual/small group bully intervention is an important part of the bully-proofing curriculum in pretraining aggressive children in healthy thinking patterns and social problem-solving skills. This prepares them to be more receptive to learning during the classroom instruction component of this program. Skill development can be individualized and embarrassment minimized in the small group setting. The activities are fun and stimulating in order to keep these children involved in the change process.

Chapter Nine will show ways to effectively impact bullying and aggressive behavior with the school's discipline plan, policies, and philosophy.

The community's involvement in recognizing and supporting a "no-bullying" position cannot be overemphasized. The importance of and approaches to collaboration with parents, as a critical component of the bully-proofing program, will be addressed in Chapter Ten.

CHAPTER NINE

EFFECTIVE PROSOCIAL DISCIPLINE

Chapter Eight, Changing the Bullies, presented an individual/small group format for working with bullies to change the behavioral, cognitive, and emotional patterns that make them high risk for future social and legal problems. Another way to impact these volatile and self-defeating patterns is through effective discipline. During staff training, a review of the school's current discipline plan was recommended in order to integrate it with bully proofing concepts and language. This chapter presents a description of how to conduct a discipline plan review and revision. In addition, a discipline philosophy is presented with these critical elements:

- ◆ Adults are nonreactive yet responsive

- ◆ Use of prosocial consequences

- ◆ Use of consequences that teach empathy, correct social thinking, social problem solving, and how to be part of a caring community

- ◆ Taking advantage of teachable moments

- ◆ Striving for shared control

- ◆ Involvement of the caring majority of students

- ◆ Protecting all students from retaliation.

Several disciplinary tools that are consistent with bully-proofing are also described in this chapter:

- ◆ School discipline reports focusing on clear assessment of the problem

- Steps for nonreactive discipline
- Student incident reports (primary and intermediate forms)
- Rituals developed by the school
- Letters from peers.

Review and Revision of Discipline Plan

It is important to integrate a school's disciplinary policies with the bully-proofing program. Bully-proofing is a climate change program that aims to create an atmosphere of safety and caring at a school. Adults implementing discipline are key to affecting school climate and are critical to setting the tone in a school. In elementary schools, initial discipline is handled in the classroom. More severe situations for discipline are handled by the administration. Most elementary schools have a disciplinary plan that specifies behavioral infractions and the consequences to be applied. After staff training in bully-proofing, the disciplinary plan needs to be reviewed to incorporate bully-proofing language and consider the principles for effective discipline discussed on the following pages. The review of the discipline plan can be done by an existing committee, for example, the school safety committee, or by the bully-proofing cadre. Any revisions and a final proposed disciplinary plan should be reviewed by all staff.

The discipline plan review committee should consider questions such as:

What is our definition of discipline?

What are the characteristics of the kind of student we'd like to shape our students into?

What are the misbehaviors that require discipline?

Why do students misbehave in each of these ways?

What standards can staff agree upon?

The review committee should refer to earlier materials from this book in designing their discipline plan, such as:

- Handout/Transparency 4-14: *Bully-Proofing Your School* Strategies
- **Handout/Transparency 4-15:** Ideas for Consequences
- **Handout/Transparency 4-17:** Ideas for Reinforcers
- **Handout/Transparency 4-18:** Key Characteristics of an Effective School Policy
- **Handout 5-28:** Conflict Resolution Steps (Intermediate)
- **Handout 8-6:** Correct Social Thinking
- **Handout 8-18:** Anger Contract
- **Handout 8-19:** Steps for Solving Social Problems

Discipline is defined by the American Heritage Dictionary as "training that is expected to produce a specified character or pattern of behavior, especially that which is expected to produce moral or mental improvement." Many teachers are surprised by this definition because discipline is commonly associated with punishment and behavior control. Years of psychological research show that punishment can suppress behavior but does **not** change behavior or teach other alternative behaviors. Positive reinforcement is a more effective behavior change strategy as it allows children to get attention and to gain power for positive behaviors. All students deserve and need attention.

It is critical that schools develop clear rules and expectations. Rules are the factors of external control, such as "no running in the halls." Expectations are ways of showing respect for the school by controlling yourself.

Principles of Effective Discipline

How a student responds to discipline is important information in designing an intervention. Students make mistakes and about one-third of them correct their behavior with discipline and are not in serious difficulty again. Another third require a tighter rein and close supervision for the first disciplinary action to be meaningful. The final third need redirection as well as practice with replacement behaviors; without this specific assistance, they will continue with the "mistakes kids make." Specifically, students who are engaged in acts of continual physical or verbal aggression and/or alienation of other students require detailed and intensive redirection relating to bullying. These students are obsessed with power and need a clear message to stop, plus held with ways in which they can get their need for attention and power met in more appropriate ways.

Nonreactive Discipline

Handout 9-1

The first disciplinary principle is that adults try to stay calm and non- reactive in disciplining bullies. Bullies can quickly get an emotional reaction from most adults. Watching a child hurt and provoke an- other child creates anger and a feeling of wanting to take a pound of flesh in return. Yet handling bullies in a emotional way is ineffective. Handout 9-1, Strategies to Use with Bullies, recommends using a no-nonsense, matter-of-fact, keep it brief, no long discussions approach with bullies. This style minimizes the adult's emotional reactions and the opportunity for the bully to engage in a discussion about the "injustice" he or she was dealt.

The following steps of nonreactive discipline are shown in Handout 9-2:

Handout 9-2

1. State your belief that the child can be a positive leader at the school and has the ability to be a good citizen.

2. State the behavioral infraction and remind the student of school rules and values.

3. State the consequence and any parameters.

4. State the follow-up plan.

Following these steps also assists the adult in remaining calm and minimizes overreacting emotionally.

Handout/Transparency 4-17

Prosocial Discipline

The second disciplinary principle is to use prosocial consequences as much as possible. Bullies are a difficult population of students to discipline. They hook adults quickly into power battles and control struggles. Giving bullies consequences that involve positive actions and then quickly reinforcing them for the positive behaviors is the most effective way to interact with bullies. The usual discipline policies that involve punishment and isolation (time in the principal's office, suspension, expulsion) only reinforce the antisocial child's poor relationship skills and view that adults are adversaries to be avoided. A preferred approach is to tell children that when their behavior has a negative or hurtful effect on others in their community, they must correct it with positive acts. Thus, consequences that require positive, prosocial actions are employed. Students learn that it usually takes three positive acts to undo a negative, hurtful act. Refer to Handout/Transparency 4-17, Ideas for Consequences, for specific suggestions of prosocial consequences. Teach the bully positive ways to get attention and have power rather than engaging in power struggles that go nowhere.

Consequences That Teach

Principle three of an effective disciplinary philosophy is to use consequences that teach, make the child think, and ultimately change behavior, rather than fear-inducing consequences that suppress behavior. Emotional intelligence is a helpful concept in showing what it is that we want our consequences to teach.

Handout 9-3

Emotional Intelligence   The concept of emotional intelligence (Goleman, 1995) is helpful in understanding what skills bullies need to learn. As shown in Handout 9-3, Emotional Intelligence—Five Factors, emotional intelligence can be broken down into five skill areas: knowing and labeling what one is feeling, knowing how to calm and soothe oneself when emotions run high, knowing how to motivate oneself, developing empathy, and knowing how to respond to emotions in others.

The thinking errors (Samenow, 1992) of bullies that were discussed in Chapter Eight obviously interfere with the development of emotional intelligence. A disciplinary program that teaches bullies emotional intelligence will be much more effective than a punitive one. The use of incident reports as a disciplinary tool attempts to teach these five skill areas by asking the child to describe the bullying behavioral incident by focusing on his or her feelings as well as those of the other children involved in the incident.

Emotional Coaching Gottman (1997) has developed some guidelines on how parents can raise emotionally intelligent children. He describes one of the stumbling blocks for parents as, "Much of today's popular advice to parents ignores the world of emotion. Instead, it relies on child-rearing theories that address children's misbehavior, but disregard the feelings that underlie that misbehavior" (p. 15). This is true of teacher training too. It is important for teachers to become skilled at questioning why students misbehave and identifying the underlying emotional process. Teachers need support from each other to do this.

Handout 9-4, Strategies for Developing Emotional Intelligence in Children, lists ways teachers can promote emotional intelligence in their students. For Gottman (1997), emotional coaching is the cornerstone for how parents can develop emotional intelligence in their children. Teachers can also effectively use this emotional coaching model of interacting with children around disciplinary issues.

Handout 9-4

Teachable Moments

A fourth discipline philosophy is to maximize teachable moments. These are opportunities when a child is much more open to learning because of aroused emotion or repeated experience. Crisis breeds opportunity and opportunity breeds change. Be ready for these windows of opportunity and know how to recognize them. The following vignette will illustrate this concept. A fifth-grade student who consistently defies rules such as wearing a seat belt when riding in a car has an older cousin who is severely injured in a motor vehicle accident, more severely because of not wearing a seat belt. The fifth grader is upset and somewhat dumbfounded. This is a teachable moment.

Shared Control

A fifth principle for effective discipline is that of shared control. Shared control is like authoritative parenting versus authoritarian parenting where the adult has all the control and laissez-faire parenting where the child is given all the control. Often school discipline is administered with the mind-set that the adult has and should control the child. Yet it is just this kind of struggle for control that engages an antisocial child and reinforces thinking errors. An approach to discipline that uses the concept of shared control and that welcomes input from the child being disciplined is advocated.

It is important for teachers to support and challenge each other in developing this principle in their philosophy and practice of discipline. Sometimes, adults talk a good line about shared control but the practice differs. A story to illustrate this point involves a residential treatment program where children and staff went camping. When it came time to set up camp, staff questioned children about where they'd like to camp. Several children suggested a location, staff said "Let's talk about it," and children said, "I guess we're not camping here."

Using the Caring Majority

A sixth disciplinary principle is based on changing a school's climate by shifting the silent majority of students into an empowered, caring majority. This is described in detail in Chapter Six. Utilizing this powerful force for change can be part of an effective discipline plan. Teachers can mobilize the caring majority in their classroom to suggest disciplinary ideas. For example, "John has continued to say cruel things to other students. Could some of you who are in the caring majority help me think of what it is John needs to learn and how we as a class might teach it?" Caring majority students have suggested things like being mentored by a caring student or doing community service.

Another way the caring majority of students can be utilized is in giving feedback to the bully. One way of giving feedback is via letter so the bully's emotional reaction can be monitored. This will be described in more detail as a disciplinary tool.

Tools for Effective Discipline

Steps for Nonreactive Discipline

Handout 9-2

A first tool for discipline is following the four steps described in Handout 9-2, Steps for Nonreactive Discipline, when determining consequences for a bully. These steps need to be practiced by staff. Using role plays at a staff meeting can be a fun way to practice. A discipline report describing the nature of the conflict and who was involved is always indicated. This is for the use of the staff and adults. One incident report for the use of the student, along with the staff, is described in the next section.

Incident Reports

Handout 9-5
Handout 9-6

A second tool for disciplining bullies is the use of incident reports to teach bullies emotional intelligence. Handout 9-5 is the primary version of the incident report, and Handout 9-6 shows the intermediate version of the incident report. After a behavioral incident, the bully fills out the questionnaire about the incident and goes over it with the discipline facilitator who interviews and questions. The adult can reinforce the student for taking responsibility for his or her own actions and for showing empathy to another. The adult can also use the incident to teach about thinking errors, for example, "I talked to Jim and he said he was feeling really hurt by what you said to him, but you wrote down that he was feeling fine." When a student cannot complete all of the incident report, this may be a diagnostic of difficulties with labeling and identifying feelings in self and others. Such a child may be incapable of social problem solving and require help with early building blocks of emotional intelligence.

Development of Rituals

It is important that a school develop rituals that can be used when students fall from grace to welcome them back when amends are made. An example is a celebration for a child who learns the most and improves most in caring behavior that year. Rituals can be developed around discipline and disciplinary steps as well.

Using Letters from Peers to Impact the Bully

A fourth tool for effective discipline uses the caring majority to give bullies feedback with letters. This classroom exercise has proved to have an impact on bullies. The teacher or facilitator asks all the students in the class to write a letter to another class member who had done something mean to them or whom they have seen do something mean to someone else. Students are told that the goal of the exercise is to learn how to give good feedback and to learn about the effects of our behavior on others. The facilitator explains that the letters will be reviewed and shared with students privately.

The letter must be addressed to that person and the student has to sign his or her name. There is no anonymity; this encourages students to take responsibility for their feelings and to write the letter in a constructive way. The facilitator instructs the students in how to give good feedback, using "I" messages, by sharing how the mean behavior made them feel, by specifying how they want that peer to change, and by empowering change with encouragement. The facilitator then gathers the letters, sorts them privately, and then discreetly calls down students who had several letters or a very significant letter addressed to them. Bullies usually receive many letters and that sheer number can have impact.

Examples 9-7 and 9-8 show how articulate and poignant this process can be. It provides a powerful window for the facilitator to work with the bully on thinking errors and developing empathy.

Example 9-7
Example 9-8

Stages of Climate Change

There are three stages of climate change, and disciplinary policy must be flexible to work through all three stages. The first stage of climate change involves clear expectations and rules. Discipline focuses on making sure students understand the rules and consistent enforcement of the rules through consequences.

The expectations are reinforcers for correct behavior, such as getting adult help or respecting others. The second stage of climate change involves skill development, and discipline will rely on emotional coaching and use of incident reports.

Emotional coaching encourages the staff and parents to retrain and redirect through clear, specific messages about correct behavior. Incident reports provide a format for the students to take personal responsibility for creating a discipline problem.

The third stage of climate change is empowering students, and discipline relies on shared control and emphasis on the caring community. An expectation is that students can and are responsible for not only their behavior but also for the behavior of others. This stage requires on-going attunement by the staff through the development of rituals, use of the caring majority, reinforcement of responsible, respectful students, and responsive adults to correct the behavior of those who disrupt the caring community.

Remember, the goal is a "safe, respectful, inclusionary environment so teachers can teach and students can learn."

HANDOUT 9-1
Strategies to Use With Bullies

◆ Use a no-nonsense style

◆ Use prosocial consequences

◆ Give brief clear description of unacceptable behavior and consequence

◆ Do not have a long discussion of the situation

◆ Correct the bully's thinking errors

◆ Identify the victim's emotions

◆ Build empathy for the victim

◆ Rechannel power—do not try to suppress

◆ Set the culture for your school through the caring majority

HANDOUT 9 - 2
Steps for Nonreactive Discipline

1. State your belief that the child can be a positive leader at the school and follow expectations.

2. State the behavioral infraction and remind the student of the school rules and values.

3. State the consequence and any parameters.

4. State the follow-up plan.

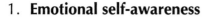

HANDOUT 9-3
Emotional Intelligence—Five Factors

1. **Emotional self-awareness**
   - Capacity to label feelings
   - Understanding cause-effect of emotions
   - Having preferences and opinions
   - Finding the right fit of hobbies, friends, job, marital partner, etc.
   - THE CORNERSTONE

2. **Emotional self-regulation**
   - Able to soothe self
   - Able to seek and use help/support from others
   - Able to recover from emotional distress
   - Capacity to wait
   - Sense of humor

3. **Self-motivation**
   - Able to set and work toward realistic goals
   - Able to sustain attention and get into "flow" state
   - Able to persist when there is a setback
   - Optimism, hope

4. **Empathy**
   - Able to recognize emotions in others, take on their social perspective
   - Shows concern and caring for others
   - Shows thoughtful and kind behavior toward others

5. **Relationship skills**
   - Skill in honest expression of own emotions
   - Skill in reading/receiving emotions of others
   - Can apologize when wrong, gives compliments and appreciation
   - Can compromise and problem solve with others
   - Sense of humor

Goleman, Daniel. *Emotional Intelligence: Why it Can Matter More than IQ.* N.Y.: Bantam Books, 1995.

HANDOUT 9-4

Strategies for Developing Emotional Intelligence in Children

1. Value emotions and their purpose as guides in living, as part of an internal compass.

2. Encourage children to have preferences, opinions, hobbies that make them unique.

3. Model, model, model. Strive to develop your own emotional intelligence and share it.

4. Be an emotional coach for EQ skill development:

   ◆ "It looks like you are feeling . . ."

   ◆ "Your behavior communicates . . ."

   ◆ "I'd feel . . . if I were in your shoes."

   ◆ "Your feelings are O.K., but your behavior needs to be appropriate."

   ◆ "Let's think of all the possible solutions to that problem."

5. Stories can set up powerful conceptualizations. Encourage children to read and discuss stories, to tell stories, and to have heroes.

6. Talk to children about everyday examples from home, school, and the news that demonstrate intelligent and unintelligent ways to handle emotions.

7. Set behavioral limits to help children learn to manage their feelings.

8. Encourage quiet time and time for reflection. Try out calming music or wrap in a blanket.

9. Teach strategies for managing emotions:

   ◆ cool-down/time-out

   ◆ relaxation

   ◆ self-talk

10. Help children think of what will soothe their distress.

11. Use written communication to slow down emotions. Write notes back and forth.

12. Allow mistakes and encourage ease in admitting and learning from them.

HANDOUT 9-4 (continued)

13. Watch for teachable moments. See crises in your child's life as opportunities.

14. Don't bail children out. Encourage them to take responsibility.

15. Teach children to be media literate. Limit television watching and show them what "spin" is.

16. Encourage positiveness (2 positives before a negative).

17. Having pets, babysitting, and community service all help in developing empathy.

18. Give feedback about how you feel being with him/her, what he/she could do to increase rapport, ask what you could do.

19. Praise/reward kind, caring behavior.

20. Coach children in how to be a good friend.

HANDOUT 9-5
Incident Report (Elementary Version)

Name _____   Date _____

Elementary School _____

Grade _____   Teacher _____

INCIDENT REPORT

What happened? _____

_____

_____

_____

I felt	**Happy**	**Sad**	**Angry**	**Scared**
	☺	☹	😠	😮

Could you have stopped yourself?   ☐ YES   ☐ NO

Did you remember to stop and think?   ☐ YES   ☐ NO

How did you make yourself feel better? _____

_____

How do you feel now? _____

_____

How do you think you handled yourself?   **Not So Good** |__|__|__|__|__|__|__| **Good**

Has this happened before?   ☐ YES   ☐ NO

How often?   ☐ Every day   ☐ Once a week   ☐ Once a month

How did the other person feel?	**Happy**	**Sad**	**Angry**	**Scared**
	☺	☹	😠	😮

Can you think of something else you could have tried? _____

_____

Who could have helped? _____

_____   _____
Student Signature   Adult Signature

Incident Report (Intermediate Version)

Name _____   Date _____

Elementary School _____

Grade _____   Teacher_____

INCIDENT REPORT

(to be completed by child, then reviewed and discussed with adult)

Describe what happened: _____

_____

_____

_____

Your feelings:

1. How did you feel during the incident? _____

   Why? _____

   _____

   _____

2. What were good choices and what were bad choices in how you acted? _____

   _____

   _____

Controlling yourself:

1. How much control did you feel you had over yourself during the incident? _____

   _____

   _____

2. How are you calming yourself now? _____

   _____

3. How do you usually calm yourself down? _____

   _____

4. When you are upset, how long does it usually take for you to calm yourself down?

   _____

HANDOUT 9-6 (continued)

Your plan:

1. What do you think about how you handled yourself in this situation? _____
    _____
    _____

2. Give examples of when you get into similar types of situations. _____
    _____
    _____

3. What would you like to change about the way you handle these kinds of problems?
    _____
    _____

4. What will you try to do next time? _____
    _____
    _____

Other's feelings:

1. How do you think the other person(s) felt during the incident? _____
    _____

2. What things could you say to the other person(s) that would help them feel better?
    _____
    _____

Handling the situation:

1. What would be some fair ways to solve this incident? _____
    _____
    _____
    _____
    _____

2. What things could you do now to handle the situation? _____
    _____
    _____

_____   _____

Student Signature   Adult Signature

Date: _____

E X A M P L E   9 - 7
Student Letter from Peer—Name-Calling

5-18-98

Dear Robbin

I am bothered by the way you always say I talk like a man,
not to say your a bad person, but it does get on my nerves.
I also don't like the way you say I love Stacy, because it
bothers me alot. Another thing that not only angers me, but
other people to, is you call us mental, I would also like you
to stop calling me person, I would like to be addressed my
name and not person. I also don't like the way you say I
am dum when I make a mistake. I don't like the way you
say I write like woman, because boys can have good
handwriting to. All in all, I would appreciate it if you would
stop pestering me with my ways.

Sincerely,
Austin

May 18

Dear David,

I do not like it when you call me names. It hurts my feelings when you do. The phrase, "Tub of lard" hurts my feelings very much. So does fatso. Yes, I may be big, but I am not the fatest kid in the school. My mom should know because she works for Weight Watchers.

From,
Kenneth

CHAPTER TEN

COLLABORATION WITH PARENTS

Working effectively with the community of parents is an important and integral component of a successful bully-proofing program. The development of a clear message from the school to the parents regarding bullying is a fundamental first step. A strong, clear position that bullying behavior will not be tolerated must be communicated to parents in order to build collaborative relationships between the school and home.

In the staff training component of this program (Chapter Four, Session 6) a plan for working with parents should have been developed. This plan should specify: (1) how parents will be informed about the classroom curriculum and kept apprised of developments with the bully-proofing program (suggestions include community meetings, newsletters/fliers, PTA involvement, telephone calls/meetings with staff members), (2) how parents should inform the school staff of a situation in which their child is being bullied, and (3) how parents will be informed when their child is bullying.

Many parents may have attended the orientation presentation to introduce the adoption of the *Bully-Proofing Your School* program, and all the parents will have received a letter inviting their participation in that presentation which briefly explained the program. Beyond those initial communications to parents, the ongoing message should not only specify behaviors that will not be tolerated, but should also educate parents about bullying and victim behaviors and strategies for handling each. The philosophy to be communicated should be one of working together to create a safe school environment with children exhibiting appropriate behaviors.

The parents should also be informed, with specific details, about the classroom curriculum. Strong assurances must be given to the parents that none of their children will be individually identified or labeled as either victim or bully.

Parents appreciate being informed of who at the school they can contact if they are concerned that their children are experiencing bullying. The staff training plan should specify a contact person for both parents of victims and parents of bullies. This person might be the classroom teacher or someone else, such as the facilitator, an administrator, or a member of the school's mental health team.

Overall, it is critical that the school take a position that no one benefits when harassment and destructive conflict are allowed to take place. Parents of bullies need to hear the same message that their children are hearing: "Bullying behavior is not allowed."

Periodic updates are encouraged, in which parents are kept informed about the progress being made with the program as well as educated about teaching their children appropriate skills for avoiding and defending against bullying behavior, both physical and verbal. Parents can help their children to become stronger and less vulnerable to attacks from other children, especially if they feel the support of the school staff toward providing a safe environment that allows learning to take place.

There are two "Golden Rules" to keep in mind when meeting with parents:

◆ **Most parents feel that their child is the victim.**

   Even when bullying behavior has been documented, the majority of parents will argue that the victim was provocative and therefore caused the difficulty to arise.

◆ **It is essential to meet with concerned parents individually.**

   Avoid, at all costs, bringing both the parent(s) of a bully and the parent(s) of a victim involved in a conflict together. If you do so, the conflict is likely to escalate with each set of parents defending their child and no solution reached. The parents of bullies and the parents of victims are dealing with entirely different problems; both need your assistance, but in very unique ways.

   Specific guidelines for working collaboratively with both the parent(s) of a bully and the parent(s) of a victim are presented in the following two sections of this chapter.

The Parent(s) of a Bully

Parents and the school staff must work together to ensure that the school is a safe and caring environment. If a school staff truly believes that a certain child is a bully, it is not only their responsibility to stop the bullying and to protect the victim(s) but to inform the parent(s) of the bully.

First of all, decide who the right person in the school is to approach the parent(s) of the bully. It may not necessarily be the child's classroom teacher or the principal or other administrator. It might be the facilitator of this program, the school counselor, or the student's former teacher who established rapport with the parent(s) the previous year. The best person is the one the parent(s) are the most likely to have respect for, to trust, and to feel is on their side rather than against them. It is also important not to "gang up" on the parent(s) by approaching them with multiple members of the school staff.

You should expect that the first reaction the parent(s) of a bully are likely to have when contacted is one of anger and defensiveness. They frequently feel that their child was provoked and that the bullying behavior was justified by the provocation. **Do not argue with this understanding of the problem**. A far more effective approach is to **remind them of the school's goal of creating a safe and caring environment** for all and that **solving problems with aggression is not a good solution regardless of the justification**. Let them know in no uncertain terms what the school's policy is regarding bullying and what the consequences of bullying behavior will be for their child.

There are three main points to remember when dealing with the bully as well as with the bully's parent(s):

1. Take a no-nonsense approach—bullying will not be an acceptable behavior within the school.

2. Set clear expectations for behavior and consequences for bullying behavior.

3. Have as little dialogue and discussion about the bullying behavior (i.e., excuses, justification) as possible.

While a no-nonsense stance should be taken with bullying behavior, it is critical that the parent(s) of the bully leave an initial meeting regarding their child with a sense of collaboration and rapport with the school staff. Emphasize the concept of assisting their child to learn how to have power without using aggression or bullying. Explain the idea of practicing and rehearsing appropriate behaviors as a more effective learning tool than punishing the incorrect behaviors. Finally, establish together some behavioral lesson plans for home so that their child will be reinforced in both the home and school environment for appropriate and caring behaviors. Parents of bullies often need guidance in responding to their children empathetically while still setting limits and reinforcing appropriate behaviors.

> **RESOURCE GUIDE**
>
> See "Books for Parents" for sources of information on intervention and discipline for parents.

There are three important skills to encourage the parent(s) to practice:

1. Trying to identify their child's feeling, need, or motivation when an inappropriate behavior occurs (e.g., "You just said something very cruel to your brother. I wonder if you were feeling jealous that he got new shoes and you didn't?").

2. Setting a limit on the behavior (e.g., "It is **not** O.K. in our family to make someone else feel bad when you feel jealous.").

3. Teaching alternative behaviors that are acceptable ways to express the feeling (e.g., "It **is** O.K. for you to say that you don't like feeling left out and to ask us for some new shoes for yourself," or "It **is** O.K. to tell your brother that it hurts your feelings when he brags and carries on about his new shoes and to stop it," or "It **is** O.K. to tell your brother that you feel jealous and want something for yourself and would he let you play with something of his to help you feel better.").

The Parent(s) of a Victim

The school may not have to reach out to the parent(s) of the victimized child. Instead, the school staff is likely to find the parent(s) contacting them, angry and upset that their child has not received protection from bullying within the school. In these conversations, emotions often run high, preventing calm dialogue and the feeling of mutuality between the parent(s) and the school.

Before these types of contacts occur, it is far better to let the community of parents know about the school's policy regarding bullying and to offer parents guidelines about who to approach and when to approach the school. **It is healthy and normal for parents to be advocates for their child.** While the school may traditionally tend to view these vocal parents as overprotective, it is important to remember that **victimized children usually do not have the skills to stop the bullying on their own. They need an advocate, and their parents are going to fill that role if the school staff does not.** Consequently, it is critical that the school set a tone (and communicate it to parents) of caring and protection; only then can the parents step aside and feel comfortable that the problem will be handled within the school.

While active concern on the part of the parents is quite common with victimized children, occasionally parents may not recognize the symptoms of victimization in their own child. The following characteristics assist in identifying victims, and can be communicated to the parent(s) if any apply to their child:

◆ A child who misses a great deal of school or makes multiple trips to the nurse's office may be attempting to avoid a bullying situation.

◆ A child who avoids the cafeteria or playground may be attempting to avoid a bullying situation.

- Sometimes a drop in a child's academic performance thought to be due to a learning problem is actually the result of bullying.

- A shy child, a child who stands on the sidelines during activity time, a child who appears isolated and/or depressed during school, is the type of child most likely to be picked on and bullied.

Victimized children are not likely to tell an adult themselves; the school staff must take responsibility for identifying these children and letting them know that someone cares and will keep them safe. Part of that process is contacting the victim's parent(s). Talking with the parent(s) and listening to their input can be very revealing. Often information is shared that helps the school staff to understand the reasons why that individual child is being bullied.

In particular, the parents of victims should be asked about the three most common triggers of victimization by peers:

- **Inhibition and shyness that is temperamentally based.**

  Some children are naturally shy and have been that way their entire life. These children are inhibited in general about approaching others or being evaluated by others. These children lack the necessary social skills for effective peer interaction (and benefit greatly from coaching). They are also likely to have overprotective parents who have naturally looked out for them during much of their life because of their inherent shyness.

- **Trauma or loss of a significant magnitude, resulting in anxiety and fear surrounding peer interaction.**

  These are children who have been hurt in life; they are afraid and anxious much of the time. They protect themselves by withdrawing; they are overly sensitive and easily hurt. Small amounts of teasing can retrigger earlier trauma and result in further withdrawal which, sadly, often has as a consequence increased bullying and rejection by peers.

  Children with significant learning disabilities, physical disabilities, and/or social processing difficulties can also be classified in this group. These children are not inherently shy, but their past history or unique circumstances cause high anxiety and fearfulness.

- **Physical weakness or petite size, especially in boys.**

  Physically weak or small boys are extremely prone to victimization. Family dynamics surrounding these characteristics can often become significant factors as well. Physically weak boys, for instance, are more at risk to be rejected by their fathers who often are critical and distant toward them. Mothers, on the other hand, tend to protect their sons when they are not of strong stature.

All three of these categories of children require protection within the school environment. While addressing the family dynamics or individual personality characteristics can help, that alone will not stop victimization without strong support and caring from the staff within the school.

Working together as caring adults in the lives of these children is the kindest and most effective approach to preventing victimization. While the school staff are doing their part, the socially inhibited child can often be assisted by a social skills groups in which interactional skills are taught, practiced, and reinforced (see Chapter Seven). The traumatized child may benefit from individual or supportive group psychotherapy. Learning disabled and physically disabled children may be helped by a strongly supportive home environment as well as an educative approach to their peers at school designed to build compassion and understanding of their disability. Finally, the physically weak child can occasionally be assisted by skill and strength development such as a karate or judo class. Some children will resist these types of assistance and these students' special contributions, be it a musical talent, hobby, or unusual interest, must be identified and capitalized on within the school setting.

The parents of victimized children are frequently overinvolved and overly protective of their children. These parents are usually compassionate and quick to identify with their children's emotional pain. Rather than criticizing their protective stance, it will be most helpful for the school to assist the parents in gradually restructuring and reshaping their ways of offering protection to their children. Simply asking concerned parents to trust that the school will keep their children safe is unlikely to be successful. In reality, their children have **not** been kept safe within the school and the parents have no reason to trust that they will be in the future without specific responses from the school staff that help them establish such trust.

Parents of victimized children will need frequent communications, in person or in writing, as to how playground time or lunchtime (two times when children are most vulnerable to bullying) went for their child. A "behavioral journal" that is sent home each Friday can be a helpful tool. The victimized child might have an identified social skill to practice each week within both the home and the school environment. A daily log could be kept within the journal of the number of times the child was observed displaying the identified skill. The parent(s) will value and

appreciate these written remarks. And while this procedure may be time consuming initially, it will frequently offer the parent(s) of the victimized child the reassurance they need that someone is looking out for their child and that the parent(s) and the school are a team working together for the growth and well-being of the child.

Handout 10-1 provides some specific strategies to prevent and cope with bullying behavior that parents of victimized children can review with and reinforce in their children. It is helpful to provide this handout to parent(s) at the initial meeting for their future reference, explaining that these skills will be taught to their child within the school as well.

Handout 10-1

What Parents Can Do . . .

How to Find Out If Your Child Is Being Bullied

What to look for:

- Excuses for not wanting to go to school
- Unexplained bruises
- Torn clothing
- Need for extra school supplies or money
- Continually "loses" belongings and school supplies
- Problems sleeping/nightmares
- Sudden loss of appetite
- Sudden academic problems
- Secretive/sullen/temper outbursts
- Ravenous after school—Ask Why: someone may be taking lunch or money
- Rushes to bathroom after school—Ask Why: your child may be frightened to use bathroom at school due to threats
- School reports frequent visits to the nurse with mysterious complaints, especially after recess (may be to avoid or need for nurturance)

If You Suspect a Problem

- Make it a habit to talk to your child about school
- Ask pointed questions such as "Who is a bully in your class?" "Who bothers kids at recess and on the bus?"

HANDOUT 10-1
Tips for Parents of Victims to Give Their Children

1. **Don't react emotionally.**

   Assist your child in knowing who the safe people are within the school to go to when bullied. Help them practice not showing strong emotions in front of the bully. This only excites the bully more. Instead, tell them to quickly go to someone identified as safe.

2. **Be assertive.**

   This works best if the bully is alone and not with a group of other children who will give him or her strength. If assertiveness is appropriate, tell your child to simply state that he or she does not like the bullying behavior, that it is not allowed, and that he or she intends to tell someone if it does not stop.

3. **Stay with others.**

   Reinforce for your child that bullies are most likely to act aggressively with a child who is alone.

4. **Do something unexpected.**

   This is especially effective if the child can turn the bullying situation into something humorous. Encourage your child's sense of humor and creative problem-solving skills.

5. **Own the put-down.**

   Remind your child that a bully often does not know what to do or say next if the victim simply agrees with him or her.

HANDOUT 10-2
How to Help: Steps to Bully-Proof Your Child

1. Let the school know your safety worries immediately.

2. Keep a record of time, date, names and circumstances to show a pattern of harassment.

3. Urge your school to adopt a clear conduct code that enforces strict penalties for students who break the rules against bullying.

4. Teach your child self-respect—confident kids are less likely to become a victim.

5. Let your child know it is O.K. to express anger if done appropriately.

6. Encourage friendships—there is strength in numbers.

7. Arrange weekend play dates to promote friendships.

8. Build social skills early.

9. Help shy kids with social skills training—role play together situations that have occurred previously.

10. Explain the difference between telling and tattling. Tattling is when you report something just to get someone in trouble. Telling is when you report that you or someone else is in danger. (Verbal abuse and being excluded are dangers too.)

11. Stress the importance of body language—a "victim stance" may attract bullies.

12. Teach your child effective skills for making friends such as how to share, compromise, apologize, use "I" statements, change the topic to avoid conflict, and use a "diplomatic" approach.

13. Teach your child alternative responses—**HA HA, SO** (**H**elp, **A**void, **H**umor, **A**ssert yourself, **S**elf-talk, **O**wn-it).

14. Don't advise either ignoring or physically attacking the bully.

What to Do If You Find Out Your Child Bullies Other Youngsters

◆ Evaluate whether the behavior might be modeled from parents. If not, is bullying of a younger sibling tolerated? Family therapy may be needed if patterns are difficult to change.

◆ Do not use physical punishment for discipline; that encourages a child to humiliate and hurt others. Instead, remove privileges or add jobs around the house.

◆ Provide as much parental (ors substitute parental) supervision as possible.

◆ Put an immediate stop to any bullying you observe. Always have the child act in a more appropriate way.

◆ Emphasize praise and positive feedback. Reward the child for caring and appropriate behaviors.

CHAPTER ELEVEN

COMING FROM AND GOING TO SCHOOL

A caring community stretches from home to school. Being part of that community means going out the door in the morning without worrying about safety, teasing, or harassment. Listening to children, few have this carefree world. Walking alone, waiting at the bus stop with others, or riding a school bus are all situations that feel scary. Kids report feeling entrapped, alone, vulnerable, with no one to turn to and no one who will listen. They do not feel safe, and many dread the coming from and going to school; those are the worst parts of their day.

Waiting at the bus stop with 20 other students—the school bus environment poses unique problems. There is one driver with a job to do that does not involve managing conflict or even being able to watch for problems. A group of children of multiple ages and grade levels ride together yet have no relationship with each other at any other time in their school day. Furthermore, many students act out their "rites of passage" on the bus. Drivers feel helpless, victims feel powerless and frightened, and bullies feel powerful—they have an atmosphere in which harassment, intimidation, and creating fear is easy. The audience is there, the adult is preoccupied, and a target for bullying is easy to spot.

A caring community includes the bus driver and riders. The goals are:

◆ to empower the drive

◆ to extend the caring community to the bus

◆ to have students monitor their own behavior and that of others

Steps to Develop a Caring Bus Community

Step 1.   A "Welcome" Breakfast for the Drivers

- The drivers are welcomed as part of the caring community in the school.

- Each is acknowledged and thanked for doing a most difficult job.

- The drivers give a brief description of their backgrounds. Often some are retired teachers or former business owners. Some have been career bus drivers. Frequently, they are frustrated. Their job is not easy.

- An overview of the bully-proofing program is explained. The importance of the drivers in the development of the caring community is emphasized.

A sense of community can be developed by encouraging the drivers to learn the names of each student on their bus and to greet them as they board. They are also asked to introduce themselves to the children. Being anonymous breeds bullying. Knowing a person's name is a beginning step in building a caring community.

Handout 11-4

It is recommended that the bus driver survey be administered if the school wishes formal data or a sense of the bus environment. (See Handout 11-4: Bus Driver Survey.)

Step 2.   Develop a Comprehensive Plan to Build a Caring Community on the Bus

- A second meeting is scheduled. This can be another breakfast with coffee and doughnuts or an afternoon tea with cookies and juice.

- Group problem solving is done, focusing specifically on ways to improve communication between the driver, the children, and the bully-proofing cadre at the school.

Handout 11-5

- Drivers are included directly in discussions of how to extend bully-proofing to the bus. Student fears are shared and drivers' problems are listened to. These are derived from the rider's survey (see Handout 11-5). Ideas are discussed regarding problem situations and interventions.

Letter 11-3

- Behavioral expectations on the bus are agreed to. A parent letter outlining the bus rules is developed. See Letter 11-3.

- Behavioral warning forms are introduced (see Handout 11-2). Referrals or warning forms are turned into an adult staff member at the drop-off point. Bus referrals are acted on immediately.

- Seating charts are discussed and drawn up for those drivers who want them.

◆ Drivers and riders are provided with a way to nominate each other for demonstrating caring behaviors on the bus. Drivers are given copies of the Caring Community acknowledgment sheet and are encouraged to award these to any students showing caring behaviors. See sample nomination form—Handout 11-1.

Handout 11-1

These are turned into the main office where they are entered into a drawing every Friday when approximately ten sheets are randomly selected to be read over the loudspeaker. All entries, read or not, are acknowledged by the principal and returned to the students with a piece of candy attached to the form.

◆ Opportunities to attend bully-proofing sessions and to meet with the bully-proofing cadre or classroom facilitators are made available.

Step 3. Bus Reward Program

◆ A system is established for tracking the behavioral warning forms and the caring community nomination forms from each bus. This enables the school to keep a record of the buses with the most and least problems.

◆ A reward program is established for the buses with the fewest referrals and for those with the most improvement. These have included:

◇ Gift certificates to the school store

◇ A special treat at lunchtime

◇ School supplies

◇ No homework pass for one night

◇ Extra credit in one class

◇ Computer time

◆ Create ways to acknowledge bus drivers for a job well done. These may include:

◇ Announcement over school loudspeaker

◇ Children thanking the driver personally with cards, notes, or drawings

◇ Mention in the school newspaper

◇ A "Caught You Caring" award for the driver

HANDOUT 11-1
Nomination Form

_____ **Caring Community**
(Name of School)

I, _____, would like to recognize the caring behavior

of _____. This person helped to make a safe and

caring school environment by: _____

_____

_____

_____

Date: _____

HANDOUT 11-2
Behavioral Warning Form

Name _____

Bus Number _____   Date _____

The problem that happened today was

Disrespectful and rude behavior   _____

Not following the instructions of the driver   _____

Food on the bus   _____

Not in assigned seat   _____

Use of profanity   _____

Other _____

_____   _____
Driver's Signature   Student's Signature

This section is to be completed by the student

1. Describe the problem that happened today.

2. What could you have done differently?

LETTER 11-3
Bus Safety Program

Dear Parent(s):

The _____ School District wants all children to feel safe while in the school environment. The bus ride to and from school is an important part of your child's school day. Everyone at _____ School is working toward safety on the bus and we would like you to join us in the effort.

We have selected your child's bus as a pilot bus for a new safety program. _____ staff members are meeting with students on bus _____ and representatives from transportation four times this month. During these homeroom sessions, students will work on building a caring community and becoming advocates for one another. Students will be asked to participate in various cooperative activities and to share information and create strategies with staff members. At the end of the pilot sessions, the _____ staff will assess the program and begin planning for bus transportation in the fall. We hope that the students involved in the pilot will provide useful suggestions and begin assuming positive leadership roles for next year. The new program will complement the existing bus rules and reinforce the fact that riding the bus is a privilege. Staff, students, parents, and community members will all need to participate in creating safer bus rides for _____ students. Please take time to speak with your child and encourage his/her participation in the pilot program. To get this conversation started, we have listed the existing bus rules below.

Bus Rules

Students must:

1. Follow the bus driver's directions the first time they are given.
2. Be seated whenever the bus door is closed.
3. Keep hands, feet, books, and objects to themselves.
4. Avoid getting involved in physical altercations or fights.
5. Refrain from bringing any weapons or facsimiles on the bus.
6. Avoid swearing, making rude gestures, teasing, or putting down other people.
7. Use classroom voices (moderate tone and volume) on the bus.
8. Avoid throwing anything off the bus or putting any part of their bodies outside the bus.
9. Refrain from smoking, chewing tobacco, eating, or drinking on the bus.
10. Avoid bringing anything alive or dangerous onto the bus.
11. Avoid bringing skateboards, roller skates, or roller blades onto the bus.

Thank You!

HANDOUT 11-4
Bus Driver Survey

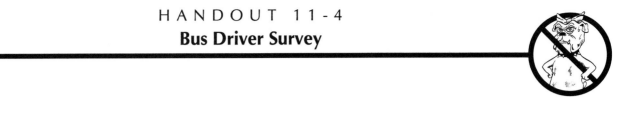

Years of experience: _____   Circle: Male   Female

Thinking about the past month, please circle your response to each statement:

Never true	Hardly ever true	Sometimes true	Often true	Almost always true	Always true
1	2	3	4	5	6

1. Children feel safe on my bus.   1 2 3 4 5 6

2. I have seen students hit, kick, push others.   1 2 3 4 5 6

3. I have heard students call names or say mean things.   1 2 3 4 5 6

4. I have seen a group of children join in bullying a child.   1 2 3 4 5 6

5. Disruptive students take up too much of my time.   1 2 3 4 5 6

6. If a student is being bullied or picked on, most of the students ignore it.   1 2 3 4 5 6

7. Students let me know when other students are causing problems.   1 2 3 4 5 6

8. There are clear disciplinary guidelines for bus drivers.   1 2 3 4 5 6

9. My administrators support me in dealing with students.   1 2 3 4 5 6

10. I like being the bus driver for this group of students.   1 2 3 4 5 6

11. I know the names of the students on my bus.   1 2 3 4 5 6

12. The biggest problem in my job as bus driver is:

_____

_____

HANDOUT 11-5
Bus Rider Survey

Grade: _____   Circle: Male   Female

Thinking about the past month, please circle your response to each statement:

Never true	Hardly ever true	Sometimes true	Often true	Almost always true	Always true
1	2	3	4	5	6

1. I feel safe on the bus.   1 2 3 4 5 6

2. I have been hit, kicked, or pushed on the bus.   1 2 3 4 5 6

3. I have often seen students hit, kick, or push others on the bus.   1 2 3 4 5 6

4. I have been called names or other mean things on the bus.   1 2 3 4 5 6

5. I have often heard students say mean things and call names to others on the bus.   1 2 3 4 5 6

6. I have seen a group of children join in bullying a child.   1 2 3 4 5 6

7. The bus driver is friendly.   1 2 3 4 5 6

8. Students who misbehave on the bus take a lot of the bus driver's time.   1 2 3 4 5 6

9. Other children help if they see someone being bullied or picked on on the bus.   1 2 3 4 5 6

10. Students try to make everyone of the bus feel included.   1 2 3 4 5 6

11. I like riding the bus to and from school.   1 2 3 4 5 6

12. The thing I like most about riding the bus is:

    _____

13. The thing I like least about riding the bus is:

    _____

MAINTAINING AND SUPPORTING THE CHANGE

Parents and schools working together offer the greatest assurance for the future well-being of all children socially, emotionally, and educationally.

Children cannot thrive in an environment of fear. Ultimately all children are affected when bully-victim problems go unaddressed. The victims feel humiliated, fearful, and some are physically tormented and hurt. The caring majority of children, those who stand by and watch, are affected as well. Some are secretly afraid of being targeted themselves; others are left feeling guilty and remorseful for not protecting the victimized children. The bullies also come out as losers. Research (Eron, 1987) has found that a boy who is a bully at age eight is three times more likely to be convicted of a crime by age thirty and less likely than others to finish college and locate a good job. Girls who bully are more likely to raise children who bully.

Bully-victim problems, like other serious problems such as chemical dependency and domestic abuse, tend to perpetuate if left unaddressed and cycle from generation to generation. Parents and schools together can stop this cycle by providing a safe, nurturing school environment for all children.

REFERENCES

Binswanger-Friedman, L. & Ciner, A. (1991, November). Unpublished material presented to Graland School, Denver, Colorado.

Eron, L. (1987). Aggression through the ages. *School Safety,* Fall, 12–16.

Goldstein, A. & Glick, B. (1987). *Aggression replacement training.* Champaign, IL: Research Press.

Goleman, Daniel (1995). *Emotional Intelligence.* New York: Bantam Books.

Gottman, John (1997). *Raising an emotionally intelligent child.* New York: Simon and Schuster.

Greenbaum, S., Turner, B., & Stephens, R. (1989). *Set straight on bullies.* Malibu, CA: Pepperdine University Press.

Hodson, J. (1992). Bullying in schools: Mainstream and special needs. *Support for Learning,* 7(1), 3–7.

Huggins, P. (1994). *Building self-esteem in the classroom: Intermediate version.* Longmont, CO: Sopris West.

Huggins, P. (1993). *Teaching friendship skills: Intermediate version.* Longmont, CO: Sopris West.

Huggins, P. (1993). *Teaching friendship skills: Primary version.* Longmont, CO: Sopris West.

Kreidler, W.J. (1984). *Creative conflict resolution.* Glenview, IL: Scott Foresman.

Lee, F. (1993, April 4). Disrespect rules. *The New York Times Educational Supplement,* p. 16.

Lewis, D.O. (1992). From abuse to violence: Psychophysiological consequences of maltreatment. *Journal of the American Academy of Child and Adolescent Psychiatry,* 31, 383–391.

Olweus, D. (1991). Bully/victim problems among school children: Basic facts and effects of a school based intervention program. In D. Pepler & K. Rubin (Eds.), *The development and treatment of childhood aggression.* Hillsdale, NJ: Lawrence Erlbaum.

Paley, V.G. (1992). *You can't say, you can't play.* Cambridge, MA: Howard University Press.

Prelutsky, J. (1984). *The new kid on the block.* New York: Scholastic.

Samenow, S. (1984). *Inside the criminal mind.* New York: Random House.

Samenow, S. (1989). *Before it's too late: Why some kids get into trouble and what parents can do about it.* New York: Random House.

Shure, M. & Spirack, G. (1978). *Problem solving techniques in childrearing.* San Francisco, CA: Jossey Bass.

Spirack, G., Platt, J., & Shure, M. (1976). *The problem solving approach to adjustment.* San Francisco, CA: Jossey Bass.

This Resource Guide is divided into seven major sections: (1) Videotapes and Films for Educators and Parents, (2) Videotapes and Films for Students, (3) Books for Educators, (4) Books for Administrators, School-Based Teams, and Specialists, (5) Books for Parents, (6) Books Primary for Students, and (7) Books for Intermediate Students. The videotapes and films to be used for students are identified for use with early or late elementary levels within their descriptions. Most entries are annotated so that you can select resources according to your specific needs. For example, if your class is working on Session 3 of the classroom curriculum, you would want to select stories that build empathy for the victim. Sessions 5 and 6, on the other hand, offer strategies for the caring majority to support the victims and books incorporating this type of content material would be best used for these sessions.

It is important that you select the films, videotapes, and stories shared with the students with care. Some of the materials designated for the later elementary aged students could traumatize a first or second grader. Similarly, some of the content depicted in certain videos is graphic and upsetting both to young children as well as to children who may have experienced a similar bullying situation in their own lives. If content of any of the Resource Guide entries is particularly explicit, a "caution" is provided. It is recommended that you first view or read anything with a caution prior to sharing it with either the students or the staff.

Videotapes and Films for Educators and Parents

Bus Discipline. (1992). Distributed by Sopris West, 4093 Specialty Place, Longmont, CO 80504.

A four-tape set that presents information on setting policies that are positive, trains drivers in management, shows teachers how to support safe policies, and gives a step-by-step process for solving behavior problems.

Cafeteria Discipline. (1995). Distributed by Sopris West, 4093 Specialty Place, Longmont, CO 80504.

Foundations: Establishing Positive Discipline Policies. (1992). Sopris West, 4093 Specialty Place, Longmont, CO 80504.

Helps school staff design policies and procedures that create a solid base of positive behavior management techniques. Includes three text volumes and six videotape sessions.

How I Learned Not To Be Bullied. (1997). Sunburst. 101 Castleton St. Pleasantville, NY 10570. 1-800-431-1934.

Easy to learn strategies for elementary aged children to use when bullied.

Managing Acting-Out Behavior: A Staff Development Program. (1992). Distributed by Sopris West, 4093 Specialty Place, Longmont, CO 80504.

A two-video set that teaches teachers, school administrators, and service providers how to cope successfully with explosive behavior, physical aggression, verbal abuse, severe tantrums, open defiance, and insubordination.

Michael's Story: The No Blame Approach. (1990). Lame Duck Publishing, 71 South Road, Portshead, Bristol BS20 90Y.

Produced in England, this video introduces a step-by-step, teacher-led program that has been successful in the English schools for helping victims and stopping perpetrators of bullying behavior.

Playground Discipline. (1991). Distributed by Sopris West, 4093 Specialty Place, Longmont, CO 80504.

A two-video set that trains teaching and playground staff in setting up a safe playground environment and designing consistent and effective expectations and clear procedures. Specific playground scenes very effectively show how to interact with students, deal with crises, implement consequences, and deal with fighting. A very helpful video for training playground aides.

Set Straight on Bullies. (1988). National School Safety Center, 4165 Thousand Oaks Boulevard, Suite 290, Westlake Village, CA 91362.

An 18-minute video that presents the story of a young boy victimized by a bully. The video is designed to educate school staff and students that bullying is a problem that adversely effects everyone within a school environment if it is tolerated.

Stamp Out Bullying. (1990). Lame Duck Publishing, 71 South Road, Portshead, Bristol BS20 90Y.

Produced in England, this video illustrates a training workshop in an English school that was the result of a 14-year old girl's suicide attempt following a bullying incident.

Videotapes and Films for Students

CAUTION ▶

Broken Toy. (1992). Summerhill Productions, 846 1/2 McIntire Avenue, Zanesville, OH 43701.

A 25-minute video that depicts a number of realistic scenarios in the life of a 12-year old boy who is ridiculed and physically assaulted at school. Not only is the home life of the victim portrayed, but the main bully's family is also depicted. While the story builds empathy for the victim, the content is dramatic. The ending, however, restores hope. The goal of this video is to build awareness and compassion in the bullies by showing them how much emotional damage their behavior can cause. For grades 5 and up. Preview before using.

Bullyproof (1997). Future Wave, Inc., 105 Camino Teresa, Santa Fe, NM 87505. (505) 982-882; fax: (505) 982-6460.

For younger children, a puppet show program is available that includes a portable stage, sound-track tape, curriculum, and supplies for creating a performance. For older children and teens, a rap and roll opera is available on video.

". . . but names will never hurt me" (1997). Kids Hope, 206 Bascomb Springs Court, Woodstock, GA 30189-3550. 1-800-465-4758.

A video-based program for grades 1–6 that helps children discover the value of treating others with kindness and respect. A step-by-step study guide is included. It is a powerful story about an overweight girl who struggles with acceptance until one individual stands up for her and sets an important example of Caring Community behavior.

In Harm's Way. (1996). Agency for Instructional Technology, Box A, Bloomington, IN 47402-0120. (800) 457-4509.

A 15-minute video to help students deal with bullies or name calling. Program also includes teacher's guide, song book, audio cassette with 17 songs. Recommended for grades 3–5.

The Choice. (1981). Phoenix/BFA Films, 2349 Chaffee Drive, St. Louis, MO 63146. (314) 569-0211. (800) 221-1274.

Available as a video or filmstrip, this is the story of how three boys struggle with their relationship when a new boy attempts to enter their group. The film is a good example of bully-victim relationships and of how the caring majority can be helpful.

Coping With Bullying. (1991). James Slanfield Company, Drawer G, P.O. Box 41058, Santa Barbara, CA 93140.

◄ CAUTION

A three-video set with a teacher's guide to help students understand and recognize bullying behavior. Various assertive responses are demonstrated as ways to respond to bullying. Recommended for grades 6 and up.

Hopscotch—Revised. (1987). SVE, 6677 North Northwest Highway, Chicago, IL 60631-1304. (800) 829-1900.

This video is the animated story of a boy who wants to make friends and tries showing off his prowess, parading his possessions, being noisy and disruptive, acting tough, and flattering other children. Finally, he stops playing roles and is accepted. Recommended for grades K–6.

Standing Up For Yourself. (1986). Phoenix/BFA Films, 2349 Chaffee Drive, St. Louis, MO 63146. (314) 569-0211 or 1-800-221-1274.

Part of the *Taking Responsibility* series of tapes, this video reminds the viewer that some attempts to be assertive will not be successful and that sometimes it is necessary to get help from adults. This tape is excellent reinforcement of the HA HA SO strategies. Recommended for grades K–6.

Books for Educators

Asher, S. & Gottman, J. (Eds.). (1981). *The development of children's friendships.* Cambridge, MA: Cambridge University Press.

Beland, K. *Second step.* Committee for Children, 2203 Airport Way South, Ste. 500, Seattle, WA 98134. 1-800-634-4449.

A curriculum guide for teaching empathy problem solving and anger management from pre-school through eighth grade.

Borba, M. (1989). *Esteem builders.* Rolling Hills Estates, CA: Jalmar Press.

This self-esteem curriculum is designed for grades K–8, and presents specific ideas for improving student achievement and behavior as well as the overall school climate.

Borba, M. & Borba, C. (1978). *Self-esteem: A classroom affair.* Oak Grove, MN: Winston Press.

Center for Applied Psychology. (1993). *Face your feelings! A book to help children learn about feelings.* King of Prussia, PA: Author.

Diamond, J.A. (1996). *Friendship note paper.* Denver, CO: Great Eye-deas Press.

This book describes a curriculum project appropriate from kindergarten through the elementary years. The project is multifaceted and the children successfully learn many skills including what a friend is, how to be a good friend, how to work together on a project, and how to carry that project to the community in the form of a fund-raiser.

Drew, N. (1987). *Learning the skills of peacemaking.* Rolling Hills Estates, CA: Jalmar Press.

This creative activity guide for elementary-aged children assists them in learning self-awareness, understanding of others, and mediation skills.

Goldstein, A. & Glick, B. (1987). *Aggression replacement training.* Champaign, IL: Research Press.

Presents a ten-week long training session for teachers or mental health staff to use for anger control with adolescents, specifically, but could be adapted for elementary aged students. A guide to moral training is also included.

Greenbaum, S., Turner, B., & Stephens, R. (1989). *Set straight on bullies.* Malibu, CA: Pepperdine University, National School Safety Foundation.

Presents statistics on bullying in the schools as well as guidelines for recognition of bullies and victims. Prevention strategies for changing the attitudes and actions of adults and students alike are provided.

Hoover, J.H. & Oliver, R. (1996). *The bullying prevention handbook: A guide for principals, teachers, and counselors.* Bloomington, IN: National Education Service.

This book is a wonderful resource for addressing bully-victim problems during the preadolescent and adolescent years. Sound research is provided that documents the middle school years as the worst in terms of the intensity of bullying experienced. A comprehensive approach that promotes prevention through education.

Huggins, P. (1990). *Teaching cooperation skills.* Longmont, CO: Sopris West.

Includes a series of lessons and experiential activities designed to teach both primary and intermediate students the skills necessary for cooperative learning to take place. Lessons focus on the skills of self-management, listening, collaborative problem solving, and leadership. Students learn to resolve conflicts through negotiation and compromise.

Huggins, P. (1991). *Creating a caring classroom.* Longmont, CO: Sopris West.

A collection of strategies designed to promote mutual support and strength connections in the classroom. Included are: (1) getting acquainted activities, (2) classroom management procedures, (3) a personal/social behavior scale and behavior improvement strategies for students with special needs, (4) a relaxation training program, and (5) a large collection of activities for establishing a nurturing classroom community. Designed for use with both primary and intermediate students.

Huggins, P. (1993). *Helping kids handle anger* (2nd ed.). Longmont, CO: Sopris West.

Includes lessons designed to enable both primary and intermediate students to acknowledge, accept, and constructively express anger. Students learn: (1) to use inner speech to inhibit aggressive behavior, (2) to use thinking skills for choosing constructive behavior when angry, (3) appropriate language to express anger, (4) a variety of techniques to release energy after anger arousal, (5) ways to defuse the anger of others, and (6) a model for resolving classroom conflicts. Role-plays and puppets are utilized to encourage active student involvement.

Huggins, P. (1999). *Helping Kids Handle Conflict.* Longmont, CO: Sopris West.

Students come to understand that they possess the power to manage their anger and conflicts by using the simple *Stop, Think, and Pick a Plan (STP)* process. They master skills such as ignoring, using chance, stating what they want, and making a deal. *STP* techniques are then applied to real-life situations. Grades 1–3.

Huggins, P. (1998). *Helping Kids Handle Put-Downs.* Longmont, CO: Sopris West.

Students learn: the art of ignoring; surprising antagonizers by "agreeing" with them; disarming antagonizers with humor; and deflecting verbal aggression with "crazy compliments." These strategies win respect and de-escalate conflict. Students also learn to use self-encouragement to dispel the hurt of put-downs and maintain their self-respect. Includes lesson presentation instructions and reproducibles. Grades 1–6.

Huggins, P. (1993). *Teaching friendship skills (Primary and Intermediate versions.)* Longmont, CO: Sopris West.

This version contains all new lessons and supplementary activities. Students identify behaviors in others that attract them and behaviors that alienate them. They examine their own behavior and determine changes they need to make in order to gain friends. They learn how to curb physical and verbal aggression. They discover that the secret to making friends is to make others feel special and practice specific ways to do so. They learn the value of sharing and how to give sincere compliments and apologies.

Huggins, P. (1994). *Building self-esteem in the classroom (Primary and Intermediate versions.)* Longmont, CO: Sopris West.

This version contains all new lessons and activities. Students refine their self-descriptions and acquire an appreciation for their uniqueness. They are introduced to the concept of multiple intelligences and learn a process by which they can determine their own strong intelligences. They learn the cognitive skill of self-encouragement, which enables them to respond to mistakes, failures, or put-downs in a manner that maintains their self-esteem. They learn to take responsibility for their school success by using self-statements to motivate and coach themselves through academic tasks.

Huggins, P. (1994). *Helping kids find their strengths.* Longmont, CO: Sopris West.

Designed to enable students to identify and utilize their strengths. Based on pioneering research by Bernard Haldane, Ph.D., and the Dependable Strengths Project Team at the University of Washington. Students build self-esteem not by positive thinking, but by analyzing experiences they're proud of for clues regarding their core strengths. Students share their good experiences, then utilize teacher and peer input to "tease out" the strengths that helped them create those experiences. They learn a large strength vocabulary and use their expanded self-identity as a springboard for new successes. In helping others find their strengths, students develop a respect for diversity.

Iowa Peace Institute. (1992). *Fostering peace.* Grinnell, IA: Author.

A comparison of nine different conflict resolution approaches for use with both elementary and high school aged students.

Jackson, N.F., Jackson, D.A., & Monroe, C. (1983). *Getting along with others: Teaching social effectiveness to children.* Champaign, IL: Research Press.

Includes a program guide and activities packet. The program covers 17 social skills and the steps required to teach them. Each lesson includes role plays, relaxation training, activities, and homework assignments.

Jenson, W.R., Rhode, G., & Reavis, H.K. (1994). *The tough kid tool box.* Longmont, CO: Sopris West.

A companion piece to *The Tough Kid Book,* provides teachers with straightforward, classroom tested, ready to use (reproducible) materials for managing and motivating tough-to-teach students.

Kaufman, G. & Raphael, L. (1990). *Stick up for yourself: Teacher's guide.* Minneapolis, MN: Free Spirit Publishing.

A comprehensive guide to a ten-part course that correlates with the book by the same title. Blends self-esteem and assertiveness with activities for a full year in the classroom. Recommended for grades 4–8.

Kreidler, W. (1984). *Creative conflict resolution.* Glenview, IL: Scott Foresman.

Presents techniques for creating a caring classroom environment. Exercises for assessing the students' behavior as well as concrete activities for promoting cooperation are specifically presented. Grades K–6 are covered.

Lavigna, G.L. & Donnellan, A.M. (1986). *Alternatives to punishment: Solving behavior problems with nonaversive strategies.* New York: Irvington.

Lee, J. (1993). *Facing the fire: Experiencing and expressing anger appropriately.* New York: Bantam Books.

A guide to understanding and expressing anger. Demonstrates ways to constructively face anger and experience it without losing control or hurting yourself or someone you love.

Loescher, E. (1991). *Peacemaking made practical: A conflict management curriculum for the elementary school.* Denver, CO: The Conflict Center.

A practical curriculum with over 50 lesson plans in developing an awareness of the feelings of self and others, social skills, and problem solving. All of the content is designed for the elementary level student and many clever applications of conflict resolution are included for the K–3 classroom.

McGinnis, E. & Goldstein, A.P. (1984). *Skillstreaming the elementary school child.* Champaign, IL: Research Press.

The program covers 60 specific prosocial skills such as saying thank you, asking for help, apologizing, dealing with anger, responding to teasing, and handling group pressure. Addresses the needs of students who display aggression, immaturity, withdrawal, and other problem behaviors.

Paley, V.G. (1999). *The kindness of children.* Cambridge, MA: Harvard University Press.

This book explores children's impulsive goodness. It contends that although each child comes into the world with an instinct for kindness, it is a lesson that must be reinforced at every turn. Paley showcases a collection of gems about children's spontaneous acts of goodness.

Paley, V.G. (1992). *You can't say, you can't play.* Cambridge, MA: Harvard University Press.

Details an experimental year in the kindergarten classroom of Vivian Paley, an innovative teacher and educator, who introduces the rule "You can't say, 'You can't play.' " Not only are the voices of the children heard as they adapt to this new order, but those of the older fifth graders observing the process are shared as well.

Peace Education Foundation, 1900 Biscayne Blvd., Miami, FL 33132-1025. (305) 576-5075.

An educational organization devoted to teaching children creative and nondestructive ways to handle conflicts. Curriculum guides, family support materials, and school-based training available.

Prutzman, P., Stern, L., Burger, M.L., & Bodenhamer, G. (1988). *The friendly classroom for a small planet.* Philadelphia, PA: New Society Publishers.

Presents techniques for nonviolence, cooperation, and problem solving for grades K–6 developed by the Reconciliation Quakers and used by more than 20,000 teachers and parents.

Rhode, G., Jenson, W.R., & Reavis, H.K. (1992). *The tough kid book: Practical classroom management strategies.* Longmont, CO: Sopris West.

A resource for both regular and special education teachers, providing research-validated solutions designed to maximally reduce disruptive behavior in tough kids without big investments on the teacher's part in terms of time, money, and emotion. The solutions also provide tough kids with behavioral, academic, and social survival skills. It contains a wealth of ready-to-use information and lists other commercially available, practical resources for teachers who want more.

Rubin, A. (1980). *Children's friendships.* Cambridge, MA: Harvard University Press.

A wonderful book that traces friendships developmentally from the preschool aged child through adolescence.

Schmidt, F. & Friedman, A. (1985). *Creative conflict solving for kids grades 4–9.* Miami, FL: Peaceworks.

Activities for use with the upper elementary grades.

Shapiro, L. (1993). *The building blocks of self-esteem: Activity book.* King of Prussia, PA: Center for Applied Psychology.

Sprick, R.S. (1981). *The solution book: A guide to classroom discipline.* Ohio: Science Research Associates. 1-800-468-5850.

STOP Violence Coalition, 9307 W. 74th St., Merriam, KS 66204. (913) 432-5158.

An organization devoted to preventing interpersonal violence through public awareness, education, and promotion of alternatives. Material available for all ages.

Trovato, C. (1987). *Teaching kids to care.* Cleveland, OH: Instructor Books.

A guide to understanding and developing a prosocial environment both within the classroom as well as within the home. Specifically focuses on ages 2–6 with special chapters on disabilities and ethnic differences.

Walker, H.M. (1995). *The acting-out child* (2nd ed.). Longmont, CO: Sopris West.

Wilt, J. & Watson, B. (1978). *Relationship builders.* Waco, TX: Educational Products.

Books for Administrators, School-Based Teams, and Specialists

Black, D.D. & Downs, J.C. (1993). *Administrative Intervention: A school administrator's guide to working with aggressive and disruptive students* (2nd ed.). Longmont, CO: Sopris West.

Provides the school administrator with a step-by-step approach and proven procedures to intervention—from the "out of control" stage through successful reentry into the classroom.

Phillips, V. & McCullough, L. (1992). *Student/staff support teams (SST).* Longmont, CO: Sopris West.

Presents a collaborative approach to solving individual student and building-level problems. SSTs are designed to assist teachers in dealing with students who are at risk and tough to teach.

Sprick, R., Sprick, M., & Garrison, M. (1992). *Foundations: Establishing positive discipline policies.* Longmont, CO: Sopris West.

Helps school staff design policies and procedures that create a solid base of positive behavior management techniques. Includes three text volumes and six videotape sessions.

Sprick, R., Sprick, M., & Garrison, M. (1993). *Interventions: Collaborative planning for students at risk.* Longmont, CO: Sopris West.

A program for anyone who has responsibility for helping regular class-room teachers develop plans for decreasing misbehavior and increasing student motivation. It is a must for administrators, school psychologists, teachers working on mainstreaming, school counselors, Student/Staff Support Team (SST) members, mentor teachers, and any other education professional engaging in collaborative problem solving. Includes a *Procedural Manual,* 16 intervention booklets, and an optional 20-cassette audio tape album.

Walker, H.M. & Severson, H.H. (1992). *Systematic screening for behavior disorders (SSBD).* Longmont, CO: Sopris West.

An easy to use, accurate, and inexpensive solution to the problem of early identification of at-risk students. Provides an effective process to screen and identify K–6 students at risk of developing serious behavior problems.

Books for Parents

Blechman, E. (1985). *Solving child behavior problems at home and school.* Champaign, IL: Research Press.

Canter, L. & Canter, M. (1988). *Assertive discipline for parents.* Santa Monica, CA: Lee Canter and Associates.

Dosick, W. (1995). *Golden rules: The ten ethical values parents need to teach their children.* San Francisco: Harper Collins.

Eyre, L. & Eyre, R. (1993). *Teaching your children values.* New York: Simon and Schuster.

Fleischman, M. (1983). *Troubled families: A treatment program.* Champaign, IL: Research Press.

Frankel, F. (1996). *Good friends are hard to find.* Los Angeles: Perspective Publishing.

Specific steps for parents and children to follow together for handling problems in friendships.

Garber, S.W., Garber, M.D., & Spizman, R.F. (1990). *If your child is hyperactive, inattentive, impulsive, distractible: Helping the ADD/hyperactive child.* New York: Villard Books.

Golant, M. & Crane, B. (1987). *Sometimes it's okay to be angry: A parent/child manual for the education of children.* Indianapolis, IN: OK Press.

Goleman, D. (1995). *Emotional intelligence.* New York: Bantam Books.

Greer, C. & Kohl, G. (1995). *A call to character.* New York: Harper Collins.

James, J. (1990). *You know I wouldn't say this if I didn't love you.* New York: Newmarket Press.

Chapter Seven of this book presents helpful information about the principles of verbal self-defense and effective come-back statements that parents can teach their children.

Samenow, S. (1989). *Before it's too late: Why some kids get into trouble and what parents can do about it.* New York: Random House.

This book describes the thinking patterns of antisocial children and shows parents how they might inadvertently be facilitating the antisocial behavior. Easy to read and understand, this book is full of good ideas for parents and professionals alike.

Schulman, M. & Mekler, E. (1994). *Bringing up a moral child: A new approach to teaching your child to be kind, just and responsible.* New York: Doubleday.

A variety of ideas for building empathy, fairness, and moral development in children from birth through adolescence.

Seligman, M. (1995). *The optimistic child.* New York: Harper Perennial.

Shure, M.B. (1994). *Raising a thinking child: Help your child learn to resolve conflicts and get along with others.* New York: Holt.

Trovato, C. (1987). *Teaching kids to care.* Cleveland, OH: Instructor Books.

A guide to understanding and developing a prosocial environment both within the classroom as well as within the home. Specifically focuses on ages 2–6 with special chapters on disabilities and ethnic differences.

Books for Primary Students

Alexander, M. (1981). *Move over, twerp.* New York: Dial Books.

An enchanting story showing the resourcefulness of a young boy who employs humor to solve a bullying problem. The victim is very endearing—a great caring majority book. Unfortunately, this book is out of print. Visit your library for a copy.

Bennett, W.J. (ed.) (1995). *The children's book of virtues.* New York: Simon & Schuster.

Classic stories, verses, poems, and fables are organized around different themes, each of which teaches a value. Courage, compassion, and honesty are just a few of the character values the book covers. It is short, easy to read, and a wonderful way to impart values through the timeless tradition of reading and storytelling.

Berenstein, S. & Berenstein, J. (1982). *The Berenstein Bears get in a fight.* New York: Random House.

In this popular story, Brother Bear and Sister Bear learn that sometimes even people who love each other get in fights, and that these are normal occurrences.

Berenstein, S. & Berenstein, J. (1993). *The Berenstein Bears and the bully.* New York: Random House.

Sister Bear has trouble with a bully. Brother Bear tries to help her learn coping strategies. The story has a positive outcome.

Boyd, L. (1991). *Baily the big bully.* New York: Puffin Books.

This story wins by persuasion, showing a bully that it is more fun to be a friend. Go to your library for this one—it is out of print.

Brown, M. (1990). *Arthur's April fool.* Boston: Little, Brown & Co.

Arthur's April Fool's surprise is almost spoiled by a bully.

Browne, A. (1989). *Willy the wimp.* New York: Knopf.

How to be gentle and kind without being a victim.

Browne, A. (1991). *Willy and Hugh.* New York: Knopf.

Carlson, N. (1983). *Loudmouth George and the sixth grade bully.* New York: Puffin Books.

How George, with the help of his friend Harriet, thwarts an older and larger boy from stealing his lunch. How to support a victimized child through friendship is the theme of this story.

Carlson, N. (1988). *I like me.* New York: Viking.

An appealing little book about taking care of and valuing yourself. This book would be especially helpful for victimized children.

Carlson, N. (1997). *How to lose all your friends.* N.p.: Puffin Books.

An easy to read picture book that teaches without preaching to young children about the importance of interpersonal skills. Readers experience why no one cares to play with a child who won't share, bullies, never smiles, and whines.

Cohen, M. (1987). *Liar, liar pants on fire.* New York: Young Yearling Books.

A boy who is new to his class tries to fit in by bragging.

The editors of Conari Press (1994). *Kids' random acts of kindness.* Berkeley, CA: Conari Press.

The refreshingly tender stories written by children remind the readers of the vital and joyful role that kindness can play in our lives.

Conta, M. & Reardon, M. (1974). *Feelings between friends.* Chicago, IL: Children's Press.

Fourteen photographically illustrated stories explore feelings and moods in relationships between children.

Crary, E. (1983). *My name is not dummy.* Seattle, WA: Parenting Press.

How to deal with put-downs.

Cummings, Carol (1991). *Tattlin' Madeline.* Edmonds, WA: Teaching, Inc.

This excellent book helps children learn the difference between tattling and reporting.

de Paola, T. (1979). *Oliver Button is a sissy.* New York: Harcourt Brace Jovanovich.

A young boy's coping with a put-down. This story builds empathy for being different and will help the caring majority understand.

Doleski, T. (1983). *The hurt.* Mahwah, NJ: Paulist Press.

What happens to a young boy who hides his feelings and hurt.

Guffe, T. (1991). *Bully for you.* New York: Child's Play.

Why it's not a good idea to be a bully. A wonderful book for overly aggressive, young children tempted to bully others.

Heine, Helme (1982). *Friends.* New York: Aladdin Paperbacks.

This story follows a group of animal friends through a typical day together. It emphasizes the importance of caring, sharing, and being fair because that is what good friends do. The illustrations and story are precious. This book is useful in defining friendship.

Henkes, K. (1991). *Chrysanthemum.* New York: Greenwillow Books.

A kindergarten-aged mouse is teased upon entering school because of her unusual name. The resolution is weak, but the story is engaging and builds empathy for the victim.

Kellogg, S. (1990). *Best friends.* New York: Dial Books for Young Readers.

Many themes of friendship are covered in this wonderful story: creating fantasies to be accepted, loss of a friend, renewal of a friendship, as well as compromise and sharing.

Moser, A. (1988). *Don't pop your cork on Mondays.* Kansas City, MO: Landmark Editions.

Moser, A. (1991). *Don't feed the monster on Tuesday.* Kansas City, MO: Landmark Editions.

A wonderful book that presents valuable information to children about the importance of self-esteem. Practical approaches are presented that children can use to evaluate and strengthen their sense of self-esteem. A very practical guide to taking small steps toward success. Recommended for grades K–5, and definitely recommended for victimized children.

Moser, A. (1994). *Don't rant and rave on Wednesday.* Kansas City, MO: Landmark Editions.

Naylor, P.R. & Malone, N.L. (1994). *The king of the playground.* N.p.: Aladdin Paperbacks.

Kevin, with his dad's help and encouragement, learns how to overcome his fear of Sammy, the self-appointed "King of the Playground."

Petty, K. & Firmin, C. (1991). *Being bullied.* New York: Barron's Books.

A young school-aged girl encounters a female bully who calls her names, teases, and scribbles on her papers. She tells her mom about her problem and she gets help from her teacher, who protects her from the bully.

Walker, A. (1991). *Finding the greenstone.* San Diego, CA: Harcourt Brace Jovanovich.

A touching story about a boy finding compassion for others both from within himself and from the spirit of care given to him by his community. A strong book for helping the caring majority create a caring environment for all.

Wells, R. (1973). *Benjamin and Tulip.* New York: Dial Books.

A charming little animal story in which the bully is a girl and the victim is a boy. The situation resolves when they encounter a bigger problem that affects them both.

Wilt Berry, J. (1984). *Let's talk about fighting.* Chicago, IL: Children's Press.

A "self-help" book for young children that provides alternatives to fighting.

Zolotow, C. (1969). *The hating book.* New York: Harper Collins Children's Books.

A little girl knew her friend hated her but she didn't know why until she finally got up courage to ask why they were being so rotten to each other.

Zolotow, C. (1982). *The quarreling book.* New York: Harper Collins Children's Books.

A short story about how a quarrel can grow bigger and bigger until it hurts many people. For the youngest elementary children, this book builds an understanding of how aggression can spread unless stopped. A beginning guide to empower the caring majority.

Books for Intermediate Students

Adelman, B. & Hall, S. (1970). *On and off the street.* New York: Penguin USA.

Bennett, W.J. (ed.) (1995). *The children's book of virtues.* New York: Simon & Schuster.

Classic stories, verses, poems, and fables are organized around different themes, each of which teaches a value. Courage, compassion, and honesty are just a few of the character values the book covers. It is short, easy to read, and a wonderful way to impart values through the timeless tradition of reading and storytelling.

Bosch, C. (1988). *Bully on the bus.* Seattle, WA: Parenting Press.

A terrific book that allows the reader to select from different options of how to handle a bully encountered on the school bus. For example, the victim can decide to fight back or to ask a friend for help by turning to different pages to learn the outcome. Children eventually read all the options, curious to find out which one proves the most effective. Many good ideas are presented for victimized children.

Burnett, Karen Gedig (1999). *Simon's Hook.* Roseville, CA: GR Publishing. P.O. Box 1437, Roseville, CA 95678, or www.grandmarose.com.

A book about teases and put-downs.

CAUTION ▶   Byers, B. (1981). *The 18th emergency.* New York: Puffin Books.

A 12-year old boy is tormented by the school bully for belittling him. His parents are of no help nor is his best friend, who is also frightened of the bully. Eventually he is beaten up by the bully.

Carrick, C. (1983). *What a wimp!* New York: Clarion Books.

Story of a fourth grade boy who moves to a new school following the divorce of his parents. He is harassed daily by a bully as he walks home from school. Finally, he decides to just let the bully beat him up. Surprisingly, the bully does nothing. The caring majority will understand what it feels like to be bullied after reading this book.

Cohen-Posey, K. (1995). *How to handle bullies, teasers, and other meanies.* Highland City, FL: Rainbow Books, Inc.

Why bullies and teasers act that way, how to deal with bullies and prejudice, and how to defend oneself against bullies.

Coombs, K. (1991). *Beating bully O'Brien.* New York: Avon Books.

A fifth grade boy is physically assaulted by a girl bully on his way home from school. His dad makes him feel like a sissy for not defending himself, but the boy is a viola player and he does not want to hurt his hands. When the bully's older brother attacks the boy, the girl bully intervenes and helps him. He later learns that she gets beaten up at home by her older brother. A good caring majority book as the main character is very likeable.

Estes, E. (1944). *The hundred dresses.* New York: Harcourt Brace Jovanovich.

A Newberry Honor story that will touch hearts: about the humiliation that results from teasing among elementary-aged girls. A good story to empower the caring majority.

Kaufman, G. & Raphael, L. (1990). *Stick up for yourself.* Minneapolis, MN: Free Spirit Publishing.

A guide to assertiveness and positive self-esteem. Discusses problems such as making choices, learning about and liking yourself, and solving problems. Recommended for grades 4–8. A wealth of ideas for victimized children.

Millman, D. (1991). *Secret of the peaceful warrior.* Tiburon, CA: H.J. Kramer.

An older mentor teaches a school-aged boy how to thwart a bully by hiding his fear and side-stepping his physical advances. Somewhat unrealistic, as the boy and the bully become friends in the end.

Naylor, P. (1991). *Reluctantly Alice.* New York: Atheneum.

Story of a seventh grade girl who is made fun of in class, tripped in the halls, and hit by flying food in the cafeteria thrown by another girl and her cohorts. When each student in class must select someone to interview, the girl chooses the bully. The girls eventually come to know each other better and the bullying stops.

Pfeffer, S.B. (1979). *Awful Evelina.* Morton Grove, IL: Albert Whitman.

Rochman, H. & McCampbell, D. (1993). *Who do you think you are? Stories of friends and enemies.* Boston, MA: Little, Brown and Co.

A collection of short stories about friendship—being a friend, being let own, being picked on, and being cared about. A great book for enlisting the empathy of the caring majority.

Romain, T. (1997). *Bullies are a pain in the brain.* Minneapolis, MN: Free Spirit Publishing, Inc.

This handbook approach offers children tried-and-true ways to deal with bullies as they laugh along with the author's jokes and cartoons. This book also provides help to kids who are bullies and want to change.

Stolz, M. (1963). *The bully of Barkham Street.* New York: Harper Collins Children's Books.

 CAUTION

The main character in this story is the bully. He is a sixth grade boy who is the oldest and biggest in his classroom. His family rarely listens to him and often threatens to take away his only friend, his dog.

Wood, W. & Wood, A. (1975). *The sandwich.* Toronto, Canada: Kids Can Press.

A wonderful story that employs humor and cleverness in solving a situation of being made fun of because of ethnicity. This book shows how to support the victim.